LORDSHIP, REFORM,
AND THE
DEVELOPMENT OF CIVIL SOCIETY
IN MEDIEVAL ITALY

Publications in Medieval Studies

LORDSHIP, REFORM, AND THE DEVELOPMENT OF CIVIL SOCIETY IN MEDIEVAL ITALY

The Bishopric of Orvieto, 1100–1250

DAVID FOOTE

University of Notre Dame Press
Notre Dame, Indiana

Copyright © 2004 by University of Notre Dame
Notre Dame, Indiana 46556
www.undpress.edu
All Rights Reserved

Manufactured in the United States of America

Library of Congress Cataloging-in-Publication Data
Foote, David, 1960–
    Lordship, reform, and the development of civil society in medieval Italy :
the bishopric of Orvieto, 1100–1250 / David Foote.
        p. cm. — (Publications in medieval studies)
    Includes bibliographical references and index.
    ISBN 0-268-02871-0 (hardcover : alk. paper)
    ISBN 0-268-02872-9 (pbk. : alk. paper)
    1. Catholic Church. Diocese of Orvieto (Italy)—History—To 1500.
2. Church and state—Italy—Orvieto Region—History—To 1500. 3. Orvieto
Region (Italy)—Church history.   I. Title.   II. Publications in medieval
studies (Unnumbered)
                    BX1547.O78F66 2004
                    282'.45652'09021—dc22

                                                            2004011375

    ∞ *This book is printed on acid-free paper.*

FOR
GAIL, AMY, AND SARA GRACE

CONTENTS

ACKNOWLEDGMENTS

THE ARCHIVAL RESEARCH FOR THIS BOOK WOULD NOT HAVE been possible without a Fulbright Fellowship, a Reed-Smith Research Fellowship, and a Humanities Research Grant from the University of California, Davis. I would like to thank the many people in Orvieto who extended such a warm welcome to me. Dom Luigi Farnese of the Archivio Vescovile made the episcopal registers easily accessible. Marilena Rossi Caponeri, the director of the Orvietan Archivio di Stato, responded to my many requests for information and for help with paleographic problems with kindness and patience. The staff of the Archivio di Stato was equally patient and helpful. I would also like to thank Lucio Riccetti, the expert on all things Orvietan, for his hospitality and advice. I am greatly indebted to a host of colleagues and friends. William Bowsky, Carol Lansing, Maureen Miller, and Tom Noble gave generously of their time. In addition to their careful reading of the manuscript and wonderfully perceptive comments, their encouragement and support sustained the project at critical moments in its development. Likewise, Paula Findlen, Joan Cadden, Barbara Rosenwein, and Marcia Colish devoted considerable effort and care in reading and commenting on the manuscript. I greatly appreciate the help and moral support of many others along the way, including Hans Hummer, John Strickland, Marshall Crossnoe, Duane Osheim, George Dameron, Patrick Geary, and Stanly Godbold. Finally, and most important, this book is dedicated to my wife and daughters, Gail, Amy, and Sara, who have labored alongside me with love and patience throughout the long process of researching and writing, all the while helping me to maintain perspective and reminding me what is truly important. This book is also dedicated to my parents, Marshall and Joan Foote, for their undying love and support.

THE BISHOPS OF ORVIETO

Guilielmo (1103–1136)

Ildibrando (1140–1155)

Gualfredo (1156–1157)

Guiscardo (1157–1159)

Milo (1159–1161)

Rustico (1168–1175)

Riccardo (1178–1202)

Matteo (1202–1211)

Giovanni (1211–1212)

Capitano (1213–1228)

Ranerio (1228–1248)

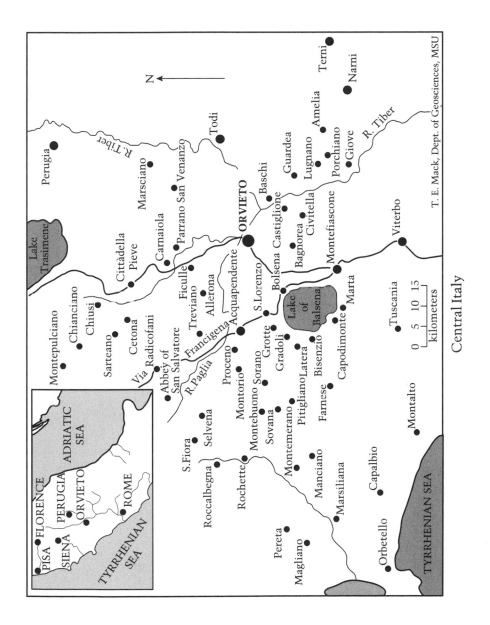

Central Italy

T. E. Mack, Dept. of Geosciences, MSU

xiii

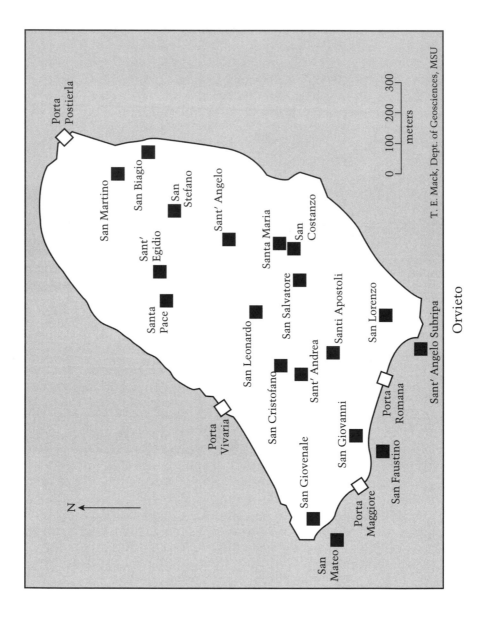

N ←

Porta
Postierla

San Martino

San Biagio

San
Stefano

Sant' Angelo

Sant'
Egidio

Santa Maria

San
Costanzo

Santa
Pace

San Salvatore

Santi Apostoli

San Lorenzo

San Leonardo

San Cristofano

Sant' Andrea

Porta
Vivaria

San Giovenale

San Giovanni

Porta
Romana

Sant' Angelo Subripa

Porta
Maggiore

San Faustino

San
Mateo

0   100 200 300

meters

T. E. Mack, Dept. of Geosciences, MSU

Orvieto

INTRODUCTION

THE FORMATION OF A CIVIL SOCIETY

In a recent article, "the sources of civil society in Italy," Edward Muir attempts to "grope through the historical mists" to answer a question of fundamental importance for historians of medieval and early modern Italy. "How did the inhabitants of north-central Italy employ collaborative solutions [as opposed to coercive solutions] to eliminate the political violence of families and factions in their communities?"[1] In other words, how does one explain the development of civil society in medieval and early modern Italy? This is the central question for this study of the Orvietan bishopric.

Because historians tend to think of the development of civil society as a fundamentally secular process, choosing a bishopric as a venue for exploring this topic requires some justification. I would argue that as one seeks to understand the development of civil society in medieval Italy, the tendency to exclude ecclesiastical institutions from the equation constitutes part of the mist through which one must grope. There are two closely related issues at stake—the relation between sacred and secular and the relation between personal power and institutions. The first is a question of interests—the extent to which religious and political interests informed each other.

The second is a question of process—identifying mechanisms that translated religious interests into political interests and vice versa. This book follows the lead of historians like Robert Brentano, whose work serves to remind us of the church's importance in the life of medieval Italian cities. Concerning the dichotomy between sacred and secular, Brentano writes, "the border between the two quietly shades into nonexistence, into the complexity of life lived by physical beings susceptible to spiritual aspirations and to the different complexity of spiritual acts performed with physical furniture."[2] He describes changes in thirteenth- and fourteenth-century Rieti that resulted from this interpenetration of sacred and secular as "a normalization, perhaps even civilization, certainly bureaucratization"—in sum, the formation of civil society.[3]

The concept of bureaucratization leads us to the second important issue—the relative weight of institutions and personal power in medieval society. One cannot fully appreciate the relation between sacred and secular aspects of society without a proper evaluation of the role of ecclesiastical institutions as mechanisms that facilitate the interpenetration of religious and political interests. While Muir does not acknowledge a role for episcopal institutions in the development of civil society, he offers a wonderfully perceptive comment that points to the importance of institutions such as bishoprics. "What we are searching for are not so much origins but the elements of a feedback process that reinforced civic culture at many different levels."[4] My central claim is that bishoprics were among the most important of these feedback mechanisms. Indeed, as one examines the development of episcopal institutions, one is looking at civil society in process, for the bishopric was the place where Orvietans contested and negotiated the political and religious ideals that would shape their community.

Such an approach represents something of a departure from traditional studies of Italian bishoprics. Muir's distinction between origins and feedback processes offers a helpful framework for articulating the distinctiveness of this approach. It is largely the question of origins that has defined the place of bishoprics in the historiography of medieval Italian cities. Scholars have called attention to the unique role that many bishoprics played in the formation of the communes, or city-states. Some of these studies focus on the temporal power of Italian bishops within the city in order to explain the origin of the urban ruling class and the early development of communal institutions.[5] Other studies have focused on the bishopric's political power in the countryside and its role in the city's conquest of the *contado*, or surrounding countryside, over which the city claimed political authority.[6] While these studies shed considerable light on bishoprics during the period of early communal formation, they are interested in the development of episcopal institutions only to the extent that they are helpful in understanding the origin of the communes. It is often the case that bishops are important characters in the prologue to the story of the communes, but they are banished to the margins of the central narrative. Once the question of origins has been addressed, the significance of bishoprics for understanding Italian cities has been exhausted.

The banishment of episcopal institutions to the margins of the central narrative reflects a more general shift in Italian historiography over the last several decades away from institutions and toward *Personenforschung*, or a study of ruling elites.[7] While this shift has been tremendously fruitful, it runs the risk of undervaluing the role of institutions in medieval society. John Najemy has commented on the tendency of many studies of late-medieval Florence to dismiss institutions as a facade that masked the more immediate and personal exercise of power.[8] I will argue that institutions, far from being mere facades, are mechanisms that regulate the competition for power. As such they shape the nature of power in a society and reflect the interests underlying this power. To use Muir's terminology, they are feedback mechanisms. If we examine episcopal institutions from this perspective, it becomes apparent that a narrative of the development of civil society in medieval Italian cities is not complete without the bishopric as one of the central characters.

LORDS, PRIESTS, AND PROPHETS

Bishoprics profoundly influenced the development of civil society in medieval Italy because they were in the right place at the right time. Italians were engaged in a fierce struggle to define the nature of secular and ecclesiastical authority between the eleventh and thirteenth centuries. For reasons that I will explain, bishoprics were among the principal institutions for regulating the constantly evolving interaction between the spiritual ideals of their respective communities and patterns of lordship. It was from the intense struggle between religious values and secular lordship that civil society emerged in medieval Italy. It is worth making a few general observations about the relation between lordship and ecclesiastical reform in medieval Italy and concerning the bishopric's role in regulating this relation.

At first glance, the task of ecclesiastical reform seems relatively straightforward. During the mid-twelfth century Bernard of Clairvaux wrote to his former pupil, Pope Eugenius III (1145–1153), admonishing him to beware of the trappings of power and wealth that too often diverted the papacy from its spiritual mission. He exhorted Eugenius to be mindful that the pope was the heir of St. Peter. "This is Peter, who is known never to have gone in procession adorned in jewels or silks, nor covered with gold, nor carried on a white horse, nor accompanied by a knight, nor encircled with servants clamoring about him. But without these things, he believed it was sufficient that the command of the savior be fulfilled, 'If you love me, feed my sheep.' In these [other] things, you are a successor not of Peter, but of Constantine."[9]

The host of reformers that became such prominent features in the political and ecclesiastical landscape during the eleventh and twelfth centuries feared that worldly political and social structures had penetrated and corrupted the sacred community of the church and its evangelical traditions. This evaluation of the eleventh- and twelfth-century church has made its way into modern scholarship with the concept of the "feudal church." According to this model, the political and economic conditions of the High Middle Ages left the church hopelessly entangled in aristocratic patronage networks that violated ecclesiastical liberties and gave the nobility a monopoly on ecclesiastical offices and benefices.

Without denying the deleterious influence that secular lordship could exert upon the church, I attempt to present a more nuanced description of ecclesiastical reform as a process of adjustment between ecclesiastical institutions, the church's evangelical traditions, and the ever-changing patterns of lordship. Max Weber's model of prophetic religions offers a helpful place to begin.[10] According to Weber, prophetic religions like Christianity find their origin in a charismatic figure bearing a revelation from God. Once the prophet is gone, however, the followers are left with the difficult

task of interpreting the revelation—and guarding it from misinter-
pretation. A priestly bureaucracy emerges as the interpreter and
guardian of authentic charisma. Thus the priest succeeds the charismatic figure of the prophet and becomes the authoritative interpreter
of the prophetic message.

A tension between prophetic charisma and priestly bureaucracy
permeates prophetic religions like Christianity, as prophets and
priests struggle to control the balance between charisma and institutional authority. Despite this tension, charisma and bureaucracy
are not mutually incompatible. One cannot exist without the
other. The charismatic message, if it is not to dissipate like a mist,
must become institutionalized. Likewise, the priestly bureaucracy
becomes lifeless without charisma.[11]

There is, however, more to reform than this dialectical relation
between prophets and priests. Ecclesiastical institutions, which
were designed to serve as guardians of charisma, stood in dialectical
relation to the political and economic structures of society as well.
From at least the fourth century, the church depended on emperors,
kings, and public officials to protect its interests and its status as a
guardian of charisma. At the same time, secular rulers leveraged
their own political power through their access to ecclesiastical institutions, resources, and charisma. Using Weber's language of ideal
types, the priest thus stood in dialectical relation to both the secular
lord and the prophet. Any adjustment in one relation required an
adjustment in the other.

This trilectic between lords, prophets, and priests was one of the
defining characteristics of Italian society between the eleventh and
thirteenth centuries. The period of communal formation coincided
with one of the most intense periods of reform activity in the history
of the church. At the same time that a variety of political actors
sought to use the bishopric as a framework for constructing a new,
urban-centered lordship, a host of reformers sought to use the bishopric as a tool for imposing their evangelical ideals on the local
church. In effect, the bishopric was a field for a multidirectional tug-
of-war among a variety of political and religious actors, all competing for access to episcopal institutions in pursuit of their interests
and in their quest to implement their ideal of an ordered society.
Such an approach to bishoprics as institutions allows us to move
beyond the question of origins and to recognize more clearly the

dialectical relations between secular and spiritual and between persons and institutions.

While I seek to move beyond the question of origins, I do not ignore it. Indeed, the question of origins points to the historical reality in which the aforementioned theoretical reflections are grounded. Following the collapse of the Carolingian state during the tenth and eleventh centuries, bishoprics emerged as one of the most important substitutes for public authority until the emergence of the communes. The bishop's diocesan authority defined the territory over which the communes would later claim political jurisdiction. Episcopal institutions, as the nucleus around which urban interests coalesced, schooled the nascent commune in collective action and administrative techniques. I examine the Carolingian and post-Carolingian roots of these developments in considerable detail in later chapters. For now it is important to reflect more generally on the role of the Carolingian state in structuring relations of power, and on what it means to say that bishoprics functioned as a substitute for it.

Chris Wickham, in his contribution to the recent debate on the feudal revolution in *Past and Present*, offered an insightful analysis of the dialectic between Carolingian institutions and local lordship.[12] While local lords exercised a de facto power based on their armed retainers and political clients, it was still in their interest to connect themselves to the Carolingian state, which gave them access to power that would not have been available to them based solely on their private resources. The Carolingian state thus functioned as a tool for local lords to enhance their own power. At the same time, Carolingian institutions such as *placita*, or public tribunals, established norms that constrained local lordship. Lords who sought to leverage their power through the state had to adapt their behavior to its norms.

Wickham used Pierre Bourdieu's concept of *habitus* to describe this constraining mechanism.[13] According to Bourdieu, *habitus* is an internalization of external power relations. Through repeated involvement in institutions such as Carolingian *placita*, political actors develop an intuitive sense of the possible—what they can and cannot accomplish, or get away with, as they pursue their political and economic interests. The ability, or at least possibility, of local political actors to appeal to an extra-local judicial tribunal created a sense of restraint in the consciousness of local lords. This sense of the possible that directs and constrains political and economic interests is what Wickham refers to as "norms" and what Bourdieu calls a *habitus*. Muir's feedback mechanism belongs to the same semantic field—it is the mechanism that generates norms or *habitus*.

After the collapse of Carolingian authority in Italy, bishoprics emerged as one of the most important generators of norms. As urban elites sought to expand the city's control over the *contado*, the diocese presented itself as the most effective framework for accomplishing this goal. It became the institution through which urban ruling families competed to define the city's jurisdiction. This had important implications for the bishopric. Any individual or group that sought to further its interests through the bishopric, as if it were a field for a multidirectional tug-of-war, felt the collective pull of others seeking to do the same. As a result, there was a very real sense in which the bishopric acted upon—or tugged back at—them. At the risk of complicating the metaphor, the bishopric was more than a neutral field where contestants came to compete. Its own traditions were part of the tug-of-war. For example, the spiritual traditions of the bishopric leveraged the competition in favor of those groups who could cast themselves as reformers or defenders of authentic charisma. While the spiritual traditions of the bishopric could leverage the tug-of-war, they were not above it. The intense struggle between competing groups profoundly changed the bishopric's spiritual ideals.

By recognizing the unique position of the bishopric as a field where a variety of political and religious interests competed, and as a guardian of spiritual traditions, one can better understand why the boundary between sacred and secular "quietly shades into nonexistence" in Italian cities. Urban culture emerged with a set of norms that were deeply infused with spiritual ideals, in part because those competing for political power through the bishopric felt the pull of reformers seeking to use the bishopric to leverage religious interests, and vice versa.

ORVIETO

Orvieto, the picturesque Umbrian hill town that offers the setting for this book, is located approximately one hundred kilometers north of Rome in the northwestern corner of the patrimony of St. Peter, that is, the territory stretching across central Italy over which the papacy claimed political jurisdiction.[14] In certain respects, Orvieto was a typical medium-sized central Italian city. The city's population approached a peak of 14,000 to 17,000 people at the end of the thirteenth century.[15] It is not possible to estimate the size of the population before this date, but patterns of settlement provide unmistakable evidence that by the early twelfth century, Orvieto was a city in bloom.

Although typical in many respects, Orvieto quite literally stood above other cities in the region. Perched atop a volcanic plateau eighty meters above the valley where the Paglia flows from the Tiber, the city was an impregnable fortress. It controlled the valuable grain-producing region of the Val di Lago to the south. Its political influence extended northwest to Acquapendente, which controlled an important section of the Via Francigena, a heavily traveled trade and pilgrim route leading from Rome to Siena and on to France. Rulers had considered the Via Francigena strategically important throughout the Middle Ages. For example, the Lombards chose Lucca as the capital for Tuscany, in part to command the Via Francigena. The road continued to play an important role in that city's politics.[16] For the Orvietans, it was the road that connected local and international politics. Orvieto struggled with popes and emperors throughout the twelfth and thirteenth centuries to control the portion of the Via Francigena that ran through the western portion of their *contado*.

ORGANIZATION OF THE BOOK

The Orvietan bishopric emerged as the principal forum for political competition because it served two important functions for the early commune. It gave the commune its territory, and it schooled the commune in administering it. The first five chapters of this book examine the first function, while the remaining chapters focus primarily on the second. Chapter 1 discusses the Carolingian roots of these developments by examining how Italian bishoprics emerged as centers of urban coalitions looking to conquer their *contado*, or surrounding countryside. Chapters 2 through 5 focus on the bishopric's role in Orvietan territorial expansion during the twelfth century, and the political and religious tensions that resulted, as the bishopric's political entanglements came into conflict with its reform traditions. The remaining chapters, which cover the first half of the thirteenth century, explore how the bishopric and commune developed innovative methods of written administration and record keeping in their quest to renegotiate the relation between the community's religious ideals and political interests. The topic of written administration leads naturally to a discussion of sources.

SOURCES

The principal sources on which I rely are Registers A, B, and C, which are housed in the Archivio Vescovile di Orvieto. With the exception of a few entries in Registers A and C, all of the episcopal records dating before 1248 are contained in Register B. These documents are more than sources. As artifacts of episcopal administration, they are an integral part of the history itself, marking a fundamental transformation in the bishopric and the political and religious dispositions of the Orvietans. As early-thirteenth-century bishops began to pay more attention to their diocese, they commissioned notaries to preserve episcopal documents in the form of registers. The three episcopal registers that form the core of this book are monuments to the influence of legal professionals on the bishopric.

Because the process of enregistering episcopal documents began only in the early decades of the thirteenth century, relatively few eleventh- and twelfth-century documents have survived. When the bishopric first comes into view in the early twelfth century, it is little more than a dance of shadows. The details that one would like to know are often hidden from view. Nevertheless, one can still discern much form and movement, due in large part to the survival of records of oral testimony in a boundary dispute between the bishops of Orvieto and Sovana. In 1194 Pope Celestine III appointed two judges to gather evidence for the claims of each bishop. The judges interviewed fifty-seven witnesses, who reflected on the development of the dispute over the course of the century. These testimonies, which were copied into Register B, provide rich insight into an otherwise poorly documented period in the history of Orvieto.

The number of documents increases dramatically by the early decades of the thirteenth century. Although there are still significant gaps, most noticeably between 1213 and 1228, the bishopric comes into view much more clearly. The increase in the number of documents is no accident. By commissioning notaries to compile registers, the Orvietan bishops made a concerted effort to preserve documents in order to administer their own property more effectively and to assert their authority over the diocese more forcefully. Bishops Giovanni (1211–1212) and Ranerio (1228–1248) each compiled extensive inventories of episcopal property and monitored the movement of this property by recording sales, purchase, and rental contracts. They documented the collection of tithes, the confirmation of clerical appointments to local churches, and disputes with rebellious monasteries, all in an effort to bring the diocese more firmly under their control. In sum, we can observe the thirteenth-century bishopric more clearly because the bishops themselves were paying more attention to it, or at least paying attention to it in more sophisticated ways.

When printed editions of documents from the registers exist, I have cited them immediately following the citation of the register. There are three sources that contain printed editions of documents from the register. In the nineteenth century, Luigi Fumi compiled an edition of Orvietan documents dating from the eleventh to the fifteenth century.[17] Although Fumi was principally interested in the history of the commune, he provided editions of most twelfth-century episcopal documents, largely because practically no twelfth-century communal documents have survived. As extant communal documents become more abundant beginning in the early thirteenth century, his interest in episcopal documents practically disappears. More recently Marlene Polock has edited the records of the boundary dispute between Orvieto and Sovana.[18] Thanks to Fumi and Polock, practically all of the twelfth-century episcopal documents are available in printed editions. As for thirteenth-century documents, Pericle Perali printed an edition of notes that Bishop Ranerio wrote in the margins of Register B.[19] Otherwise, the vast majority of episcopal documents after 1200 do not exist in printed editions.

In addition to Registers A, B, and C, I have used registers of the cathedral chapter and commune. Various edited texts complement these archival sources. The *Passio Beati Petri Parentii Martiris* and the "Processus Canonizationis B. Ambrosii Massanii" are important narrative sources for the development of the commune's political and religious culture. Finally, I have used numerous papal documents and biographies to shed light on papal interests in Orvieto, a crucial aspect of the history of the Orvietan bishopric.

FROM CHARISMA TO BUREAUCRACY: ORVIETO AND HIGH-MEDIEVAL EUROPE

The implications of this book reach far beyond Italian cities to address issues that are central to one of the defining developments of high-medieval Europe. Between 1100 and 1250, the chronological boundaries of this study, Europeans rulers sought to expand territorial authority and centralize jurisdiction through innovative bureaucratic mechanisms. At the same time, the feverish activity of clergy and laity produced one of the most intense periods of ecclesiastical reform in the history of the church. This competition and cooperation between lords, priests, and prophets resulted in a fundamental transformation in medieval European society, which several historians have recently characterized as a transition from charisma to bureaucracy. Michael T. Clanchy has called attention to the emergence of a literate mentality, which included the habit of using written documentation, as an important manifestation of this transformation. In his description of Henry II's growing reliance on documents, Clanchy writes, "Henry II used a system of standardized writs to automate and depersonalize the legal process. Without being aware of it, Henry had achieved what Weber describes as 'the routinization of charisma.'"[20] One can see similar efforts toward written administration and bureaucratization in France under Philip II.[21]

The historian C. Stephen Jaeger described the transition from eleventh- to twelfth-century intellectual culture in similar terms— from charismatic to intellectual—noting that this transition was part of a more fundamental transformation that included "an essential shift in the exercise of political power . . . from itinerant to 'administrative kingship' and in church administration from . . . 'charismatic leadership' to canonical procedure in the election of bishops and abbots."[22] In the sphere of church administration, one might add the Fourth Lateran Council as the culmination of an attempt to routinize the charisma that eleventh-century reformers sought to infuse into the church. Jaeger characterized this broad transformation from charisma to bureaucracy as "crisis control."[23] The disintegration of the Carolingian Empire caused the crisis. As Europeans responded to the crisis, they weighed the relative merits of embodied charisma and authority—in the cathedral master, the king, and the priest—and the routinization of this charisma in the text and bureaucratic institutions—in the summa, the writ, canonical legislation, city-states, and national kingdoms. During the twelfth and thirteenth centuries, an increasing number of Europeans chose the latter over the former. This transformation from charisma to bureaucracy, whether in Italy, France, or England, was nothing other than the development of a civil society—the development of institutional mechanisms for regulating private power and generating norms that would provide a basis for social order. A careful local study that focuses on the development of episcopal institutions has much to add to an understanding of the growing preference for the text and bureaucratic institutions over the person, for so many aspects of the transformation from charisma to bureaucracy—territorial expansion, ecclesiastical reform, bureaucratic innovations, and written administration—collided within the institutional field of the bishopric.

CHAPTER ONE

CAROLINGIAN BEGINNINGS

ELEVENTH- AND TWELFTH-CENTURY ITALIANS WERE ENGAGED
in a quest for order. Admittedly this is true of every society that has
ever existed. Nevertheless, there are times when a society's political
institutions disintegrate to such an extent that the quest for order
becomes all-consuming and frustratingly elusive. Such was the condition of central and northern Italy between the late ninth and twelfth
centuries. A Carolingian system, which preserved many elements of
the preceding Lombard system of rule, prevailed until the death of
Louis II in 875. After his reign, Carolingian institutions began to disintegrate, inaugurating a reconfiguration of Italian politics and society
that continued into the early thirteenth century. Communal formation represents the culmination of this process of reconfiguration.

The difficult period between the collapse of Carolingian authority and communal formation was filled with violent and seemingly
interminable conflicts. One can, however, detect order emerging
from the chaos. These conflicts were part of a multilevel process of
political formation in which bishops—allied with urban elites—
competed with signorial lords for local authority, while popes and
German kings competed and sometimes cooperated to create a
broader territorial state to replace that of the Carolingians. During

13

this transitional period, when popes and kings were too weak to restore order, bishoprics emerged as the most useful institutions for rebuilding public authority at the local level. The enduring influence of bishoprics on communal political and religious culture finds its origins in the period of episcopal lordship that bridged Carolingian Italy and the world of the communes.

Bishoprics emerged as substitutes for Carolingian authority by the early eleventh century because they performed two important functions for their nascent urban communities. First, a bishopric's diocesan jurisdiction and landed wealth made it the most useful tool for local urban elites to expand their authority over the surrounding countryside. Second, bishoprics tutored early communes in the art of administration by virtue of their close working relation with notaries and judges. In order to understand how bishoprics assumed these functions, this chapter will examine the role of bishoprics in the Carolingian state and trace the development of notaries and judges from the Carolingian period.

THE ITALIAN KINGDOM UNDER THE CAROLINGIANS

Central Authority in the Early Middle Ages:
Challenges and Strategies

The fundamental challenge for early medieval rulers was to gain consent from local ruling elites. This proved to be a formidable challenge for the early medieval state because of the nature of the transition from the later Roman Empire to the successor kingdoms. On the one hand, the state entered the early Middle Ages greatly simplified and weakened. The land tax, which allowed the Roman Empire to expropriate the lion's share of surplus wealth, disappeared by the Lombard period. Much of the civilian bureaucracy, from the highest offices in the imperial court to local city councils, was absorbed into a military command structure that was an amalgamation of Roman and barbarian military institutions. The limited rights that cities retained, including administration of common land and public works, care of churches, and local defense, passed to bishops.[1] On the other hand, an entirely new aristocracy emerged with fewer incentives for granting their consent to the state. The senatorial aristocracy disappeared in the midst of the Lombard invasion. Some senators met a violent end while others fled to Sicily or to the East. In their place, military commanders emerged as the ruling elite. Their power, like that of the old senatorial class, was based in landed wealth; but this landed wealth—and hence their power—was more localized.

These developments made it difficult for early medieval kings to maintain centralized authority. With the disappearance of a land tax, the bulk of Italy's surplus wealth in the Lombard region remained at the local level and was concentrated in the hands of the new class of aristocratic warriors. Lombard dukes, who represented the most serious threat to royal authority, could, and did, act independently of the state when it served their interests. The first half-century of Lombard rule in Italy is a testimony to this fact. In the areas that remained under Byzantine control, there was a militarization and localization of the aristocracy as well. The tendency toward localization of power, however, was not as pronounced. The essential difference was that many Roman public institutions, including the land tax, remained in effect.[2]

Lombard kings learned to manage these challenges to centralized authority remarkably well by the early seventh century. Agilulf (590–616) moved aggressively against northern dukes and gained the upper hand. Strong kings like Rothar (636–652) and Liutprand (712–744) were able to maintain this hard-won advantage, in part by using the *gastaldate* as a counterweight to ducal authority. They prevented dukes and *gastalds* from establishing hereditary control over their offices.[3] The army was composed of *arimanni*, a class of free peasant warriors that owed military obligations directly to the state, unmediated by lordship or feudal obligations.[4]

Lombard kings fortified central authority with an increasingly sophisticated system of law and administration. Rothar's edict of 643 formed the basis of one of the most highly developed bodies of Germanic law.[5] As kings like Liutprand introduced elements of Roman procedural law, such as testimony and written documents as forms of proof, Lombard law increased in subtlety and sophistication. Pavia, the capital of the kingdom, was home to a sophisticated court and had become a cultural center under the patronage of cultivated kings.[6] Perhaps because these strategies proved sufficient, or because the relation between Lombard rulers and the church developed rather slowly, Lombard kings were not inclined to use ecclesiastical institutions as a tool for state building. Bishops had no recognizably public function apart from their role in the ecclesiastical hierarchy. They had little influence at the royal court. Lombard kings did not concern themselves with calling councils to deal with ecclesiastical matters.[7]

The Lombard State and the Carolingians

When Charlemagne conquered the Lombard kingdom in 774, he took over a state that was, arguably, stronger and more sophisticated than his own. He maintained the capital at Pavia and continued to rule through Lombard institutions and Lombard law.[8] He allowed most of the Lombard ruling class to remain in place as well. Rather than remove Lombard officials immediately, he changed the composition of the ruling class by attrition. It was fortunate that the Carolingians inherited such a strong state, for until the reign of Louis II (844–875), their attention often was distracted by events north of the Alps. Charlemagne visited Italy four times between the conquest in 774 and his death in 814 (in 776, 780–781, 786–787, and 800–801). In 781 he crowned his four-year-old son, Pippin, subking of Italy. Thus, for approximately a decade, Charlemagne ruled Italy through a group of loyal Frankish aristocrats serving as guardians for Pippin. Pippin ruled until 810, when his son Bernard succeeded him. Bernard rebelled in 817, fearing that his position was not as secure under his uncle, Louis the Pious, as it had been under Charlemagne. When Bernard finally submitted in 818, Louis the Pious had him blinded. Bernard died from the wounds and Lothar assumed the crown of Italy. Lothar's attention was diverted from Italy as well, as his reign was punctuated by a series of rebellions against his father. One of the largest waves of Frankish immigration to Italy came in 834, after Lothar's second rebellion against his father failed. Lothar was allowed to return to Italy, where he had to find estates and offices for his supporters, who had lost positions and wealth north of the Alps. For this reason, the gradual transformation of the ruling class from Lombard to Frank culminated during Lothar's reign.[9]

Despite the distractions that often prevented Carolingian rulers from focusing their attention on Italy, they built upon the strengths of the Italian kingdom. By the middle decades of the ninth century, loyal Frankish aristocrats had largely replaced Lombard dukes and *gastalds*. The royal fisc was solid, as Carolingian kings rarely granted land to followers from their Italian possessions. When Lothar rewarded his supporters in 834, he did so largely by secularizing ecclesiastical land. Carolingian kings built upon the foundation of Lombard legislation and made important innovations in the administration of justice. Charlemagne, Pippin, and Lothar legislated on a wide variety of topics in their Italian capitularies. General legislation, such as the capitulary of Herstal, *Admonitio Generalis*, and the capitularies of 803, 805, and 818–819, made a strong impression in Italy as well. The Carolingian kings held assemblies in which Lombard aristocrats and bishops participated in making policy.[10]

Carolingian Innovations: Ecclesiastical Policy and Judicial Administration

While Charlemagne kept the Lombard state intact, he introduced important innovations in the ongoing struggle to maintain central authority. In contrast to Lombard kings, the Carolingians found it expedient to use ecclesiastical institutions as a buttress for the state. They worked hard to strengthen secular institutions as well. For the purposes of this book, the most important of these efforts was the development of a class of secular legal professionals that were entrusted with the exercise of justice.

Carolingian ecclesiastical policy was grounded in political realities. While Lombard kings allowed little room for the church in royal administration, a convergence of interests between bishops and military aristocrats at the local level made it increasingly difficult to ignore the importance of ecclesiastical institutions. The clearest and earliest examples of this convergence are found in regions under Byzantine control, especially Ravenna and Rome, where bishops transformed the local military aristocracy into a network of clients by leasing ecclesiastical property to them.[11] While the church suffered during the early Lombard period, it began to rebuild its landed wealth during the seventh century. By the early eighth century, the interests of bishops and local Lombard officials had converged as well. For example, the Lombard *gastald* of Siena, along with local *exercitales*, vigorously defended the bishop's claims to baptismal churches located in a disputed region between the dioceses of Siena and Arezzo. While the Lombard court had little interest in ecclesiastical affairs, local officials and military aristocrats could no more afford to be indifferent about diocesan boundaries than the bishop.[12] Likewise, the close relationship between Lombard aristocrats and Luccan bishops in the early eighth century was responsible for a period of rapid growth in the diocese of Lucca.[13]

When Charlemagne took over the Italian kingdom in 774, he realized that the church could play an important role as a buttress for royal power. On a general level he felt that political unity and religious/cultural unity went hand in hand. Therefore he made great efforts to reform the clergy and make them an integral part of the state.[14] He also recognized the natural convergence between local aristocratic power and ecclesiastical property. After all, his ancestors built their dynasty, at least in part, on such a convergence. Thus, Charlemagne and his successors recognized the necessity of managing this convergence lest it compromise royal authority at the local level.[15]

Immunities provide a good example. Charlemagne and his successors granted numerous immunities to bishoprics and monasteries throughout Italy, forbidding public officials from exercising justice and exacting fines or other dues and services of a public nature from a bishopric's or monastery's property and dependents.[16] While the Carolingian policy of granting immunities was not new—the policy dates back to the Merovingians—it assumed a new dimension and significance in the ninth century as ecclesiastical landowning grew through royal and private donations. Carolingian rulers had two closely related goals as they granted immunities. First, they recognized that local officials often behaved aggressively toward the church, seeking to expand their families' wealth and power by gaining control over ecclesiastical property.[17] A grant of immunity would provide a measure of protection to the local church. At the same time, Carolingians attempted to reduce the threat to royal authority posed by families seeking to exploit ecclesiastical property to build a strong base of local power. Immunities enhanced episcopal power at the local level, but it is worth noting that this power was already firmly rooted in the military aristocracy's convergence around the bishop. Immunities conferred a public sanction to the bishop's power in order to channel it toward the state.

While Charlemagne incorporated bishops into some aspects of the state's ruling apparatus, he limited it in others. In judicial administration, he chose to rely on a class of lay professionals. He laid a foundation for improvements in the administration of justice in both the Frankish and Italian kingdoms with the institution of *scabini*, a permanent body of assessors chosen by *missi* to accompany the count on his judicial circuit. They were instituted north of the Alps in the 770s in order to replace the Merovingian *rachimburgii* with a more highly qualified body of legal assessors.[18] In Italy, where they appear more frequently by 810, *scabini* gradually replaced officials variously known as *sculdahis*, *locopositi*, and *lociservatores*, who performed judicial and policing functions under the authority of the local *gastald*, who was himself a royal administrative and judicial officer.[19] The level of training for *sculdahis* often was low. As late as the mid-eighth century, many *sculdahis* were unable to sign their names to documents issued by tribunals. Instead, they indicated their presence by making a cross next to a notarial formula, which included the phrase *signum manus* plus their name.[20]

The initial impact of the reform was slight—those who were formerly designated as *sculdahis* simply changed their title to *scabini*. The long-term impact was significant. Italian *scabini* became an increasingly knowledgeable body of legal professionals during the course of the ninth century. Counts, bishops, or *missi* who presided over tribunals increasingly assumed an honorary role, contributing solemnity to the tribunal by their presence, but not taking an active role in the judicial process. The real work of applying the law and rendering judgment increasingly fell to *scabini*. By the late ninth and early tenth centuries, *scabini* were typically notaries, a clear indication of the extent to which local tribunals had become professionalized.

A look at the diminishing role of bishops and clergy in judicial administration highlights Carolingian efforts to entrust the exercise of justice to lay professionals. In criminal matters, the bishop's role in the eighth century was confined, as one might expect, to overseeing men in clerical orders and to addressing questions of moral conduct, such as illicit unions and the conduct of widows.[21] The bishop's role in lay justice was to pronounce canonical penances for crimes, such as murder and perjury, that were tried in the count's tribunal. Counts, in turn, were expected to enforce penitential sentences and excommunications.[22] One area in which the bishop's sphere of activity widened was the right to conduct inquests. The task of

conducting inquests into criminal offenses among the local population originally belonged exclusively to local judges, acting on behalf
of the count.[23] By the beginning of the ninth century, bishops were
given the task of conducting inquests into criminal offenses as
well.[24]

Italian *placita*, or tribunals, provide an especially interesting picture of how the role of bishops and clergy in judicial administration
diminished over time, as Charlemagne's successors fostered the
development of lay notaries and judges. The vast majority of surviv-
ing *placita* record land disputes that were brought before the local
tribunal of a count, bishop, or other local representative of royal
authority.[25] Until the mid-ninth century, it was not uncommon for
placita to be held in the bishop's residence, or *domus ecclesie*, with
the bishop presiding over a tribunal composed of clerical *scabini* and
scribes/notaries. In some cities, such as Lucca, Pisa, Milan, Verona,
Florence, and Siena, the bishop's *domus* was practically the only
place where *placita* were held.[26] *Placita* held in the bishop's residence represent the perfect convergence of form and function. This
domus, a fortified house attached to the bishop's church with no
architectural features that would distinguish it as an ecclesiastical
structure, was modeled after residences of lay nobles. It was, in
effect, the architectural expression of the bishop's position as one
who had assumed the burdens of secular power.[27]

Control over *placita* began to shift from bishops to counts and
dukes during the early decades of the ninth century, reaching its culmination by the mid-ninth century.[28] Several developments contributed to this shift. This is the period when the insertion of
Frankish aristocrats into the ruling class of the Italian kingdom
reaches its culmination. Those families that came to Italy during
Charlemagne's reign had firmly established their roots by this time.
Moreover, Lothar returned to Italy in 834, or rather was banished
there, following his unsuccessful rebellion against his father. A host
of Frankish aristocrats, in need of offices, followed in his train.
Lothar, in particular, seems to have promoted the shift toward secular *placita*.[29] Equally important was the fact that Charlemagne's judicial reforms had matured by the mid-ninth century. *Scabini* had
become a group of lay professionals—usually notaries—that performed the essential functions of the tribunal under the presiding
official. Clerical *scabini* virtually disappeared by the late ninth cen-

tury. While some *placita* continued to be held in the *domus ecclesie*, most were held in the *curtis ducalis*, or court of the count or duke.[30] Thus, while bishops played a large role in *placita* until the early ninth century, Carolingians gradually limited their role by increasingly assigning the administration of justice to a class of lay professionals.

Notaries constitute one of the most important classes of lay professionals to emerge under the Carolingians. Because they will play such an important role in episcopal administration and communal formation, it is worth looking at early developments in the Italian notariate from the later Roman Empire through the Carolingian period. In the later Roman period, private documents were written by *tabelliones*, who worked at *stationes* in the market or public square. Unlike imperial notaries or other professional writers working for members of the imperial bureaucracy, *tabelliones* were not officials of the state. Nevertheless, public officials closely regulated them. Those who wanted to preserve records of testaments or private contracts could have a *tabellio* draw up a document and have it deposited in a public archive. *Tabelliones* continued to function in the Middle Ages in areas outside of Lombard control, most notably Ravenna and Rome.

There was little continuity with Roman institutions in Lombard regions, although bishops continued to have their documents redacted by episcopal notaries, who were usually members of the diocesan clergy. Episcopal notaries redacted private documents as well, but these private documents carried no official authority. Rather, private parties simply hired them as men who were skilled in the art of producing documents. Indeed, the Lombards did not place any legal limitations on who could produce documents. Therefore, in addition to episcopal notaries, a wide variety of lay writers produced private documents. Some of these writers designated themselves as scribes or notaries; others bore no designation at all. The only notaries with a public function, the *notarii regis* attached to the king, did not produce private documents.[31] As eighth-century Lombard kings became increasingly concerned with the probative value of private documents, they focused their attention on regulating the content of documents rather than the class of people who produced them.[32] Nevertheless, it appears that a group of public scribes were beginning to emerge by the final decades of the Lombard kingdom.[33]

Building upon these developments, Carolingian kings devoted attention to creating a stable class of notaries and a consistent framework within which written documents could be used. Lothar instructed his *missi* to choose notaries who were trained in law and whose reputations were beyond reproach.[34] The request that notaries be trained in law was not entirely unrealistic, as legal training, admittedly at a rudimentary level, was probably available as part of the study of rhetoric at the palace school. Charlemagne brought Dungal, an Irish scholar, to preside over a palace school at Pavia. It was there, and in the royal chancery, that the highest grade of notaries—variously designated as *notarii domini regis, notarii domini imperatoris,* or *notarii sacri palatii*—probably received their training. These royal notaries sat as judges and redacted documents throughout the kingdom as they accompanied royal *missi* on their circuit.

In addition to the royal notaries attached to the palace, Charlemagne established a group of notaries whose activities were firmly rooted in the county. In his *capitulare missorum* of 803, he commanded *missi* to appoint notaries as well as *scabini* for each locality.[35] In Italy, unlike the areas north of the Alps, a permanent body of comital notaries emerged.[36] In contrast to royal notaries, they could not redact documents beyond the boundaries of the county without the count's permission. They were commanded to write their documents in the presence of the count or his representatives (*scabini* or vicars). In special cases—for example, when the person for whom the notary redacted the document was sick and could not come before the count or his representatives—the notary could redact a document without a comital official present; but he had to take it immediately to the bishop, the count, or the count's representatives to have it officially acknowledged as authentic. Otherwise, notaries were exhorted not to make documents in secret.[37]

Recognizing that such tasks required more broadly diffused educational institutions, Lothar tried to establish a system of regional schools at Turin, Cremona, Florence, Verona, Fermo, and Vicenza. It is unlikely that this legislation produced significant results. Nevertheless, it is clear that rudimentary training was available beyond the royal palace in cathedral schools and scriptoria in places like Verona, Lucca, and Arezzo.[38] This training provided a sufficient level of familiarity with the law to allow a growing number of *scabini* to be drawn from the notariate.

POST-CAROLINGIAN ITALY

Carolingian kings lost their ability to control these developments in the episcopate and judicial apparatus by the late ninth century. In 882 Charles the Fat presided over a council of Italian bishops in Ravenna alongside Pope John VIII. After the council he issued a diploma to the bishop of Arezzo. The diploma addressed the problem of local officials that violated ecclesiastical immunities by demanding free men living on church lands to attend their *placita* and to render public dues and services. Similar diplomas issued on the same occasion to Verona and Cremona indicate that these problems were not isolated to Arezzo.[39] The tools that had proved useful for maintaining order in the eighth and early ninth centuries escaped royal control, leaving local politics to develop in an increasingly autonomous fashion. After decades of civil war, central authority disintegrated and counties fragmented into urban-centered episcopal lordships surrounded by a host of signorial lords in the countryside that fought to build quasi-public authority upon the fragments of the old county.

Civil War and the Disintegration of Royal Authority

Louis II was the last Carolingian king to rule the Italian kingdom effectively. He came to Italy in 844 to rule as subking under his father, Lothar. In 850 he assumed the imperial title, but he continued to devote his attention to Italy. He ruled from Pavia through a well-developed bureaucracy. The royal fisc remained strong throughout his reign. Louis continued to issue legislation and was able to call the aristocracy to arms on numerous occasions. He led expeditions against the Arabs in southern Italy in 846 and 848. He successfully mustered troops for campaigns in Benevento in 848 and 866. *Missi*, counts, and bishops behaved like functionaries of the state for the most part. His attempts to impose order on the chaos of southern Italy, however, provoked a response, as Benevento, Salerno, Naples, and Spoleto allied against him. He was taken prisoner by Adelchis of Benevento in 871. Deeply disappointed by the failure of his policies in southern Italy, he died four years later without a male heir.[40]

After Louis's death in 875, the Italian kingdom began to disintegrate under the absentee rule of Charles the Bald and Charles the Fat, whose attentions were consumed by civil war and Viking raids north of the Alps. The inability of Charles the Fat to meet these challenges led to a rebellion of western Frankish aristocrats, who chose Odo, the count of Paris, as king of the west Franks. In Italy, the deposition of Charles the Fat in 887 was followed by over seventy years of civil war and instability, which saw a dizzying array of contenders vying for the throne.

The first two contenders were Berengar of Friuli and Guy of Spoleto, both descendents of Frankish aristocrats who had settled in Italy and established close relations to the throne by marrying Carolingian brides. It looked as though Berengar I had consolidated his hold on the throne in 898 with the death of Lambert of Spoleto, who had continued to press his claim to the throne after his father's death in 895. When Hungarians raided in northern Italy in 899 and destroyed Berengar's army, Italians began looking for a more power-ful protector, offering the crown to Louis of Provence in 900. Be-rengar disposed of Louis by 905 and ruled unopposed until the final years of his reign, despite his continued inability to provide protection against the Hungarians. Opposition against Berengar mounted once again in 920, when he hired Hungarian mercenaries to strengthen his army. Magnates in the northwest called upon Rudolf II, king of Burgundy, who defeated Berengar in 923. One year later, Berengar was assassinated, perhaps in response to the sack of Pavia by the Hungarians. Rudolf lasted only one year before Italians called on Hugh of Arles to assume the throne.

Hugh made a concerted effort to rebuild royal authority, but the process of disintegration had advanced too far to be reversed. Support for Hugh among lay aristocrats quickly faded, as Hugh rewarded members of his own family at their expense. When threatened from the north by Arnulf of Bavaria, Hugh had to rely almost entirely on bishops. Such support was not sufficient to withstand the assault of Berengar II of Ivrea, the grandson of Berengar I. Although Berengar had married Hugh's daughter—part of Hugh's strategy of rebuilding royal authority through family connections—he was forced, in 941, to take refuge from Hugh at the court of Otto the Great in Germany. In 945 he crossed the Alps and gathered sufficient support among Italian aristocrats to force Hugh to flee to Provence. Following the death of Hugh in 947 and Hugh's son, Lambert, in 950, Berengar II was able to consolidate his hold on the throne.

Only one year later, Otto I descended into Italy and had himself crowned king of Italy. Otto had several compelling reasons for coming to Italy. In 950 Berengar had Hugh's widow, Adelaide, imprisoned, recognizing that if Adelaide were to remarry, her husband would have a legitimate claim to the throne. Her imprisonment outraged a faction of Italian nobles, as well as Adelaide's brother, Conrad, king of upper Burgundy, who appealed to Otto for help. Italy had already gained Otto's attention, for dukes from the southern portions of his kingdom, such as Arnulf of Bavaria, had meddled in Italian affairs, seeking to build an independent base of authority. Otto descended into Italy in 951, put Berengar to flight, married Adelaide, and assumed the throne. Given Otto's inability to remain in Italy, due to pressing concerns in Germany, Berengar was able to work his way back into Italy as subking under Otto's overlordship. Berengar soon began to assert his authority too independently, drawing Otto back to Italy in 962. Otto removed Berengar and had himself crowned emperor.[41] Although he was considered a strong ruler, Otto could only make his influence felt in Italy when he was physically present. The political center of gravity in Italy had become intensely local.

The Fragmentation of Local Authority:
From County to City and Countryside

Damage to royal authority caused by civil war is already apparent in the records by the first decade of Berengar I's reign. Royal legislation stops after 898. The only documents flowing out of the royal chancery were diplomas that granted privileges to a variety of aristocrats and prelates. In Berengar's diplomas, one can see the kingdom melt away. Unable to count on support from public officials amidst fierce competition for the throne, he began to parcel out royal resources in order to build a reliable network of support.[42] He gave away royal estates, forests, judicial rights, and tolls from roads, ports, and markets. He granted numerous charters that allowed bishops, monasteries, and lay aristocrats to construct castles, in part to compensate for his inability to provide adequate defense against the Hungarians.[43] He confirmed old charters of immunity and granted new charters to loyal supporters, including numerous bishops. In the most extensive of these grants, he relinquished all fiscal rights and gave complete immunity to the bishop of Cremona for the territory encompassing the city and a five-mile stretch of countryside surrounding the city.[44] By the time Berengar died in 924, he had impoverished the royal fisc and hastened the fragmentation of the counties throughout the kingdom. Jurisdiction within the city increasingly fell to the bishop, as in the case of the bishop of Cremona. *Incastellamento* charters, which granted the right to build castles, reinforced the fragmentation of authority in the countryside among competing lay and ecclesiastical lords.[45]

Developments in judicial administration provide an interesting picture of the attempt and ultimate failure to arrest this fragmentation. As royal authority weakened in the late ninth century, Carolingian and post-Carolingian rulers sought to reinforce their authority by asserting control more directly over the exercise of justice. Because early Carolingian rulers often were unable to focus their attention on Italian affairs, it should come as no surprise that they rarely presided over tribunals in person. From Charlemagne's reign to that of Louis II, it was customary for Carolingian kings to receive requests for royal justice and to delegate the resolution of disputes to bishops, counts, or *missi*, who acted as royal representatives. By the 880s Charles the Fat, Berengar I, Hugh, and Lothar presided over a growing number of *placita*.[46]

Equally important for attempts to reassert royal authority through judicial administration was the appearance, around 850, of a new class of royal judges that emerged from the royal notaries connected to the palace. These judges bore the title *iudex domini regis/imperatoris*, possibly indicating a *cursus honorum*, whereby the king officially recognized a group of royal notaries as an elite group of legal experts by virtue of their training at the palace school in Pavia.[47] As early-tenth-century kings sought to resist the disintegration of royal authority, they attempted to establish control over local judicial administration by replacing local *scabini* with *iudices domini regis*. In northern Italy and Tuscany, the process of substitution was largely complete by 960. Likewise, royal notaries began to replace comital notaries, as they settled in northern Italian and Tuscan cities during the late tenth century and redacted a growing number of court documents and private contracts. Comital notaries disappear by the eleventh century.[48]

Despite these attempts to bolster centralized authority over judicial administration, local forces ultimately prevailed. By the mid-tenth century, and certainly by the reign of Otto II, the title *iudex domini regis*, as well as the title *notarius domini regis*, began to proliferate, indicating that instead of filling the kingdom with judges and notaries trained in Pavia, kings began to recruit locally trained judges and notaries. The geography of *placita* reinforces the impression that judicial administration was drawn into the logic of local autonomy. By the late tenth century, practically all *placita* over which kings or royal officials presided were held outside city walls. Court sessions inside the city were increasingly held in private houses of prominent citizens, often judges. This important development in the geography of *placita* reflects the fact that during the late tenth and early eleventh centuries, royal, ducal, and comital palaces were often relocated outside the walls of the city, an indication that both royal authority and the county as a unit of jurisdiction were losing their control over cities.[49]

Important changes in the redaction of private documents offer another indicator of the fragmentation of public authority. Royal judges and notaries were only nominally subordinated to the sovereign by the early eleventh century. The locus of authority that conferred validity upon private documents shifted from the administrative and judicial apparatus of the emperor, king, or count (of which the notary was a functionary) to the notary himself. The notary became the source of *publica fides*, that is, any document that the notary executed was legally valid, regardless of whether it was executed in the presence of a royal or comital official.[50] This growing autonomy is manifest in a fundamental transformation in the form of private notarial documents.[51] The change in form was characterized by a shift from the *charta* to the *instrumentum*. The *charta*, the typical format for private documents in the early Middle Ages, was written in the first person and contained subscriptions or autographs of the principal actors and witnesses. The autographs contained in the *charta* and the execution of the document in the presence of a royal or comital official offered assurances of its authenticity. The *instrumentum* followed the style of the *notitia*, or judicial record, which was written in the third person and contained only a list of witnesses, not their autographs.[52] As royal and comital authority disintegrated, notaries became the principal guarantors of a document's trustworthiness.

CENTRAL AND LOCAL AUTHORITY IN THE ELEVENTH CENTURY

These developments in judicial administration reflect the fragmentation of the county into city and countryside. Immunities and the liquidation of the royal fisc, both of which tended to benefit ecclesiastical entities, weakened both royal and comital authority. What was left of royal and comital authority was pushed into the countryside, where it continued to disintegrate in the face of signorial forces. In cities, bishoprics emerged at the center of a coalition of urban elites that included knights and legal professionals. This raises the question of why the burden of political power increasingly fell on bishoprics as central authority collapsed.

Central Authority: Emperors and Popes

It seemed as though royal authority revived under Otto I. No rivals in Italy were capable of challenging him militarily. He issued legislation and worked to restore comital authority, though his privileges to bishops were counterproductive and undermined comital authority. If the Ottonians and their Salian successors had been capable of residing in Italy, perhaps the task of rebuilding the Italian kingdom would have been successful; but German kings were too occupied with building royal authority in Germany to make their presence felt consistently in Italy. From 950 to 1050 German kings spent little more than twenty years in Italy—over half of them during the reigns of Otto I and Otto III. In their absence, kings could do little more than depend on coalitions of local magnates and cities. From the experience of Conrad II (1024–1039), it was clear that kings could not rule through local factions; rather, local factions used royal support to pursue their own local interests.[53] Not until Frederick Barbarossa came to the throne in 1152 would Italy see a concerted effort to rebuild royal authority.

In central Italy the papacy was another source of central authority that lay dormant in the eleventh century. Papal efforts to rebuild authority over central Italy in the twelfth century later would have a tremendous influence on Orvietan politics and religion; it is therefore worth looking at the papal state in the early Middle Ages and its place in the broader developments of Carolingian and post-Carolingian Italy discussed thus far. After the Lombard invasions of the late sixth century, Rome remained under Byzantine control. The Roman duchy, which stretched about ninety kilometers north and south of Rome and which bordered the independent Lombard duchies of Benevento to the south and Spoleto to the east, was under the authority of the Byzantine exarch of Ravenna. Despite significant differences between Byzantine and Lombard institutions, underlying developments in the nature of power were similar throughout Italy. Territories under Byzantine control experienced a militarization of civil authority. Nowhere was the convergence of interests between bishops and military aristocrats more pronounced than in the Roman duchy. This convergence of interests had important consequences, for as issues of doctrine and spiritual authority made the relation between popes and Byzantine emperors increasingly bitter, the Roman duchy's military aristocracy chose to support the former over the latter. The Roman duchy had become, for all intents and purposes, an autonomous state by the early eighth century.[54] This claim to autonomy received legitimacy through a series of negotiations and treaties with Pippin III and Charlemagne. Moreover, Charlemagne extended papal control beyond the Roman duchy to include much of the territory formerly controlled by the Byzantines.[55]

Especially important for our purposes is Charlemagne's decision to extend the boundaries of the Roman duchy into Lombard Tuscany. Because this region included Orvieto, it is worth taking a closer look at its political boundaries. The Lombards established two duchies in Tuscany when they took control of central Italy in the late sixth century: Lucca in the north and Chiusi in the south. The duchy of Chiusi included Orvieto. To the south lay Roman Tuscany, which constituted the northern territory of the duchy of Rome.[56] The boundary separating Lombard from Roman Tuscany remained fluid throughout the early middle ages. Shortly after Charlemagne conquered the Lombard kingdom in 774, he detached a portion of southern and coastal Lombard Tuscany, including Orvieto and Sovana (a town that will play an important role later in this book), and added it to the Roman duchy.[57] Charlemagne kept the remainder of the Lombard kingdom for himself and his successors.

Central authority in the papal state deteriorated earlier than in the Italian kingdom. By the first decade of the tenth century, while

Berengar was consolidating his hold on the throne, Theophylact, a leader of the Roman military aristocracy, established his control in Rome and over the papacy. Apart from occasional interventions by Ottonian rulers, Rome and the papacy remained under the control of local families until the emergence of the reform papacy 150 years later. Roman ambitions became more localized in the process. Evidence suggests that public officials from Rome continued to exercise at least a degree of authority in Campagna and Sabina, but the papacy possessed neither the resources nor the administrative structure to enforce its authority beyond these regions.[58] This is certainly the case in the northern patrimony. In 817 Louis the Pious confirmed earlier agreements that extended papal control into Lombard Tuscany, as did Otto I in 962 and Henry II in 1020.[59] Despite the appearance of continuity suggested by these imperial confirmations, the rulers of the Italian kingdom did not consistently recognize papal jurisdiction in the portion of Lombard Tuscany granted to the papacy. For example, Sovana appears in some early-tenth-century documents as a county that recognized papal jurisdiction, while in other documents it appears without the status of a county, under the jurisdiction of Chiusi, which remained part of the Italian kingdom.[60] Orvieto drifted toward the jurisdiction of the southernmost counties of the Italian kingdom as well. Only with efforts by twelfth-century popes to rebuild their authority in Roman Tuscany did papal authority start to become a reality in Orvieto. Until then, Roman Tuscany felt the full force of the disintegration of central authority and the fragmentation of comital jurisdiction.

Local Power: Signorial Lords and Bishops

As central authority collapsed, two competitors emerged to redefine the nature of authority at the local level. The countryside fractured into a series of signorial lordships. In the city, urban elites coalesced around bishops to protect the interests of the urban community. Signorial lordship was a novel combination of landlordship, that is, the authority that a landowner exercised over his tenants, and quasi-public powers, or rights exercised over nontenants, such as the right to exercise justice and demand military service. It originated from a convergence of political and economic forces. Royal policies during the ninth and tenth centuries did much to hasten the disintegration of comital authority in the countryside. *Incastellamento* charters allowed bishops, monasteries, and lay lords to build castles that were often immune from comital authority. In Tuscany, Berengar I began to install counts in cities, where previously there had been none, in order to combat the virtual autonomy of the Tuscan marquis. Hugh and Otto I continued these policies. As a result, a new group of comital families emerged, such as the Guidi, Cadolingi, and Gherardeschi, whose power would last well into the communal period. While office holding contributed to their power, these newly created comital jurisdictions were fragile and were quickly converted into family possessions with no further connection to the state. As partible inheritance scattered public land and jurisdiction across branches of these families, the comital title became an honorary designation of status. Their real source of power was castle lordship. Thus, several paths—*incastellamento* charters, grants of immunity, and the creation of new comital jurisdictions—led to the same destination, namely, the fragmentation of public authority among a variety of rural lords, whose authority was centered on castles.[61] While the emergence of castle-centered signorial lordships was most intense in Lazio, its impact on Roman and Lombard Tuscany was significant as well.[62]

Economic developments worked in the same direction. The manorial system broke down during the tenth century as partible inheritance made the traditional system of landlordship incoherent. Portions of a single village often came under the authority of different landlords. Manors consisted of widely scattered parcels, woven into a patchwork containing portions of other manors and peasant allods.[63] While many of Berengar's *incastellamento* charters refer to the Hungarian threat as the justification for granting such privileges, it is clear that castles were also used as tools for reorganizing the countryside in response to the disintegration of the traditional manor. Holders of *incastellamento* and immunity charters, along with newly created comital dynasties, used control of castles to transform the countryside into a more coherent group of territorial lordships. Settlement patterns changed from widely dispersed groupings of peasants to concentrated settlements in and around castles.

In some cases, the formation of castle communities was a peaceful process, based on a contract between a lord and the castle community. It could, however, be violent and disruptive, creating intense competition among magnates to establish signorial lord-ships. People were uprooted, as allod holders and tenants alike were under intense pressure to surrender to the domination of castle lords. As royal and comital authority disintegrated, there were few institutional mechanisms for regulating this competition. Herein lies the importance of bishoprics for their urban communities.

Bishoprics were well positioned to function as substitutes for comital authority. In some cities in northern Italy and Tuscany, such as Cremona and Arezzo, kings officially conferred comital authority on bishoprics, hoping to use them as a local base for royal authority.[64] It was rare for bishops in central Italy to possess comital authority.[65] It would be a mistake, however, to assume that where such grants were absent, the bishopric's role in the local community was less significant. In reality, grants of comital authority did not confer a coherent comital jurisdiction, for the county had already fragmented into a plurality of jurisdictions. As is clear from Henry III's privilege to the bishopric of Arezzo in 1052, these grants simply provided official recognition for power that bishops already possessed.[66] This power was based on several factors. The diocese, as a unit of spiritual jurisdiction, was the one remaining institution that preserved the unity of city and countryside.[67] Moreover, bishops owned considerable amounts of land in the countryside. Indeed, bishops owned many of the castles in the countryside that served as a base for signorial lordship. This combination of spiritual and temporal authority, which connected a large number of rural communities to the city, made the bishopric the most effective instrument for drawing the countryside into the orbit of the city.

Bishoprics emerged at the center of a group of urban elites with an interest in extending the city's control over the countryside. It is worth taking a look at these elites who coalesced around the bishopric, for they later formed the ruling class of the early communes. In larger northern towns with more advanced economies, such as Milan, three distinct orders emerged by the eleventh century: *capitanei*, *valvassores*, and *populi*. The *capitanei* derive from the Carolingian nobility. Their ancestors were manorial lords who became royal vassals under the Carolingians and Ottonians. During the tenth century, they used castles to transform their power as manorial lords into signorial authority. They expanded their signorial authority by settling in the city, becoming episcopal vassals, and holding episcopal fiefs. In the city they maintained close relations with the cathedral chapter and exercised authority in condominium with the bishop.[68] Also from the Carolingian period *valvassores* derive from families of humbler status. Their ancestors belonged to the non-noble class of *arimanni*. While their landholding was sufficient to support their status as free men during the Carolingian period, it was not sufficient for building signorial authority. They became vassals of *capitanei* in the tenth century and began to hold smaller fiefs from the bishop as well. Although their ancestors were not nobles, they obtained noble status as *milites* and vassals.[69] The third group—the *populi*—crosses the boundary from noble to non-noble status. When sources distinguish between *cives maiores* and *cives minores*, the *capitanei* and the *valvassores* belong to the former, while the *populi* belong to the latter. The class of legal professionals that evolved from the Carolingian period straddled the boundary that divided *maiores* from *minores*. At the top of the group of non-nobles were *boni homines*, which included notaries and minor officials attached to the bishopric. Most judges belonged to the class of *maiores*, usually the lower nobility, although there were a few ranked among the *capitanei*.[70]

In the smaller towns of central Italy, it is not possible to make such fine distinctions. The most useful distinction for describing urban populations in central Italy would be that between *maiores* and *minores*. Signorial lords in central Italy usually remained in the countryside. *Maiores*—urban aristocrats in the service of a bishop or royal official—originated in the city. Nevertheless, like their northern Italian counterparts, they owned land in the countryside, had close connections with the cathedral chapter, and trained in arms and mounted warfare.[71] Notaries and judges, who straddled the boundary between *maiores* and *minores*, developed a close working relation with the Orvietan bishopric and cathedral chapter—a relation that was not uncommon for Italy, as the examples of Lucca and Arezzo suggest.[72]

Bishops and the coalitions of knights, legal professionals, and other *boni homines* that gathered around the bishopric shared a common goal—to pacify the countryside. While they were united in their goal, they were not necessarily united in their visions of order and authority. In the most general terms, one can distinguish these visions as corporate and individual. For bishops, pacification of the countryside was primarily an issue of spiritual authority. This was a corporate vision, inasmuch as spiritual authority was supposed to be exercised for the benefit of the community of believers. Violent competition between signorial lords thwarted the ability of bishops to look after Christian communities in rural churches and monasteries. Of course, bishops were also among the signorial lords competing in the countryside; but even here, issues of a corporate nature were at work. At least in theory, castles and rural land constituted the economic resources that supported the bishop's work as pastor of the people. While a corporate vision was not entirely alien to the knightly class, their motivations were more individual in nature. They were interested in pacifying the countryside in a manner that reinforced the power and wealth of their families. They fought to protect the bishop's spiritual authority because there were temporal rewards for doing so. In addition to leasing ecclesiastical property or holding it in fief, they owned land beyond the city walls and felt that by participating in the bishop's efforts to pacify the countryside, they could dictate the terms of peace in ways that were favorable to them. In contrast, the interests of the other group of laypersons that coalesced around bishops, the *minores*, reflected a more corporate vision. On the one hand, they shared the spiritual corporatism of the bishop, for they were concerned—sometimes more than the bishop—that the economic resources of the church be used for the benefit of the church community. On the other hand, they shared a political corporatism that could clash with the interests of both knights and bishops. Artisans, craftsmen, petty merchants, and notaries were part of an economic network that depended on free access to the countryside. They wanted to impose an order on the countryside that benefited a broader network of economic interests than those of knightly families. They were also wary of subordinating these economic interests to the spiritual authority of bishops and popes.

By the middle of the twelfth century, popes and emperors joined the competition as well. As popes and emperors began to rebuild central authority and gain a foothold at the local level, they too had to try to leverage their power through bishoprics.

CHAPTER TWO

BUILDING AN EARTHLY CITY

The Bishopric and Orvietan Territorial Expansion

ONE OF THE INTERESTING ASPECTS OF THIS PERIOD OF political disorder is the way in which seemingly incompatible interests converged and became practically indistinguishable. The ideal of ecclesiastical liberty motivated bishops to venture into the countryside to aggressively defend their jurisdiction. When force was necessary, bishops were able to assemble a band of knights to enforce their claims. Where did these knights come from? In some cases, rural aristocrats with inadequate resources to defend their authority decided that their most attractive alternative was to become clients of the bishop. In other cases, urban elites, who owned property in the countryside and therefore had an interest in its pacification, joined forces with the bishop. The ideal of liberty emerged in response to the political disorder of the period that sometimes left the church a prey to aggression, or at least unable to defend its claims without resort to violence. The only remedy to this situation was the construction of a new political order. The bishop's diocesan authority was one of the best means for accomplishing this order. Reform and state building became one and the same activity.

35

THE BISHOPRIC: BETWEEN POLITICAL FORMATION
AND ECCLESIASTICAL REFORM

The Church in the Countryside

The structure of the Orvietan church was fairly typical for Italy. The bishop exercised spiritual authority over a diocese, an area that encompassed the city and a broad stretch of territory surrounding it. Beyond the city walls, the bishop presided over a network of rural churches. The organization of the church in the countryside was based on *pievi*, or baptismal churches. As the name implies, the essential feature of these churches was the possession of a baptismal font. They functioned as mini-cathedral churches, or mother churches, for rural districts, exercising exclusive rights over baptisms, burials, and tithes. Each *pieve* was the center for a cluster of smaller chapels or oratories. The *pievano*, or rector of the baptismal church, appointed and supervised the clergy of the oratories and, as a symbol of his authority, celebrated mass on the feast day of the oratory's patron saint. The clergy assigned to the oratories often received their training and rose through priestly orders at the baptismal church. While *incastellamento* seems to have shifted the organizational center from baptismal churches to castles in Lazio, the system of baptismal churches remained in place in Tuscany and much of northern Italy.[1]

The bishop's authority over baptismal churches became seriously compromised in certain regions of Italy by the tenth century, Milan and Lucca offering the best-documented examples. In theory, territorial lordships and the ecclesiastical structure over which the bishop presided were responsible for distinct spheres of human activity, one political and economic, the other spiritual. In reality, they converged and often competed to order a society in which it was impossible to distinguish where religion ended and where politics began. Nowhere is this clearer than in the plight of baptismal churches during this period.

The history of the tithe is the key to understanding how baptismal churches became entangled in the politics of signorial domination.[2] The tithe was a voluntary tax before the eighth century, collected by the bishop for poor relief and the ransom of captives. The Carolingian period marked a fundamental transformation in the tithe. The capitulary of Herstal, issued by Charlemagne in 779, made the tithe essentially a public tax by making it compulsory. The Carolingians also transferred control over rural tithes from bishops to the rectors of baptismal churches. Because the tithe was mandatory, and encompassed a significant portion of the agricultural surplus, the office of the *pievano* was now worth competing for. Baptismal churches became yet another tool, along with castles and fragments of comital authority, for constructing territorial lordships. This caused considerable problems in some episcopal sees during the tenth and eleventh centuries. In Lucca the bishop's authority over most of the baptismal churches in the countryside virtually disappeared.[3] Lay control over baptismal churches is well documented for Pisa and Milan as well. The late eleventh and early twelfth centuries saw a reversal of these trends, as Italian bishops aggressively fought to regain authority over their *pievi*.

Lay control over *pievi* in the tenth and eleventh centuries, though conspicuous in several important episcopal sees, was not necessarily the rule. The bishops of Arezzo maintained control over most of their baptismal churches.[4] This seems to have been the case for the Orvietan bishopric as well. It is clear, however, that the Orvietan bishop's efforts to defend his authority over certain baptismal churches was a critical factor in the city's expansion into the western *contado* during the early twelfth century, as will become apparent in the next chapter.

The organization of the diocese by *pievi* was threatened from another direction as subordinate chapels and oratories clamored for full parish rights. By the late twelfth century, local churches increasingly gained control over tithes, burials, and baptisms. As circumstances would have it, monasteries were the chief beneficiaries of these developments. During the eleventh century, as reformers called upon the laity to relinquish control over private churches, lay aristocrats donated countless chapels to monasteries. Therefore, when these chapels began to obtain full parish rights, portions of the diocese often appeared like a network of monastic centers with satellite churches.[5] Monastic control of newly formed parishes did not necessarily work against episcopal authority. Indeed, bishops sometimes promoted these developments as a way to effectively administer the diocese.[6] Nevertheless, some monasteries stubbornly resisted the intrusion of episcopal authority into their private churches, as the bishops of Orvieto discovered in the case of the monastery of San Sepolcro in the northwestern section of its diocese.[7]

No matter how much secular lords and monasteries compromised the bishop's authority by gaining control of churches and *pievi*, the diocese remained a palpable entity in a way that the county did not. No other institution could offer such a coherent framework for rebuilding public authority.

The Church in the City

The center of episcopal authority was, of course, the urban cathedral, which was the mother church for the diocese. The bishop's church in Orvieto was the cathedral of Santa Maria. It functioned as the urban *pieve*, or baptismal church, claiming exclusive rights to baptisms, tithes, and burials within the city and in its immediate suburbs.[8] In Orvieto, as in cities like Florence, Ravenna, and Naples, the function of the urban *pieve* was shared between a complex of buildings that included the cathedral, a nearby church belonging to the cathedral chapter, and a baptistery.[9] In Orvieto, this second church was San Costanzo, located directly across the plaza from the cathedral. Until the late eleventh or early twelfth century, there was a baptistery of San Giovanni located directly behind San Costanzo. There were probably nine other churches in the city at the beginning of the twelfth century that offered liturgical services, but they did not function as parishes.[10] Only later in the twelfth century did these churches begin to compete with the cathedral to gain full parish rights.

In Orvieto, as in most Italian cities, the clergy attached to the bishop and to the service of the cathedral church were known as cathedral canons, or collectively as the cathedral chapter. In late antiquity the cathedral clergy constituted part of the bishop's household. Over the course of the early Middle Ages, they gradually formed a distinct and privileged group among the city's clergy and gained increasingly well-defined rights in the cathedral.[11] Among the important steps in this process were the reforms of the eighth-century bishop Chrodegang of Metz, who imposed a monastic regiment on the cathedral clergy of Metz. His reforms, usually referred to as the "common life," became normative for all cathedral clergy in the Carolingian Empire when they found their way into the canons of the Council of Aachen in 816. According to this rule, the cathedral clergy were to live in a cloister near the cathedral, to share common meals, and to perform the daily liturgy of the cathedral. Italian bishops with ties to the Carolingian court, such as the bishops of Arezzo, adopted the common life relatively soon after the Council of Aachen.[12] In the centuries that followed, bishops throughout Italy imposed this monastic model on their cathedral clergy, often granting them property and urban tithes as an economic foundation for their corporate activity.[13]

In Orvieto, cathedral clergy appear in documents as canons of San Costanzo. They exercised exclusive rights to officiate mass in both San Costanzo and Santa Maria, the only urban churches with full parish rights until the late twelfth century. The two principal officials for the cathedral chapter were the archpriest and archdeacon. In theory, the archpriest was in charge of the spiritual life and liturgical functions of the cathedral canons, while the archdeacon managed the chapter's property. In Orvieto the distinction between the two offices was rather fluid. At various times both the archpriest and the archdeacon actively managed the chapter's financial resources. In addition to overseeing the cathedral chapter, the archpriest and/or archdeacon usually managed the bishopric when the episcopal see was vacant, though this practice may have only begun around the middle of the twelfth century.

Over the course of many centuries, cathedral churches acquired extensive property in the city and countryside through donations and purchases. The cathedral's property, along with tithes and oblations, constituted the *mensa episcopalis*, or pool of economic resources available to support the life and work of the bishop and cathedral canons. Bishops and cathedral chapters generally held episcopal property in common during the early twelfth century, although the bishop usually exercised a greater degree of control over the management of the *mensa*.[14] By the mid-twelfth century, there was increasing pressure for a division of property between the bishop and the cathedral chapter. This division was typically a slow process, lasting well into the thirteenth century. It was also a source of considerable tension between the bishop and the cathedral chapter.

In Orvieto the *mensa* was already divided to a certain extent by the early eleventh century. In 1026 Bishop Sigifredo donated a sizable portion of the episcopal *mensa* to the cathedral chapter. The donation included seven baptismal churches, three urban churches, and property in the suburbs and countryside.[15] By donating this property, Bishop Sigifredo probably intended to provide an economic basis for the renewal of the common life among the cathedral canons.[16] The donation of 1026 was by no means a decisive division of the episcopal *mensa*. After 1026 a large portion of episcopal property remained under the joint control of the bishop and the chapter. The canons provided consent to transactions in which the bishop was involved throughout the twelfth and early thirteenth centuries, suggesting that there was still some degree of joint control over the *mensa* as late as the thirteenth century. Bishop Sigifredo's donation thus was only the first stage of a long and sometimes contentious process.

Ecclesiastical Reform and the Orvietan Church

A discussion of the cathedral chapter and the common life naturally leads to a discussion of ecclesiastical reform, for it is in the cathedral chapter that the imprint of eleventh-century reform movements is most visible in the Orvietan church. As political pressures on ecclesiastical institutions and resources intensified during the tenth and eleventh centuries, there was a growing fear that the church was becoming corrupted by worldly concerns. Reformers offered the common life as a way to protect the clergy, who were the guardians and ministers of the sacraments, from worldly contamination. In order to understand the far-reaching implications of this reform, it is worth considering its place in the broader context of ecclesiastical reform during the eleventh and twelfth centuries.

Over the past forty years, historians have abandoned the idea of "Gregorian Reform" as a useful concept for understanding the varieties of ecclesiastical reform during the eleventh and twelfth centuries.[17] There is no doubt that Pope Gregory VII's effort to firmly establish papal supremacy as a basis for securing the freedom of the church profoundly influenced the direction of ecclesiastical reform. Nevertheless, his reform program was only one of several currents, and by no means the most important or representative. Papal reform, monastic reform, clerical reform, and efforts to create a new lay spirituality were characterized by tremendous variety and creativity. Between 1049 and 1123 alone, historians of the papacy have identified as many as five distinct periods of papal reform.[18] The Lateran

Councils of the twelfth and thirteenth centuries represent yet another clear shift in papal reform efforts.[19] The examples of Cluny, Gorze, Citeaux, Chartreuse, Camaldoli, and Vallombrosa demonstrate that variety and creativity characterized monastic reform as well.

Though distinct, these currents of reform often reinforced each other. This is especially true in the case of monastic and clerical reform. As churchmen looked for ways to protect the clergy from worldly contamination, the cloistered life of the monk seemed to be the most fruitful model for reform. Reform-minded popes reinforced this tendency to use monastic models of spirituality as a measuring rod for the clergy. As a result, monastic ideals of poverty and chastity profoundly shaped lay expectations for the clergy. The anticlericalism that became so widespread during the twelfth and thirteenth centuries cannot be attributed to the moral failings of the clergy alone. It was rooted in the high expectations created by monastic and papal reformers as well.

The clergy thus felt tremendous pressure for reform from a variety of directions. The dynamics of clerical reform in Italy provide one of the best examples of this. The hermits of Camaldoli and Vallombrosa often were outspoken critics of the secular clergy. Their calls for reform resonated among the laity, who admired their austerity and spiritual commitment.[20] It is likely that the hermits of Camaldoli and Vallombrosa influenced the Milanese Pataria, one of the most aggressive lay reform movements in the eleventh century.[21] The Pataria found further reinforcement in their aggressive campaign to reform the clergy from reforming popes like Alexander II and Gregory VII.[22]

What did it mean to impose a monastic lifestyle on the clergy? This became a contentious question. For Peter Damian, who was an active promoter of Camaldoli and its founder, Romuald, the imposition of monastic spirituality on the clergy meant that they were to be chaste and poor. The common life seemed to be a natural solution to these problems. A cloistered community would protect the clergy more effectively from the temptations of wealth and sex.[23] While Damian supported the common life as a tool for reforming the clergy, he felt that the version of the common life prescribed in the Council of Aachen was too lax, for it did not include a vow of poverty. It allowed individual canons to own their own property. According to

Damian, poverty was the sine qua non of clerical reform. Private property inevitably distracted the clergy's attention from the care of souls. Moreover, the apostles themselves gave up their property to preach the gospel. If the role of the clergy was to deliver the apostolic message, how could they fulfill this task if they did not live the apostolic life?[24]

By creating a necessary link between a more rigorous version of the common life and the mission of the clergy, Damian sparked a debate over the nature of the common life. Despite the support of Damian and Ildebrand (later Pope Gregory VII), the Lenten synod of 1059 prescribed a more moderate version. It recommended that priests sleep in a common dormitory, eat common meals, and hold the revenues of the church in common (as opposed to dividing the property between the canons in the form of prebends). Nevertheless, they were not prohibited from owning other property on their own.[25] Thus there emerged two general forms of the common life during the eleventh century. The older and more moderate version, which was based on the Council of Aachen, became the official position of the papacy from the time of Alexander II (1061–1073). The stricter version, which did not allow canons to own individual property, came to be known as the rule of St. Augustine. Amidst the fervor of reform in the eleventh century, many cathedral chapters adopted the latter.[26] This change often was signified by the replacement of the archpriest by a prior, who rose above the archdeacon as the dominant figure in the chapter.[27] Bishop Sigifredo probably imposed this stricter form of the common life on his cathedral clergy, though the evidence is not unambiguous. Bishop Ranerio recalled that Bishop Sigifredo reformed the chapter according to the rule of St. Augustine. It was, however, only in the twelfth century, after another reform of the cathedral chapter, that a prior replaced the archpriest.[28]

The more rigorous version of the common life proved difficult to sustain. By the twelfth and thirteenth centuries, the clergy had largely abandoned their ascetic rigor and commitment to poverty. Even the more moderate prescriptions of the Lenten synod of 1059 were relaxed, as it became increasingly common for the canons to divide the church's property into prebends. With a few exceptions, the twelfth-century papacy lost its fervor for the common life and did little to reverse these trends.[29]

These developments had a profound effect on the laity. Eleventh-century papal and monastic reformers significantly raised the standards by which the laity measured their local clergy. The common life evoked an enthusiastic response on the part of the laity, as evidenced by donations and more active participation in the life of the local church.[30] Over time, however, the clergy's zeal for reform often diminished while expectations of the laity did not. As a result, the twelfth century witnessed another burst of anticlericalism. At times, this anticlericalism contained a strain of Donatism. Eleventh-century monastic and papal reformers focused a spotlight on the moral condition of the clergy, using the relatively narrow standards of poverty and chastity to measure the clergy's moral purity. Given this intense concern with moral purity, the laity often failed to distinguish between the sanctity of the clerical office and the personal sanctity of the cleric. Groups like the Pataria questioned the efficacy of sacraments conveyed by priests whom they considered immoral.[31] This frustration with the progress of reform, combined with the tendency toward Donatism, made the laity in the twelfth century increasingly receptive to heretical movements.

The common life and the emphasis on purity introduced another interesting and unintended tension into the dynamic between the clergy and the laity. While raising lay expectations for the clergy, the eleventh-century reform movements also heightened the desire of the laity to participate more directly in the spiritual life of the local church, as seen in the growing popularity of confraternities.[32] In other words, the laity expected both purity and engagement from their clergy. While these two qualities are not necessarily contradictory in the abstract, they are not easily reconciled when the recipe for purity was monastic withdrawal.

When the Orvietan bishopric begins to emerge in the sources in the late eleventh and early twelfth centuries, it is caught in a tug-of-war between forces of political reformation and ecclesiastical reform and between engagement and withdrawal. The vacuum of public authority dragged the bishopric into the violent contest to reconstruct a political order. Was this necessarily bad? Perhaps engagement was the path to purity. The weakness of political institutions offered a unique opportunity for the church to step into the breach and order the political world according to evangelical principles.

What better way to guarantee the church's purity than to subordinate the secular sword to the spiritual sword?

CONQUERING THE COUNTRYSIDE

Italian bishops moved aggressively into the countryside to impose order during the eleventh and twelfth centuries, gaining control of castles and drawing a growing number of signorial lords into the orbit of episcopal power. As was the case in other cities, like Lucca and Florence, bishops used a variety of methods to impose order on the countryside.[33] Fierce competition in the countryside drove many signorial lords to submit to the bishopric by donating or pawning property, or by becoming vassals and treating their property as episcopal fiefs. Urban elites cooperated with bishops in much of this activity, as they had a stake in controlling the countryside as well. This is a classic example of the early stages of European state building, when the territorial authority of medieval rulers—whether kings, territorial princes, popes, or urban ruling elites—was uneven, a patchwork of agreements by which signorial lords, villages, and cities acknowledged varying degrees of subjection to a more powerful authority.

The Competition for Signorial Domination

The political configuration in the border region of Lombard and Roman Tuscany changed drastically with the collapse of the Italian kingdom in the tenth century. Demographic and economic growth between the tenth and early twelfth centuries, combined with the breakdown of political structures, transformed settlement patterns in southern Tuscany from widely dispersed villages and estates to more concentrated settlements inside castles and small fortified towns. This concentration of settlement was especially evident along the Via Francigena, the pilgrim and trade route running from Rome to northern France. The growth of towns and cities along the Via Francigena beginning in the tenth and eleventh centuries testifies to a quickening of regional trade and a heightened interest in controlling the route.[34] The Via Francigena ran through the western portion of Orvietan territory from Bolsena and San Lorenzo in the south to Acquapendente in the north. From there it passed by the castle of Radicofani before reaching Siena (see map 1). When the Orvietan bishopric and commune first come into view in the early twelfth century, much of their activity is directed to controlling these towns and castles along the Via Francigena. This important trade and pilgrim route also becomes one of the principal axes of expansion for the papacy, as it begins to actively reclaim its jurisdiction over Roman Tuscany and the southern portion of Lombard Tuscany between the mid-twelfth and early thirteenth centuries.

The competition for power in the countryside of Roman Tuscany was fierce. The families who were most successful in establishing signorial domination entered the struggle with considerable resources, having exercised comital authority under the late- and post-Carolingian rulers of Italy. By successfully appropriating property and rights belonging to the office, these families were able to establish territorial lordships that endured long after the office of count ceased to be meaningful. The Aldobrandeschi, who would play an increasingly significant role in Orvietan history during the twelfth and thirteenth centuries, emerged as one of the wealthiest and most powerful families in southern Tuscany during the ninth century under the patronage of Louis II. As bishop of Lucca, Jeremias, an ancestor of the Aldobrandeschi, alienated a large amount of episcopal property in southern Tuscany to his family through sales and leases. Louis II appointed Ildebrando, the brother of Jeremias, as count of Roselle. A third brother was an imperial *missus*.[35] As late as the thirteenth century, members of the family exercised genuine comital authority over portions of southern Tuscany such as Roselle, Sovana, and Pitigliano. Continued imperial patronage made them more successful than other families in the region at maintaining control over these counties. Comital office, however, constituted only a small portion of the family's wealth and power, for the Aldobrandeschi controlled an extensive network of castles and estates throughout the region.

The Aldobrandeschi were only one of many families to establish a network of territorial lordships, albeit the most successful. The growing importance of private wealth as a source of power, as opposed to office holding, had a leveling effect on the rural aristocracy, creating an atmosphere of intense competition. Military might became the principal tool for establishing authority. The militarization of the region had two principal effects. For peasant cultivators, it inaugurated a new wave of concentration into fortified settlements under signorial domination. For lay and ecclesiastical lords, militarization functioned as a selective criterion, weeding out those lacking the economic resources to maintain a private army. The monastery of San Salvatore in Monte Amita, located about fifty kilometers northwest of Orvieto, offers an interesting example. The early decades of the twelfth century mark the beginning of a financial crisis for the monastery, as it proved unable to bear the expense of fortifying its holdings and maintaining a military clientele.[36] The Aldobrandeschi, on the other hand, with their massive holdings throughout southern Tuscany, possessed the resources to draw the population into fortified settlements and to create a military clientele out of lesser aristocrats who did not possess the resources to maintain their independence in such a competitive environment.

Shelter from the Storm

The fierce competition to establish territorial lordships in the countryside produced winners and losers. While the losers had no choice but to submit, they could choose among several masters. Many families decided that submission to emerging cities like Orvieto or Siena would be preferable to the overlordship of the Aldobrandeschi or other such powerful families. As clients of the bishop or city (at this time there was no distinction between the two), they gained an ally to help them preserve a measure of independence in the countryside. Thus, as Delumeau observed concerning the signorial lords in the Aretine countryside, the signorial lords in Roman Tuscany seemed to be fighting a battle in retreat.[37]

The earliest episcopal documents in Orvieto trace the gravitation of one such family into the orbit of the Orvietan bishopric. The Farolfingi were a powerful family in Chiusi and the northern region of Orvietan territory. Peter Damian referred to a Farolfo, count of Orvieto, in one of his letters.[38] It is not unlikely that Farolfo did indeed exercise comital authority over Orvieto. Given the fluid jurisdictions of southern Tuscany during the late tenth and early eleventh centuries, it is less likely that his family established a long-term claim to the office, or that the office itself survived. A certain Ranerio, "count from the county of Orvieto," appears in an Orvietan document dated 1115.[39] The awkward reference to a count from Orvieto instead of a count of Orvieto suggests that the title had become empty by the early twelfth century.

During the early eleventh century, when Farolfing power was still intact, the family apparently exercised some type of officially recognized power with respect to the bishopric. In 1026 Count Farolfo (probably Farolfo II) and his wife were among those giving counsel and consent to Bishop Sigifredo concerning a sizable donation of episcopal property.[40] Bishop Ranerio wrote in the margin of this entry that Pietro and his son Farolfo the Bald donated one hundred *scuta* to the bishopric during the episcopate of Bishop Albertino, an act commemorated by paintings in the old episcopal palace.[41] These paintings suggest that the Farolfingi inhabited an important place in the consciousness of the bishopric.

The Farolfingi were important figures in the life of the regional church throughout the eleventh century. In 1068 Ranerio II, the son of Bulgarello, appears as one of two great laymen by the side of Alexander II at a reforming synod in Chiusi.[42] In 1075 Gregory VII sent a letter to Ranerio II and several of his kin concerning the discipline of a priest in Chiusi who was living with a concubine.[43] Not all of the Farolfingi were sympathetic to the reform party. In 1062 Pepo I fought alongside Cadalus (antipope Honorius II) in Rome.[44] Regardless of the side they chose, the frequent mention of the family in a variety of eleventh-century sources testifies to their power in the region.

The early decades of the twelfth century marked an eclipse in the family's wealth and power. During this period the Farolfingi alienated a tremendous amount of property to ecclesiastical entities in the regions around Chiusi and Orvieto.[45] For example, in 1137 Count Otto, along with other family members, donated to the Orvietan bishopric a sizable number of estates, castles, and villages that he held in the counties of Orvieto, Perugia, and Todi.[46] In return, he received a countergift of one hundred lire from Cittadino Malabranca, who was acting on behalf of the city of Orvieto. There are six other episcopal documents dating between 1103 and 1139 in which the Farolfingi transferred significant amounts of property to ecclesiastical entities.[47] These agreements fall into one of two categories. One group of agreements, in which they pledged property to the bishop or a monastery, are essentially loans—an indication that the family was experiencing a financial crisis. Other documents record Farolfing donations to the bishop that were given back in fief. It is worth examining both types of agreements, for they are found throughout Italy and tell us much about the world of signorial lords in the late eleventh and early twelfth centuries.

In April 1118, Count Bernardo II and his family promised to do all in their power to protect the bishop's claims to the castle of Parrano, located approximately seventeen kilometers north of Orvieto. The bishop, in turn, promised not to alienate the castle to anyone except Bernardo, who could repurchase the castle from the bishop at any time he wished, if the bishop was willing.[48] Apparently, this agreement between Bernardo and Bishop Guilielmo is an addendum to a prior agreement—now lost—in which Bishop Guilielmo purchased the castle from Bernardo. The repurchase clause gives the agreement the character of a loan. Two months later, in June 1118, the abbot of San Pietro of Aquaorte and Ranaldo, a cousin of Bernardo, made a similar agreement. Count Ranaldo, with the consent of his family, sold the monastery of San Pietro of Aquaorte, located approximately twenty kilometers northwest of Orvieto, to Guilielmo, its abbot. The contract reserves Ranaldo's right to repurchase the monastery within twelve years.[49] Like the transaction involving the castle of Parrano, the repurchase clause effectively makes this agreement a loan.[50] These examples suggest that liquidity problems were a motivating factor behind Farolfing alienations. This was typical for signorial lords throughout Tuscany. For example, the Gherardeschi, who were caught in the middle of struggles between Pisa, Lucca, and Volterra, were forced to pawn property to the bishops of Lucca and Pisa. These bishops eventually forgave the loans, but took possession of the properties held in pledge.[51]

There were several forces that strained the wealth of signorial families during the tenth and eleventh centuries. Unlike families north of the Alps, who were becoming more patrilineal in order to hold their patrimonies intact, Italian families continued to practice partible inheritance.[52] This was less of a problem in the ninth and tenth centuries, when the comital office functioned as a center of gravity to hold family wealth and power in place. The gradual dissolution of public authority during the late eleventh and early twelfth centuries left no anchor for family identity.[53] Certain members of the family continued to call themselves counts, but it was little more than an honorary title, as indicated by the way in which the title multiplied across various branches of the family.

By the early twelfth century, the Farolfingi were breaking up into distinct branches. The pattern of Farolfing names reveals that the family as a whole had no real consciousness of itself. There is no family name to identify individuals as part of a lineage. Each person in the documents is identified by a first name attached to the name of his father (for example, "Count Bernardus, son of Count Ranerio"). In the absence of a family name, the memory of the lineage was usually very short.[54] The fragmentation of Farolfingi wealth and power in the late eleventh and early twelfth centuries was fairly typical for the families in southern Tuscany that had built their fortunes from office holding in the ninth and tenth centuries.[55]

As family wealth and power fragmented across various branches, the militarization of the region increased the financial pressure on the Farolfingi. The same burdens of maintaining castles and a military clientele that drove the monastery of Monte Amiata into a financial crisis strained the resources of families like the Farolfingi. In the midst of these unsettling changes, the family looked to the bishopric and other ecclesiastical institutions for the stability that they formerly derived from their comital office. The bishopric thus functioned as a center of gravity, drawing powerful families in the countryside into the orbit of the city.

This leads us to the second type of transaction—feudal contracts. In 1115, Count Bernardo I, son of Ranerio, "count from the county of Orvieto," along with his two sons, Ugolino and Pepo IV, surrendered the church of Santa Cristina in Bolsena to Bishop Guilielmo, who then granted the church back as a fief.[56] This contract reflects a proliferation of feudal relations in Italy during the eleventh and twelfth centuries. Feudalism was a latecomer to medieval Italy. Previously, instead of the feudo-vassalic relations based on a fief that one might find north of the Alps, Italians defined such relations within the context of traditional long-term lease agreements of emphyteusis, which could include obligations of military service.[57] During the period of signorial lordship, Italians introduced feudo-vassalic relations in a modified form as a way to impose order and definition on the chaotic landscape of the countryside. This form of feudalism, which Giovanni Tabacco calls "political feudalism," was a hybrid of vassalage/benefice and allodial conceptions of property, inasmuch as the benefice was hereditary and therefore essentially an allod. This political feudalism proved to be a flexible tool for rebuilding order in the countryside because it provided a reasonable compromise between the signorial lord's desire for autonomy and the desire of kings, popes, bishops, or monasteries to establish at least a measure of control over them.[58] By receiving the church of Santa Cristina back in fief, Bernardo received the benefit of the bishop's protection at little cost, for his rights in the church were still essentially allodial. The bishop, in return, strengthened his claim to authority over Bernardo and his heirs. In the long run, the cost of this subordinate relation would increase as the bishop's and city's territorial authority grew; but it is unlikely that eleventh- and twelfth-century signorial lords like Bernardo had the ability or the luxury of weighing long-term consequences.

THE DIOCESE AND TERRITORIAL EXPANSION

Episcopal expansion into the countryside took a variety of forms. Orvietan bishops gained complete control over castles and villages through donations. They held properties as pledges against loans—claims that they could eventually convert into absolute possession. Feudo-vassalic relations offered a foothold in more stubborn pockets of signorial domination. All of these forms belong to the bishop's authority as a signorial lord. In the long run, the bishop's diocesan authority was the most important tool for expansion into the countryside. That Bernardo held the church of Santa Cristina in fief indicates that the bishop was not simply imposing order on the countryside: he was imposing order on his diocese.

The same forces that drove families like the Farolfingi into the orbit of episcopal power also caused considerable problems for diocesan administration. Nowhere is this clearer than in the dispute between the bishops of Orvieto and Sovana over diocesan boundaries. Disputes over diocesan boundaries were nothing new to medieval Italy, as demonstrated by the celebrated dispute between the bishops of Siena and Arezzo, which was a half-millennium old by the twelfth century.[59] Nevertheless, it is no coincidence that the Orvieto-Sovana dispute erupted in the early twelfth century, during the latter stages of a period when settlement patterns were becoming more concentrated. The movement of people meant the movement of tithe payers, which activated the potential for conflict in the ill-defined border region between the two dioceses. At the center of the dispute was control over baptismal churches, along with their tithes and revenues. Given the lack of differentiation between episcopal authority and public authority during the early communal period, the dispute over diocesan boundaries appears to have been both a defense of ecclesiastical jurisdiction and an aggressive expansion of the city's political influence to the west. It illustrates how important episcopal control of baptismal churches could be for establishing political jurisdiction over the countryside and how political and ecclesiastical jurisdiction often were indistinguishable in the pre-communal period.[60]

The Evidence

The evidence for the dispute comes from an inquest commissioned in 1194 by Pope Celestine III in response to a complaint of Bishop Giordano of Sovana. The two judges appointed by Celestine interviewed fifty-seven witnesses who reflected on the development of the dispute over the course of the century. Unfortunately, the record of the final judgment has not survived, and the memory of the witnesses often is not as precise as one would like. One witness illustrates this lack of precision in a rather humorous way. He testified that twenty years earlier he had seen several priests from Acquapendente going to a synod called by the bishop of Sovana. When asked who these priests were, he responded that he did not know, because when he saw them he did not realize that twenty years later he would be asked who they were.[61] Despite difficulties presented by the witnesses' memory, these testimonies offer a valuable source for the early twelfth century, for the dispute was almost a century old by the time it reached Pope Celestine.[62]

The Dispute

The hearing in 1194 was at least the fourth time that the case had been brought for judgment.[63] The only information regarding the previous three hearings comes from passing references in the testimonies of 1194. The bishop of Orte presided over the first hearing around 1150 in

Pitigliano, which was under the jurisdiction of Count Bartolomeo, an Aldobrandeschi. There is no mention of who appointed the bishop of Orte to hear the case, but Pope Eugenius would be a reasonable guess. He was certainly familiar with the case.[64] Orvieto won this hearing on procedural grounds. In 1168–1169 the bishops of Orvieto and Sovana reached a compromise with the help of an arbitrator, but the agreement proved to be short-lived. The bishop of Sovana presented his case to Pope Alexander III at the Lateran Council of 1179. The parties reached another compromise that was soon broken.

In the opening complaint of the 1194 hearing, Bishop Giordano of Sovana (1193–1206) claimed that the bishop of Orvieto had invaded Cloiano, Grotte di Castro, Gradoli, Castel San Lorenzo, Acquapendente, and the church of Sant' Hyppolyto.[65] The jurist representing the bishop of Orvieto complained that the bishop of Sovana was unjustly collecting tithes in Grotte di Castro and that Proceno and Montorio, which the bishop of Sovana had taken, were allods of the Orvietan bishop and therefore should be returned.[66]

The places under dispute were located in two regions. Grotte di Castro, Gradoli, and Castel San Lorenzo were located to the southwest of Orvieto near Bolsena. Acquapendente, Proceno, and Montorio were located to the west and northwest. More important, Bolsena and Acquapendente were the two most important towns in Orvietan territory through which the Via Francigena ran (see map 1). It is not unreasonable to assume that control over the Via Francigena was one of the principal factors making the boundary between the two dioceses so sensitive. Episcopal expansion in Florence and Lucca focused on control of road systems as well.[67]

During the 1140s the region to the southwest around Grotte di Castro seems to have been the principal area of conflict. Around 1150 the conflict spread to the north around Acquapendente. The bishop of Orvieto first gained control over Grotte di Castro sometime during the 1140s. An inhabitant of the castle testifying in 1194 said that he witnessed the formal submission of Grotte to the citizens of Orvieto, which included an obligation to make an annual recognition payment of two *soldi* to the bishopric.[68] This submission, made to the Orvietan bishopric and commune as an undifferentiated whole, illustrates how the bishop's efforts to enforce his jurisdiction over the diocese often were indistinguishable from political-military conquest.

The submission also illustrates the importance of baptismal churches for territorial authority. Both before and after the conquest, Grotte was entangled in a confusing array of claims to the baptismal churches in and around the castle. Sometime after the submission of Grotte (probably in the late 1140s), Bishop Ildibrando consecrated San Giovanni, a new baptismal church, inside the castle. Before the construction of San Giovanni, there had been one baptismal church, San Pietro, inside the castle and two more, San Stefano and Santa Romana, outside the castle.[69] Because these three churches predated the Orvietan conquest, the construction of San Giovanni was probably intended to clarify and strengthen the Orvietan bishop's authority over the castle and the surrounding region.

There was indeed a desperate need for clarification. Jurisdiction over these churches was remarkably confusing. The baptismal church of San Pietro belonged to the monastery of San Sepolcro in Acquapendente, which was, according to one witness, directly subject to the papacy.[70] There is no record of how San Sepolcro gained ownership of San Pietro, but as noted earlier, it was not unusual for bishops to alienate baptismal churches during the eleventh and twelfth centuries. The baptismal church of Santa Romana, located outside of the castle, belonged to the bishop of Sovana.[71] Santa Romana was particularly confusing because it was not clear to the inhabitants of Grotte whether the bishop of Sovana's authority over the church was that of an owner or a bishop. San Stefano, the third baptismal church, was also located outside of the castle and was apparently under the jurisdiction of the bishop of Orvieto.[72]

It is not clear how this unusual concentration of baptismal churches occurred. The most likely explanation is to be found in a combination of factors. The two baptismal churches located outside of the castle are the oldest of the four competing churches, probably predating the construction of the castle. Santa Romana, which belonged to the bishop of Sovana, and San Stefano, which belonged to the bishop of Orvieto, represent the competing claims to diocesan authority by the two bishops. It is impossible to know which bishop and baptismal church possessed the prior claim.

The construction of the two baptismal churches inside the castle is attributable to the incessant warfare in the region, which drove people from open villages to fortified settlements and towns during the eleventh and twelfth centuries.[73] San Pietro was the first baptismal church to be constructed inside the castle. Once the baptismal church of San Pietro came under the control of the monastery of San Sepolcro, it was of no use to the bishops of Sovana or Orvieto as a basis for episcopal authority. Therefore, when Bishop Ildibrando decided to assert his authority over Grotte and its ecclesiastical district, he had two choices. He could either forcefully assert the priority of San Stefano, located outside of the castle, or he could build a new baptismal church inside the castle. The decision was not difficult. Grotte was a dynamic center attracting an influx of people. Bishop Ildibrando had to build where the people were moving.[74]

The attempt to clarify jurisdiction in Grotte was like placing a boundary marker in the middle of the ocean. The persistent agitation of violent conflict allowed nothing to remain still. Moreover, the concentration of people inside the castle raised important economic questions that were not easily resolved. If villagers from the diocese of Sovana resettled in the castle of Grotte, to whom did they pay tithes and other ecclesiastical dues? Assuming for the sake of argument that Grotte was part of the Orvietan diocese, what if certain members of the transplanted population lived in Grotte, but still owned or leased land in the diocese of Sovana? These were the economic issues that made the dispute over Grotte's baptismal churches so difficult. Priest Girardo was asked if anyone from the diocese of Sovana came to live in Grotte. He is said to have responded that "certain people came from Argazano and some came from Terzano, both of which belonged to the diocese of Sovana . . . and the heirs of those who moved are still there. And the bishop of Orvieto demanded tithes from all the aforementioned who came to Grotte, saying to them, 'give [the tithes] to me because you stay in my *castrum* and you listen to the divine office from my priests. Later, if you want to give to another, then you can do so.'"[75]

The lack of jurisdictional clarity continued to be a source of hostility and conflict in Grotte even after Bishop Ildibrando built San Giovanni. Domenico, a citizen of Orvieto, recalled that a man from Santa Romana was in Grotte, but he did not dare to collect tithes for the bishop of Sovana, because representatives of the Orvietan bishop would have killed him had he tried.[76] Thus it appears that Bishop Ildibrando exercised sufficient control over Grotte to prevent representatives of the bishop of Sovana from collecting tithes inside the castle. Those who moved from the diocese of Sovana to Grotte could still treat the bishop of Sovana as their diocesan by going outside of the castle to the church of Santa Romana. At one point Bishop Ildibrando tried to eliminate this option. Martinozzo, an Orvietan knight, recalled that he participated in an attack on the church of Santa Romana in order to prevent people from Grotte from being baptized there. "Certain people who had come from the diocese of Sovana to live in Grotte went to be baptized at the *pieve* of the bishop of Sovana, which is outside of the *castrum*. Because we did not want our parishioners to go, we went with our weapons and took the baptismal cloths from the women."[77] According to another witness, an Orvietan priest destroyed the altar with his own hands.[78] Others took the relics from the church.[79] Parte di Homodei, who took part in the attack, said that he was invited to participate by the bishop of Orvieto.[80]

In the early 1150s, Orvieto turned its attention northward to Acquapendente. Before then the bishop of Sovana seems to have exercised diocesan authority there. Genuario of Sovana testified that Acquapendente came under the control of Sovana in 1111 when Henry V went to Rome.[81] Nevertheless, by the 1140s the bishop of Sovana found it increasingly difficult to exercise his jurisdiction over Acquapendente. Without specifying any dates, Genuario recalled that Bishop Ildizo of Sovana (1126–1151) was afraid to go to Acquapendente for fear of Count Ugolino di Calmaniare, whom Ildizo had excommunicated.[82] By 1151 the bishop of Sovana seems to have lost control of Acquapendente to Bishop Ildibrando. Vinzio, an Orvietan knight, said that the church of Orvieto had exercised control over Acquapendente for forty years, placing Orvietan expansion into Acquapendente around 1154. Bishop Ildibrando probably established some measure of control over Acquapendente before 1151, for Bishop Ildizo of Sovana complained about Orvietan expansion there at the hearing in Pitigliano around 1150.[83]

The northwestern region apparently was no less chaotic than the southwest. Indeed, the problems in the two regions were strikingly similar. Communities in the Orvietan diocese were uprooted by conflict and forced to relocate. Many of these refugees settled in the castle community of Proceno, in the diocese of Sovana. The people who resettled in Proceno continued to recognize the diocesan authority of the Orvietan bishop.[84] As was the case in the southwestern corner of the diocese around Grotte, the migration of the rural population caused a confusion of ecclesiastical jurisdiction. It was a confusion that Bishop Ildibrando could not solve by a simple appeal to his spiritual authority. Therefore he called upon his knights to support his claims with the sword.

In response to Orvietan aggression along the entire border separating the two dioceses, Bishop Ildizo of Sovana raised a formal complaint against the bishop of Orvieto. Ildizo presented his case in the church of San Pietro in Pitigliano before the bishop of Orte, who was appointed to hear the case. This, the first of four attempts to settle the century-long dispute, took place around 1150.[85] The bishop of Orvieto won the case on procedural grounds. Ildibrando Uguli, a knight from Acquapendente, who was present at the case, provides the most complete testimony regarding Pitigliano. "[Ildibrando] said that he was present at the hearing between the bishops of Orvieto and Sovana at Pitigliano in the church of San Pietro in the court of count Bartolomeo. And when the bishop of Sovana was asked to take the oath of calumny, he refused to swear, even if it was a question of the major part of his diocese. And the judge of the court . . . said to Maestro Viviano, the advocate of the Orvietan bishop, who requested the oath, 'I absolve [your] party.' "[86] The calumny oath was simply a promise to present one's case honestly. It was commonly used in cases judged according to civil law. There is no indication why Ildizo refused to take the oath. Perhaps he objected to the use of the calumny oath in a case that was supposed to be judged according to canon law.[87] In any case, Bishop Ildibrando won the dispute on a procedural maneuver.

Despite Orvietan conquests to the southwest and northwest, and despite the legal victory at Pitigliano, the authority of Bishop Ildibrando was extremely fragile in these regions during the final years of his episcopate. The events surrounding the construction of the baptismal church of San Giovanni is typical of the problems that sapped the momentum from Orvietan expansion. When Bishop Ildibrando first built San Giovanni in Grotte in the 1140s, he probably hoped to clarify his diocesan authority there. Instead, the construction of the new baptismal church only led to another dispute, this time with the abbot of the monastery of San Sepolcro in Acquapendente. The abbot complained that the new church would diminish the revenues that his monastery derived from the old baptismal church of San Pietro. The dispute apparently lasted a number of years until Ildibrando compensated the abbot by granting him certain revenues from San Stefano, located outside of the castle.[88] For every two steps forward, there was at least one step back, sometimes even two or three.

Nevertheless, by the time Bishop Ildibrando died (c. 1155), his efforts to assert his diocesan authority had laid the basis for Orvieto's territorial claims all along the western border of the diocese. Perhaps the best evidence for the joint activity of the commune and the bishopric in the countryside comes from a thirteenth-century survey of communal property. In 1244 Giacomo de Ponte, the *podestà* of Orvieto, commissioned a survey of the *comunalia*, or property owned by the commune.[89] This survey is a monument recalling the importance of the twelfth-century bishopric in the early development of the commune. With a few minor exceptions, all of the city's property was located in the west. The eastern half of the *contado* belonged almost entirely to ecclesiastical entities, private owners, and local communities.[90] This concentration of communal property in the western portion of the *contado* almost certainly finds its explanation in the westward expansion led by the twelfth-century Orvietan bishops.

Creating Political Jurisdiction: Making the New Seem Old

Giovanni Tabacco writes that as expansion into the countryside approached the limits of the diocese by the second half of the twelfth century, urban communities used the concept of *civitas mater* as "the ideological cloak for that knotted tangle of pacts, conventions and violent submissions which brought the forces of the *contado* to centre on the city."[91] In Orvieto the diocese was both the tool of conquest and the ideological justification for it. In 1194 the jurist representing the bishopric of Orvieto presented twelve documents dating between 1026 and 1149 to prove that the disputed area belonged to the diocese of Orvieto. Many of these documents made no mention of the Orvietan diocese. They simply stated that certain locations belonged to the *comitatus*, or political jurisdiction, of Orvieto. Therefore the jurist argued, with no supporting documentation, that "the expression 'in the *comitatus* of Orvieto' contained in this document and others ought not to disturb the judge, as this is held in frequent use and custom in our province, that *comitatus* is used interchangeably with *episcopatus*, because the counts, as is said by our ancient ancestors, held Orvieto from the Roman church."[92] According to the jurist, *comitatus* and *episcopatus* traditionally had been synonymous in Orvieto. He could have been more precise about when and how the two terms became synonyms, but precision is not always the best strategy in a legal dispute. Hoping to compensate for weak documentary evidence, the jurist offered an interesting argument. If the disputed territory was in the county of Orvieto, it must be in the diocese as well, because the city's political jurisdiction was based on its ecclesiastical jurisdiction, as mandated by the papacy.

The argument is a curious blend of half-truths. As I suggested in the discussion of the Farolfingi, there may have been counts of Orvieto. It is even conceivable that a pope sanctioned royal appointment of this office at some point in the eleventh century, but, as noted earlier, such counties proved ephemeral. It is unlikely that such an appointment was representative of papal policy. While the papacy could claim jurisdiction over Orvieto, it could not exercise it until the mid-twelfth century. Moreover, in most cases the papacy upheld the principle that there was no necessary connection between the boundaries of dioceses and political jurisdictions.[93] The city's political jurisdiction was indeed grounded in the bishop's ecclesiastical jurisdiction, but this relationship did not date back to Orvieto's ancient ancestors: it was scarcely a century old and had been forged in the furnace of central Italian power politics.

Although the argument is not compelling, there is something profoundly true reflected in its half-truths. That the jurist strained to find a deeply rooted legal justification for the relation between the city's political and ecclesiastical jurisdiction indicates that none existed. He lived in a world only recently formed. The disintegration of the Italian kingdom in the tenth century created a gulf separating Carolingian Italy from the emerging world of the Italian communes, at least from a constitutional perspective. Eleventh- and twelfth-century cities did not inherit their political jurisdiction from the early Middle Ages. They gathered or usurped the fragments of the old political order and created something new. This is precisely what happened in the case of the Farolfingi and in the Orvieto-Sovana dispute. In the absence of a legitimate constitutional claim, many Italian cities, including Orvieto, depended on their bishops' ecclesiastical jurisdiction as the most effective tool for extending and, more importantly, justifying their political jurisdiction. Under the circumstances, the diocese presented itself as a natural field into which new political currents of the tenth and eleventh century flowed. This raised a difficult and contentious question. As the Orvietan bishops and the city's ruling elite subdued the countryside, where did ecclesiastical reform end and state building begin? To put it another way, to what extent did one compromise the other?

CHAPTER THREE

THE CONNECTEDNESS OF THINGS

Episcopal Reform and State Building

MORE THAN SEVENTY YEARS AFTER BISHOP ILDIBRANDO DIED, Bishop Ranerio wrote the following summary of Ildibrando's episcopate. "In the time of Ildibrando, who was from Valloclis, from the family of Beccario, and who was procurator of the vacant see, there was a great dispute and war between him and Archpriest Ranerio along with his [cathedral] canons, because Ildibrando was having the parish clergy celebrate the divine office in the major church, despite the canons' protests. Once the church was restored [to the canons], a certain priest Ranerio, who was a member of the bishop's family and belonged to the parish clergy, was grieved and set fire to episcopal documents."[1] In another passage Bishop Ranerio recalled, "Ildibrando . . . succeeded Guilielmo. And he had a dispute with the canons, who charged him with a lapse in the flesh. As a result he granted them episcopal property under duress."[2] In addition to this bitter dispute with the cathedral chapter, Ildibrando apparently fell out of favor with the papacy during the latter years of his reign and was exiled from Orvieto for a brief period.[3] In sum, Orvietans remembered Ildibrando as a controversial and embattled bishop.

This image of Bishop Ildibrando is surprising in certain respects. As one pieces together the scattered memories of his episcopate, he emerges as the principal architect of a powerful coalition of political and religious interests in Orvieto that aggressively expanded into the countryside. In his final years as bishop, however, Ildibrando lost a bitter dispute with the cathedral chapter over control of the episcopal *mensa*. The outcome of this dispute accounts for the overwhelmingly negative memories of his episcopate.

Ildibrando's dispute with the cathedral chapter is fascinating for several reasons. First, it offers a wonderful example of the difficulties and contingencies involved in the influence of reform ideals on local networks of political and religious interests. The implementation of reform at the local level was a catalyst for a chain reaction that proved difficult to control. Second, this dispute had profound implications for the city's political development, for the cathedral canons appealed to the papacy in their dispute with Ildibrando. As a result, resolution of the dispute was swept up in papal state building. Finally, the resolution of the dispute demonstrates that as late as the mid-twelfth century, there was still a strong tendency for state building—in this case, papal state building—and ecclesiastical reform to converge.

THE GHOST OF BISHOP SIGIFREDO

The Dispute and the Common Life

Although details of Ildibrando's dispute with the canons are lost, it is possible to follow its general development from Bishop Ranerio's comments and from testimonies taken in the Orvieto-Sovana dispute. Before Ildibrando became bishop, he was involved in a dispute with Ranerio, the archpriest of the cathedral chapter.[4] During this time Ildibrando was procurator of the bishopric, in charge of managing episcopal property during vacancies. Animosity between the two continued into his episcopate. After another dispute (or, perhaps, a continuation of the same one) that pitted Bishop Ildibrando against Archpriest Ranerio and the cathedral canons, Ildibrando revoked the right of the canons to celebrate mass in the cathedral church of Santa Maria, replacing them with clergy of the city's neighborhood

churches. According to Bishop Ranerio, the canons accused Ildibrando of a "lapse in the flesh," a charge they were able to use to
get concessions from the bishop. Sometime between 1150 and 1154,
Ildibrando was forced into exile, having incurred the disfavor of the
pope.[5] In 1154 Bishop Ildibrando restored the right to celebrate mass
in the cathedral to Archpriest Ranerio and the canons.[6] In 1156 Pope
Hadrian visited Orvieto and confirmed the possessions of the cathedral chapter. The following year he concluded a treaty with Orvieto,
recognizing the city's status as a self-governing commune under the
overlordship of the papacy.

Bishop Ranerio provides the only evidence concerning the cause
of the dispute that set this complicated chain of events in motion. He
commented, with an unmistakably sarcastic tone, "this diminution
[in the bishop's property] is known to have begun during the time of
Bishop Sigifredo, under the pretext of the canons *religio* according to
the rule of St. Augustine."[7] His skepticism regarding the religious
motives of the canons arose from his belief that this dispute marked
the beginning of a shift in power from the bishop to the cathedral
chapter. According to Ranerio, this shift in power involved a usurpation of the bishop's property by the canons during the middle years of
the twelfth century.[8] Ranerio's comments portray an important
aspect of eleventh-century reform traditions in a surprisingly negative light.

It is tempting to dismiss Bishop Ranerio's commentary on the
dispute, since he wrote his comments seventy years after the fact.
Nevertheless, there is a great deal of truth in Ranerio's argument that
Bishop Sigifredo's reforms led to a shift in power from bishop to
cathedral chapter a century later. This shift was not intentional.
Rather, it was grounded in unforeseen implications of the economic
arrangements that made the new style of common life possible.

The common life, as prescribed by the council of Aachen, was
well suited to the rural economy of the Carolingian world. Each
member of the chapter relied on servants to cultivate and manage
the property that constituted his individual prebend. While the
canons lived off of the fruit of others' work, they still had to devote
considerable attention to management and protection of their
prebends. The stricter form of common life that reformers like Peter
Damian championed required a patrimony that was easier to manage
and administer and that yielded income in currency. In order to free

the canons, as much as possible, from property management and the burdensome apparatus that came with it, bishops usually donated the most liquid and easily managed revenues of the episcopal *mensa* to the canons. It is no coincidence that the stricter form of common life was more prevalent in southern Europe, where urbanization was more developed and wealth was more mobile.[9]

Bishop Sigifredo donated seven baptismal churches, whose control over tithes and burials allowed the canons to live off of the fruits of others' labor and management. More importantly, he donated urban property and churches as well, which were more easily managed than property dispersed throughout the countryside. As a result, in comparison to the bishop's resources, the chapter's patrimony was more easily managed, consisting of assets that yielded income without a lot of overhead costs. During periods of stability, when the bishop's resources in the countryside were accessible, this imbalance was not significant. Unfortunately, peace and stability were not easy to come by in twelfth-century central Italy. As shown in the previous chapter, it could be difficult to protect baptismal churches—one of the easiest rural resources to convert into currency. It could be expensive as well. Territorial lordship was an expensive endeavor, requiring maintenance of a military apparatus. The episcopal knights who sacked Santa Romana did not offer their services for free. It is not unlikely that financial burdens of lordship drove Ildibrando to covet the chapter's portion of the *mensa*, particularly the chapter's urban property. In addition to the political instability of the twelfth century, there is yet another factor that caused the Orvietan bishops to feel the economic imbalance more acutely. Population growth and urbanization significantly increased the economic value of the chapter's portion of the *mensa*.

Urbanization and the Common Life

While it is not possible to estimate Orvieto's population before the late thirteenth century, the pattern of settlement provides unmistakable evidence of rapid growth as early as the twelfth century.[10] The institutional infrastructure of local churches provided the framework for settlement of this rapidly expanding population. In fact, ecclesiastical institutions throughout Italy were among the most important promoters of urbanization, as they realized the advantages of converting their urban holdings from agricultural lands into residential rental property. Beyond rental income, which was often nominal, conversion of cultivated space into rental property meant new parishioners, which in turn, meant more tithes, offerings, and bequests. On a more spiritual plane, rental property tightened the links between the local church and its people.[11]

At the beginning of the twelfth century, the Orvietan population was concentrated in the western and southern part of the plateau. Four or five churches in this part of the city date from the sixth century. There were probably ten churches by the eleventh century, mostly located in the southwestern portion of the city. By the late twelfth century, population was expanding into the eastern and northern portion of the city, which previously was covered with gardens, vineyards, and other cultivated spaces belonging primarily to the bishop, the cathedral chapter, and the Benedictine monastery of Santi Severo and Martiro, located just outside of the city.

It was the issue of settlement and population that made these urban churches such a contentious issue between the bishop and chapter. From thirteenth-century sources that document the bishop's and cathedral chapter's urban holdings, it is clear that the cathedral chapter was the chief beneficiary of this expansion. Roughly 80 to 85 percent of the bishop's property was concentrated in the district of Santa Maria, where the cathedral church is located. Another 10 percent was located in the San Giovanni district. The remainder was scattered across other districts. The property of San Costanzo was distributed more evenly: San Costanzo, 30 percent; San Cristoforo, 27 percent; San Lorenzo, 14 percent; Sant' Andrea 11 percent; San Salvatore, 8 percent; San Stefano, 6 percent; other 4 percent (see map 2).[12] Of these churches, San Cristoforo and San Stefano appear to be twelfth-century foundations and represent developing neighborhoods.

During the early stages of demographic growth, neighborhoods around the older churches probably benefited most from the expansion. As these spaces became more densely populated, demographic growth spilled over into new neighborhoods. The demographic expansion produced a significant economic windfall in old and new neighborhoods alike. The crucial issue was whether the bishop or chapter would reap the economic benefit. Bishop Sigifredo's imposition of the common life on the cathedral canons significantly leveraged their position, allowing them to appeal to a deeply compelling reform tradition to support their claim. The distribution of property between bishop and chapter in the thirteenth century indicates that the chapter was the clear winner, as the bishop's property was virtually confined to a single district of the city around the cathedral.

Urbanization and Parish Formation

Disputes possess a natural inclination to mate, as contending parties search for justification and/or tactical advantage in deeper principles or broader and more powerful coalitions of interests. This was certainly the case in Ildibrando's dispute with the cathedral canons. Bishop Ildibrando found an ally in the clergy of the city's churches. The alliance of the city's clergy with Ildibrando had ominous implications, for it signaled that the common life, at least as it was practiced and used by the Orvietan cathedral canons, could alienate the laity.

As is clear from other cities like Verona, potential for antipathy between urban clergy and the cathedral chapter was great. First, urban clergy were very poor, while the cathedral chapter was wealthy.[13] Imposition of the common life, which involved a significant donation to the chapter, only accentuated this economic difference. Moreover, urban clergy enjoyed little autonomy. In the city only the cathedral had full parish rights, which included the right to baptize, collect tithes, and bury the dead.[14] In Orvieto, the churches of San Costanzo, the church of the cathedral chapter, and the cathedral church of Santa Maria shared the status of urban *pieve*.

From examples in other cities where similar disputes arose, it is clear that demographic expansion only increased this tension. As districts of the city grew more densely populated, urban dwellers increasingly looked to their neighborhood churches for their spiritual needs. Important aspects of pastoral care, such as penance and celebration of mass, became attached more securely to neighborhood churches and chapels. While population growth increased the need for greater autonomy on the part of urban clergy, the cathedral chapter was unwilling to relinquish control. Thus a struggle on the part of neighborhood churches for full parish rights, which included control over tithes, burials, and other revenues, soon followed. This struggle continued into the thirteenth century. In the early stages of the struggle, associations of urban clergy emerged, as urban clerics sought to leverage their power against the cathedral chapter.[15] There was an Orvietan clerical confraternity by the 1170s.[16] Although there is no direct evidence concerning its origin, it would not be unreasonable to think that it originated in the disputes of the 1140s and 1150s.

Bishop Ildibrando thus shared an interest with urban clergy in curbing the power of the archpriest and cathedral chapter over the swelling urban population. Expulsion of the canons from the cathedral and assignment of their duties to the neighborhood clergy indicate that the bishop and parish clergy gained the upper hand in the early stages of the dispute. The balance shifted toward the chapter in the latter stages as the dispute became entangled in papal politics. Before discussing the papacy's influence on the dispute, it is worth calling attention to the far-reaching implications of Ildibrando's temporary alliance with the urban clergy. In their drive for autonomy, urban clergy reflected the interests of the laity. Indeed, lay aspirations were one of the primary forces behind development of parishes, both in the city and in the countryside. The laity's quest to establish parish rights for their neighborhood church probably was driven more from pragmatic concerns—it was their wealth that maintained the local priest—than by popular religious enthusiasm.[17] Nevertheless, the subordination of their wishes to the cathedral chapter's economic and religious interests must have created a certain amount of religious disaffection. What good was the purity of the cathedral canons if it excluded laypersons from more active participation in their neighborhood church? Even worse, as the canons lost their zeal for reform, the common life could appear as a false pretext for economic privileges, as it did to Bishop Ranerio seventy years later.

THE PAPACY, BISHOPRIC, AND COMMUNE

While Bishop Ildibrando found an ally in the clergy of the city's neighborhood churches, the canons looked to the papacy to protect the economic basis of their common life. The papacy's support of the cathedral chapter was the first in a series of formal papal interventions in Orvieto, culminating in Hadrian's treaty with the city in 1157. This treaty was essentially a pact of mutual legitimation for communal and papal state building. The Orvietans recognized papal claims in central Italy, while the papacy recognized the Orvietans' efforts to create a self-governing city-state under papal overlordship.

Papal state building in Orvieto is interesting for several reasons. First, it demonstrates the extent to which papal state builders such as Pope Hadrian IV ultimately depended on local political and religious dynamics. The papacy could not force its way into local politics. It had to patiently look for opportunities to make itself welcome. Second, and more important, it is difficult to distinguish in these agreements where religion ends and where politics begin. Hadrian's success in Orvieto depended on his ability to harmonize political and religious interests that had become incompatible. As a result, papal state building in Orvieto came as a package in which ecclesiastical order and political order were inseparable components. They remained so in Orvieto until the time of Innocent III. Before turning directly to papal activity in Orvieto, I will touch on royal and papal politics in early-twelfth-century Italy, as central authority will begin to play an important role in Orvietan politics by midcentury.

Royal and Papal Authority in the Early Twelfth Century

Cities in Roman and Lombard Tuscany developed in the absence of central authority during the eleventh and early twelfth centuries. Salian kings emerged from the investiture controversy considerably weakened in German and Italy. Their territorial base in Germany was weak. As the old tribal duchies disintegrated, new dynasties, such as the Supplingburgs, Staufer, and Zähringer built increasingly autonomous jurisdictions that were similar in nature to Italian signorial lordships, only on a larger scale.[18] Given the disintegration of royal authority in Germany, it was difficult for German kings to intervene effectively in Italy. Henry V tried to rebuild the Tuscan march as a base for imperial authority, but failed.[19] His successors, Lothar III (1125–1138) and Conrad III (1138–1152), were chosen, in large part, because they were not strong enough to threaten the growing power of the dukes. Each had to contend with rival claims to the throne. As a result, their ability to intervene in Italy was even less than that of Henry V.[20]

Papal authority in central Italy revived under the reform papacy. With the support of Beatrice of Tuscany, Gregory VII seems to have planned an aggressive campaign of state building in central Italy. He began fortifying castles and moved aggressively against those who resisted. In 1074 he sent an army against the counts of Bagnorea, just south of Orvieto. The expedition proved unsuccessful, and with the outbreak of the Investiture Controversy, plans to build up the papal state fell by the wayside.[21] For most of the first half of the twelfth century, papal authority in central Italy was as weak as that of the German kings, in large part because the Normans in southern Italy absorbed the attention of papal Italian policy.

Activity in the northwestern portion of the papal state is evident once again in the 1140s. There were two principal reasons for this renewed attention: the failure of papal policy in southern Italy and the emergence of the Roman commune. Eleventh-century popes forged a strong alliance with the emerging Norman state in southern Italy. In 1059 Pope Nicholas II conferred legitimacy on Norman conquests by investing Richard of Aversa with the principality of Capua and Robert Guiscard with Apulia and Calabria. The alliance proved mutually beneficial. Norman rulers restored much of southern Italy to papal obedience. During the investiture contest, Gregory VII leaned heavily on the Normans for support. In return, papal support conferred legitimacy on the Normans in the face of traditional Ottonian and Salian claims that southern Italy belonged to the empire.

Relations between the papacy and the Normans grew hostile by the 1120s with the emergence of Roger II, Robert Guiscard's nephew, who sought to consolidate Norman territories into a unified state, and who was less willing to defer to papal authority than his predecessors. This disturbing turn in papal/Norman relations divided the College of Cardinals into pro-imperial and pro-Norman camps and contributed to a schism that lasted from 1130 to 1138. Anacletus, the pro-Norman pope, confirmed Roger's claims to the kingdom of Sicily, Calabria, Apulia, Capua, and the duchy of Naples. Anacletus's rival, Pope Innocent II, emerged as the victorious candidate by 1137 and was determined to punish Roger for his support of the antipope. Innocent excommunicated Roger at the second Lateran Council in 1139 and led an expedition against the recalcitrant Norman ruler. The Normans routed papal forces. Roger took Innocent prisoner and forced him to confirm Anacletus's concessions. Roger continued his aggression toward the papacy throughout the 1140s, taking control of papal territory in Campagna, the southern region of the papal state.[22]

To make matters worse, Innocent II found himself at odds with the Romans as he tried to protect Tivoli against the territorial ambitions of Roman aristocrats. In 1143 the Romans rebelled. They discarded the office of prefect, through which the papacy governed the city, and placed executive and judicial authority in a newly constituted senate, which claimed the patrimony of St. Peter, both inside and outside of Rome, for itself. Further, the new Roman senate found assistance from the popular reformer Arnold of Brescia, whose denunciation of the corrupting influence of ecclesiastical property lent support to the senate's claim to the patrimony. Pope Eugenius III was able to reach a compromise in 1145, whereby the members of the senate were granted their offices by the pope. Despite this agreement, the pope had effectively lost control of Rome.[23]

Eugenius thus faced threats from the Normans and the Romans without a reliable protector. Conrad III supported the papacy, but was too weak to provide effective assistance. As Eugenius realized the need for an alternative base of power, he began to look to the northern portion of the patrimony, especially Orvieto, where the political and religious disputes that divided the city provided an opportunity for the papacy to intervene and begin building a basis of power.

Orvieto and the Papacy before Pope Hadrian IV

Although the papacy was not capable of intervening in local politics in any meaningful way before the 1150s, one can detect papal politics lurking in the shadows during the first half of the twelfth century. Ildibrando's conflict with Archpriest Ranerio and the chapter may have intersected with papal politics as early as the 1130s. Details concerning papal influence in the early stages of the dispute are meager. Priest Amideo recalled that the dispute between Ildibrando (before he became bishop) and Ranerio, the archpriest, began during a "time of error."[24] The word "error" calls to mind the papal schism of 1130–1138.[25] It is unlikely that Orvieto remained unaffected by these events. In most cities, it was not uncommon to find supporters of both popes. In Viterbo there were Innocentian and Anacletan parties until the very end of the schism. On his return to Rome in 1137,

Innocent stopped in Viterbo. His visit sparked a violent clash between the two parties.[26]

Unfortunately, there is not sufficient evidence to determine how Orvietans responded. It is, however, clear that the bishopric was vacant during the schism for an unspecified number of years. The last extant document executed by Bishop Guilielmo is dated 1131.[27] The first extant document executed by Bishop Ildibrando is dated 1140.[28] In 1137, when Count Otto donated his property to the bishopric, the see was vacant. Receiving the donation on behalf of the Orvietan bishopric were Bishop Radolfo of Perugia, Ranerio the archpriest, and Caromo the archdeacon.[29] Although there is no way to determine the length of the vacancy, its end coincided with the end of the schism. The antipope Anacletus II died in 1138. Ildibrando was bishop by 1140.

Papal politics began to emerge from the shadows to exert a more direct influence in Orvieto during the pontificate of Eugenius III (1145–1153). He was the first twelfth-century pope to make significant progress in establishing papal authority in the region. In 1147 he passed through the Orvietan diocese on his way to France. Arlotto di Berizo, one of the witnesses testifying on behalf of the Orvietan bishop in 1194, recalled that his father, along with other Orvietan knights, conducted Eugenius through the diocese.[30]

After Eugenius returned from France, he began to lay a foundation for papal authority to the northwest of Orvieto. In this effort, he benefited from the same social and demographic forces that allowed Bishop Ildibrando and the Orvietan knights to draw the countryside under the religious and political jurisdiction of the city, that is, the signorialization of power and the financial strains that militarization placed upon lay and ecclesiastical lords like the Farolfingi and the monastery of San Salvatore. In 1148 Eugenius received half of the castle of Radicofani from the monastery of San Salvatore of Monte Amiata. This transaction is among the early examples of papal efforts to create an infrastructure of castles inside the patrimony as a basis for papal authority.[31] It should come as no surprise that Radicofani lay along the Via Francigena.[32] In light of Eugenius's efforts to establish his authority to the northwest of Orvieto, one must suspect that when he crossed the Orvietan diocese with a band of Orvietan knights in 1147, it was not simply to reach the other side. The presence of Pope Eugenius in the region was not unlike that of Bishop Ildibrando. Each possessed a critical mass of power around which property, authority, and people gravitated.

In the early 1150s, relations between these two centers of power was still undefined, creating a potential for conflict. Apparently this potential was realized in 1153/1154 when Bishop Ildibrando was expelled from Orvieto because he was out of favor with the pope.[33] There is no mention of the precise reason for Ildibrando's exile. Perhaps it was Ildibrando's rejection of the common life, one of the fundamental components of the eleventh-century reform movements. Perhaps Ildibrando's aggressive territorial policies clashed with those of the papacy. One thing is clear: the cathedral chapter and the papacy found a common adversary in Bishop Ildibrando. As a result, his authority in Orvieto disintegrated. Several witnesses in 1194 remembered the latter years of his episcopate as a time of disorder. Archdeacon Dono commented that during the time of Ildibrando, it was almost a custom for priests to go outside of the diocese for ordination.[34]

When Ildibrando returned from exile in 1154, he restored the right of the cathedral canons to celebrate mass in the cathedral. The settlement included a careful definition of the rights and duties of the bishop and canons with respect to the cathedral church. The bishop retained half of the revenues derived from burials, penance, and other offerings for the episcopal *mensa*. The other half belonged to the canons. The bishop, in turn, would receive a fourth of the offerings from burials in the church of San Costanzo. The bishop had the right to confirm the canons' choice of archdeacon and *primicerius*, the official directly below the archdeacon in charge of liturgical functions of the chapter. Finally, the bishop was responsible for repairing the ceiling and walls of Santa Maria and for providing oil lamps and other ornaments for the church.[35] Bishop Ildibrando lost the battle to exclude the canons from the cathedral.

Pope Hadrian IV and the Marriage of Orvietan and Papal State Building

While it appears that Pope Eugenius had already begun to influence the course of Bishop Ildibrando's dispute with the chapter, only during the pontificate of Hadrian IV (1154–1159) did the papacy offer an effective resolution to the economic and religious tensions that

plagued the bishopric. Hadrian's intervention had far-reaching implications for both the bishopric and the commune by tying this resolution to papal state building.

When Hadrian became pope in 1154, it seemed as though political winds had shifted in the papacy's favor, reducing the urgency of
papal policy in the northern patrimony. Frederick Barbarossa came
to the throne in 1152, intent upon restoring royal authority in
Germany and Italy. Frederick's intervention in a disputed election in
Madgeburg, against the wishes of Pope Eugenius, caused early concern regarding Frederick's attitude toward the papacy. Frederick
allayed these fears when he concluded the Treaty of Constance with
Eugenius III in 1153, promising to protect the papacy against the
Romans and Roger II of Sicily. In return, Eugenius promised to crown
him emperor. Eugenius died shortly thereafter, leaving the matter of
the imperial coronation to Hadrian IV. During the summer of 1155,
Hadrian planned to meet Frederick Barbarossa in Orvieto to plan the
coronation and to discuss other pressing concerns. According to
Boso, Hadrian's biographer, Hadrian did not trust Frederick and
chose Orvieto as a secure place to await Frederick's arrival. Because
Frederick arrived in Italy earlier than expected, Hadrian feared that
he did not have time to go as far north as Orvieto, "that safest of
places," as Boso referred to it. He decided to wait in Città Castellana
instead.[36]

The meeting finally took place at Sutri. Mutual suspicion
between Hadrian and Frederick made the meeting a tense affair;
nevertheless, they renewed the Treaty of Constance and proceeded
to Rome for the coronation. Unfortunately, the ceremony went as
neither of them had planned. The Romans rioted, recognizing that
Frederick's treaty with Hadrian was against their interests. Frederick
put down the riot in brutal fashion then marched back to Germany,
without fulfilling his promise to subdue the Normans.[37]

William I, who succeeded his father, Roger II of Sicily, in 1154,
continued his father's hostile policy toward the papacy. Despite
Frederick's departure, it looked as though Hadrian would be able to
handle the Norman problem by other means. William became ill in
1155. Hadrian decided to take advantage of the opportunity by allying with the Byzantines and William's rebellious vassals. William
quickly recovered and defeated the papal forces. Like Innocent II in
1139, Hadrian found himself at the mercy of the Norman king. He

signed a treaty at Benevento in 1156, recognizing the unity of southern Italy under William, along with William's claim to his father's conquests in the southern patrimony. In return, William swore fidelity to the pope.[38]

At this point Hadrian renewed Eugenius's policy of building a new base of power in the northern patrimony. He cast his eyes toward Orvieto as the key to recovering papal claims in Roman and Lombard Tuscany. Given Orvieto's fortress-like character and its aggressive expansion to the west along the Via Francigena, Hadrian recognized that if the city did not become an ally of the papacy, it would present a formidable obstacle to papal interests in the region. One of the principal challenges for the papacy in Orvieto was to penetrate the core of interests that bound the bishopric and commune. Pope Eugenius may have already begun this process when he passed through Orvietan territory with Arlotto di Berizo's father. Nevertheless, the exile of Bishop Ildibrando indicates that relations between the papacy and the Orvietan bishop were strained as late as 1154. Furthermore, many Orvietans feared that papal authority in the region would come at the expense of their own hard-fought gains. The cathedral chapter's appeal to the papacy offered an opportunity to overcome these obstacles.

The turning point in papal-Orvietan relations came in 1156. Boso recalled that Hadrian left Benevento and headed north. He decided to bypass Rome and went to Orvieto. "It seemed good to Hadrian and his brothers to go to Orvieto and honor the city with his presence because, with great effort and diligence he had recently brought the city, which for a long time had rejected papal authority, under subjection to the Roman church. For until Hadrian's time, as was said by all, none of the Roman pontiffs had ever entered that city or exercised any temporal power there. For this reason the clergy, *popolo*, and knights of Orvieto, with all the more longing and veneration, received the pontiff and honored him in every way they could. During his stay, he was joyful and honored great and small alike with fond affection as the new family of St. Peter."[39] The great effort and diligence to which Boso referred consisted of approximately two years of negotiations and compromises to transform the political and religious interests within Orvieto into a well-defined pro-papal coalition.

This process began when Hadrian confirmed the chapter's property during his 1156 visit and took the chapter under papal protection.[40] This suggests that the Orvietan welcome mentioned by Boso was not unrelated to the ongoing dispute between the bishop and chapter. His confirmation of the chapter's property sealed the victory of the cathedral canons in their struggle to control the bulk of episcopal property in the city. There is, however, an atmosphere of religious reform in this document that tempers the canons' victory with a certain degree of humility and religious purpose. Throughout his pontificate Hadrian was deeply concerned with preserving the sanctity of the clerical order, and he saw the common life as an important tool for doing so. He issued numerous privileges to cathedral chapters in order to promote the common life.[41] His privilege to the Orvietan cathedral chapter must be understood in this context. The document recording Hadrian's confirmation of the chapter's property marks the first appearance of Rocco, the prior of the cathedral chapter, and the first time that the head of the cathedral canons is called "prior." Previously, Ranerio, whom Rocco replaced, was called the "archpriest."[42] The change in terminology probably indicates a restoration of a stricter form of common life.[43]

Given the importance of ecclesiastical property in the political dynamics of the region and the corresponding interpenetration of religious and political activity, religious reform could not be divorced from economic and political concerns. Hadrian recognized this. After his confirmation of the chapter's property, representatives of the papacy were involved in the recovery of a sizable portion of episcopal property located in Caio, property that was held in pledge by members of one of Orvieto's most powerful families.[44] Bishop Ildibrando probably pledged much of this property to pay for the military services of Orvietan knights who supported his efforts to establish episcopal authority along the western border of the diocese. The recovery of episcopal property pledged to laypersons removed the economic imbalance between the bishop and chapter that had led to their dispute in the first place.

The pledge of episcopal property to powerful families was connected to yet another critical issue, that is, the stake that the local elite had in the bishopric as the vehicle for Orvietan territorial expansion. Five months before the first recovery of property in Caio, Hadrian and the Orvietan commune came to an agreement regarding their respective roles in Orvieto and the surrounding region. The presence of Guilelmo Beccario, a kinsman of Bishop Ildibrando, as one of the consuls representing Orvieto indicates that the partisans of Bishop Ildibrando were not left out of this agreement, even though Ildibrando himself had been exiled under pressure from Hadrian's predecessor. The document of February 1157 records that "the consuls swore the fealty of liege men to the pope himself and his catholic successors, by swearing according to the oath that his other *fideles* make to him concerning papal temporalities."[45] Just as Orvietan bishops used political feudalism as a flexible tool for imposing a tolerable degree of subjection on signorial lords, Hadrian began to use similar methods to rebuild papal authority in the northern patrimony.[46]

Both parties had much to gain from this treaty. The Orvietans had created a territorial lordship with no juridical basis. Imperial diplomas dating back to Charlemagne gave the papacy de iure authority over central Italy, but the papacy lacked the power to enforce these claims. The treaty of 1157 gave Orvieto a juridical claim that its territorial power lacked and gave the papacy a tool for enforcing its de iure authority. Hadrian also allayed Orvietan concerns that a strong papal presence in the northwestern patrimony threatened their own interests in the region. He apparently assured them that, instead of blocking Orvietan expansion, he was willing to support their territorial ambitions. In the final clause of the agreement, Hadrian promised to negotiate a peace between Orvieto and Acquapendente, a city that the Orvietans had fought long and hard to control.

In sum, Hadrian's rapprochement with Orvieto was a complicated series of compromises that addressed the fundamental tension between episcopal lordship and ecclesiastical reform. He supported the chapter's reform traditions and their claim to property in the city, while compensating the bishop for this economic loss by working for the recovery of episcopal property in the countryside, which had fallen into the hands of certain powerful families. On a more fundamental level, Hadrian's treaty with Orvieto removed the potential for conflict between episcopal lordship and ecclesiastical reform by constructing a political framework that would make episcopal lordship obsolete. The burdens of territorial expansion that formerly fell on the bishopric would now fall on the papacy. Whether this was an unintended consequence of papal state building or a conscious design on Hadrian's part is unclear. Nevertheless, by officially recognizing the existence of the commune and its territorial ambitions, Hadrian effectively transferred the weight of the city's territorial expansion from the bishopric to the papacy. The city no longer depended on the bishopric to extend and to justify its political jurisdiction, at least in theory.

From Hadrian's perspective, the papal-Orvietan alliance was quite fruitful, creating a powerful center of gravity that began to draw the region connecting Roman and Lombard Tuscany into the papal orbit. This was, after all, the ultimate goal of Hadrian's treaty with Orvieto. Boso recalled that Hadrian's activity in the northwestern patrimony was one of that pope's principal successes.

He expanded the patrimony of St. Peter with great possessions and many buildings. He bought the castle of Corciano[47] from Boccaleone for 140 lire. He bought two excellent mills located next to Santa Cristina[48] from Ildibrando and Bernardino, the sons of Ugolino di Calmaniare, for 190 lire. He received Rocca di San Stefano,[49] along with half of Proceno and Ripeseno[50] in pledge for 148 lire and five soldi from the same counts, as written in the public record. Additionally he received all the land of the same counts as St. Peter's inheritance by their own voluntary donation, which is also contained in the archive. . . . He built a rampart in the castle of Radicofani, protected by towers and a deep ditch.[51]

It probably is no coincidence that Hadrian's acquisitions in this region followed his treaty with Orvieto. Nor is it a coincidence that practically all of these acquisitions came from Ildibrando and Bernardino, the sons of Count Ugolino di Calmaniare, members of a branch of the Farolfingi. Hadrian's transactions with Ildibrando and Bernardino began in October 1157 with the purchase of two mills in Bolsena.[52] Boso noted that these mills were located next to the church of Santa Cristina in Bolsena, the same church that Ildibrando and Bernardino's grandfather, Count Bernardo I, donated to Bishop Guilielmo in 1115 and received back in fief.[53] Among the witnesses to Hadrian's purchase of the two mills was Arlotto di Berizo, whose father had been among the knights who escorted Pope Eugenius across the Orvietan diocese in 1147.

On the same day, Ildibrando and Bernardino donated all of their property to Hadrian and received it back in fief. This property included Marsciano, over which Ildibrando and Bernardino retained some measure of comital authority; Collelungo; Getone; Santa Croce; Santa Lucia; Rocca di San Stefano; Ripeseno; half of Orzoli; half of Proceno; and one-fourth of Biceno. Most of this property was located in an arc that stretched from the northwest of Orvieto to the northeast, a broad band of territory where the diocese of Orvieto bordered the dioceses of Sovana, Chiusi, and Todi.[54]

Like Hadrian's treaty with Orvieto, these transactions were political compromises with a strong sense of religious purpose. The document recording the donation reads, "thus we [Ildibrando and Bernardino] concede to you these [properties] for the many and grave offenses that we often committed against you, your predecessors, and the Roman curia. And because we recognize that the aforementioned lands belong by right to blessed Peter, we freely restore them to you . . . for the redemption of our souls and the souls of our parents."[55] This transaction was both a political compromise and a religious act. Regarding their control over Rocca di San Stefano, the agreement specifies, "if you violate the truce or offend against hospitals, templars, clerics, or monks and do not pay the required penalty within fifteen days, then let Rocca di San Stefano remain under the authority and ownership of St. Peter. You will foster and serve the churches, clerics, and monks of your land just as our other *fideles* serve their churches, clerics, and monks."[56] Like Bishop Ildibrando's expansion into the countryside, the recovery of papal claims in central Italy was simultaneously a political and a religious endeavor. The work of the church could proceed only in an atmosphere of political stability.

Also like Bishop Ildibrando's expansion, the papacy capitalized on the financial strains caused by signorialization. In January 1159, Ildibrando and his brother borrowed 148 lire and five soldi from Hadrian. In return, they pledged Rocca di San Stefano, half of Proceno, and half of Ripeseno.[57] In a region where lay and ecclesiastical resources were strained, the exigencies of hard times offered a foothold for the pope, whose intervention would not have been welcome otherwise. Throughout the 1140s and 1150s, papal finances were relatively strong.[58] Because of that strength, Hadrian could purchase castles and lend money, thereby gaining control over property and drawing a circle of clients around him. In sum, Hadrian's state building was simply a larger version of Orvietan state building—a patchwork of agreements, which, with lots of effort, time, and luck, could be transformed into a more consistent territorial authority.

Pope Hadrian's achievement in Roman and Lombard Tuscany was nothing short of remarkable. He had a gift for negotiating settlements in which there seemed to be no losers. An exclusive focus on the papal perspective, however, obscures the complexity of Hadrian's achievement. His success depended on his admittance into the network of interests tugging at the Orvietan bishopric. One would naturally assume that this would have been easy for a pope. In reality, his entrance into the tug-of-war resulted from forces largely beyond his control. The disintegration of the Italian kingdom and the signorialization of power thrust episcopal lordship upon the bishopric. This new role, which Bishop Ildibrando adopted with considerable enthusiasm, changed the configuration of forces pulling at the bishopric, thus creating a tension between the financial demands of territorial lordship and the economic requirements of the cathedral chapter's common life. It was this seemingly irreconcilable tension between political, economic, and religious interests that opened the door for papacy.

Once the door was opened, Hadrian made a profound impression on Orvieto's religious and political life. Although the Orvietan jurist in chapter 2 referred to a distant past when papal fiat made the *comitatus* and *episcopatus* synonyms, it was really Pope Hadrian IV who established this order. He reinvigorated both the city's territorial ambitions and the bishopric's reform traditions, all the while establishing papal authority over the city and its surrounding region. This harmony between Orvietan territorial ambitions, papal state building, and ecclesiastical reform was nothing short of miraculous. Although this magic moment was short-lived, it became deeply embedded in episcopal consciousness as the blueprint for managing the sometimes overwhelming tensions between the economic, political, and religious interests pulling at the bishopric.

CHAPTER FOUR

THE UNTENABILITY
OF EPISCOPAL LORDSHIP

*Bishopric and Commune in
the Late Twelfth Century*

IT LOOKED AS THOUGH HADRIAN'S ACTIVITY IN ORVIETO
would reinvigorate the city's territorial expansion without creating
the tensions inherent in episcopal lordship. The papal-Orvietan
alliance did indeed provide the framework for several decades of
Orvietan expansion, although in a manner that neither the papacy nor
Orvietans could have predicted. The political order that Pope Hadrian
established never took root. Scarcely two years passed before the papal
schism (1159–1177) and the bitter struggle between Pope Alexander III
and Frederick Barbarossa plunged Italy into chaos. The fragility of
Hadrian's peace became apparent during these years. The schism
strained papal finances to its limits. Instead of purchasing castles and
lending money, the papacy began to sell castles and borrow heavily.[1]

The second half of the twelfth century was a critical period for
Orvieto and other central Italian communes. Between 1150 and 1200,
the central Italian communes came into their own. The schism was

one of the principal motors driving this process of maturation. The schism polarized the region around Orvieto into pro-papal and pro-imperial partisans. Some of Orvieto's subject territories, most notably Acquapendente, used imperial partisanship as an excuse to escape the yoke of Orvietan overlordship. On the balance, however, polarization of the region worked in Orvieto's favor, as several powerful territorial lords, who were looking for protection against imperial troops and partisans, submitted to Orvieto. This territorial expansion was one of the most notable characteristics of Orvietan history during the second half of the twelfth century.[2] The commune emerged from these tumultuous decades with a sense of self-confidence, having significantly expanded its territorial authority.

Given the political and economic strain on the papacy and the relative immaturity of the city's own political institutions, the bishopric was forced to step into the breach once again and provide a framework for much of this expansion. The results were disastrous for the bishopric. Episcopal lordship reawakened old tensions between bishop and chapter and introduced new problems, as heretics and radical reformers challenged episcopal authority.

BISHOP AND COMMUNE AT MIDCENTURY

The daily functioning of the twelfth-century Orvietan commune is largely hidden from view. Practically all that can be known about civic institutions before the late twelfth century is that consuls and a General Assembly governed the commune. The consulate was the defining institution of the early communes. Indeed, the birth of a commune is usually dated by the first mention of its consulate. Consuls were the supreme executive and judicial officials. They were generally chosen from among the urban aristocracy and served for terms ranging between six months and a year. The number of consuls was not fixed, often varying from year to year. The General Assembly was the council of all citizens.[3]

The earliest mention of the commune occurs almost as an aside in the document of 1137 recording Count Otto's donation to the Orvietan bishopric. Cittadino Malabranca, acting on behalf of the *comune civitatis*, gave Otto a counterpayment for his donation to the bishopric.[4] The first mention of the consulate occurs twenty years later, when Pope Hadrian officially recognized the commune as a legitimate political body. Pope Hadrian IV made his treaty with the *populum Urbevetanum*, or Orvietan people, represented by Rocco, the prior of the cathedral chapter, two consuls, and two nobles.[5] While these two documents do not contain an abundance of information about political and social structures of the early commune, the information that they do contain is interesting. When placed in the context of other twelfth-century episcopal documents, they reinforce several important points about the bishopric's role in the early communal period. The city's consular aristocracy, or ruling class, emerged from a group of families closely tied to the bishopric. Their political and religious interests, as well as those of the broader community, were defined, in large part, by their cooperation with the bishop in the conquest of the countryside.

When Count Otto donated his vast possessions to the bishopric in 1137, the *comune civitatis* paid the *launegild*, or countergift, which confirmed the donation as irrevocable.[6] This points to a critical function that bishops served in the early communes. When dealing with a king or count, urban elites looked to the bishopric to lend institutional identity and permanence to their collective activity, for they had yet to fashion their own institutions and gain recognition for them.[7] Otto was, in fact, placing his possessions under the control of the urban community. The bishopric was the only legally recognized institution in the city capable of representing the urban community before 1157. Therefore, the only means of making a legally binding contract with the urban community was through the bishopric.[8]

Thus the bishopric served as an institutional mechanism for collective activity by the urban elite. It should come as no surprise that the witnesses to Otto's donation constitute a group of prominent families that appear consistently in episcopal documents and emerge as a consular aristocracy during the second half of the twelfth century. Cittadino Malabranca, a witness, as well as the one who paid the *launegild*, was the father of Pietro di Cittadino, who appears in a document of 1157 holding episcopal property in pledge.[9] Pietro di Cittadino was an ancestor of the Monaldeschi, a family that dominated Orvietan politics throughout the thirteenth and early fourteenth centuries. Also among the witnesses were two brothers, Ildibrandino and Homodeo. Ildibrando's son Ranaldo was a consul of the commune in 1168. This family had a long history with the bishopric. In 1126 Bishop Guilielmo leased half of the church of Santa Cristina in Porrano to Ildibrando di Pepolo di Homodeo; his sons Homodeo and Parte; and Rapizello, the nephew of Homodeo and Parte.[10] Parte, probably Ranaldo's brother, was a knight in the service of the Orvietan bishop.[11] Another witness to the 1137 document, Martinozzo, was one of the episcopal knights that sacked the church of Santa Romana, outside of Grotte.[12] While it would be tedious to provide a long list of names and transactions, it is worth noting that other witnesses to the 1137 donation appear frequently as witnesses in episcopal transactions throughout the twelfth century.[13]

When the consulate first appears in 1157, most of the representatives have close ties to the bishopric. The four lay representatives of the commune were two consuls—Guilielmo di Giovanni Lupi and Pietro Alberici—and two nobles—Guilielmo Beccario and Nero. The family of Giovanni Lupi appears alongside the family of Cittadino Malabranca in a number of important transactions involving episcopal property. Matteo, the son of Pietro Alberici, was a cathedral canon in the late twelfth century.[14] Guilielmo Beccario was related to Bishop Ildibrando.[15] In sum, the city's ruling class emerged from a group of families closely connected to the bishopric.

The representative structure of the city in the treaty of 1157— the prior of the cathedral chapter, two consuls, and two nobles— raises some interesting points about the bishopric's relation to the commune. First, the bishopric's role as a representative of the urban community did not disappear with the emergence of the consulate, as is clear from the prominent place of Rocco, the prior of the cathedral chapter, among those acting on the city's behalf.[16] Signorial lords continued to offer their submission to Orvieto in the form of donations to the bishopric, which was a more stable and deeply rooted institution. The commune's institutional structure remained ill defined into the late twelfth century; therefore, the bishopric still had a significant role to play. A document of 1170 illustrates this point. Bishop Rustico and the consuls of the commune made provisions to allow citizens to donate property for use in maintaining a bridge.[17] The nature of this transaction is obscure. No specific bridge is mentioned, although they presumably had in mind the bridge over the Paglia. Nevertheless, this document provides an interesting description of the process by which the privilege was granted. Geizo, the master of bridges, and a group of citizens first approached the consuls concerning the security of the bridge and property donated for its maintenance. With the counsel of Bishop Rustico and the clergy, the consuls reached the decision, which the citizens then approved by acclamation. An exception clause excluded all donations that violated the rights of the *boni homines*. The transaction took place in the choir of the cathedral church of Santa Maria.

One clear point emerging from this otherwise obscure document is the immaturity of communal institutions. The role of the bishop, clergy, and *boni homines* alongside consuls, citizens, and the master of the bridge demonstrate that this privilege arose from the interaction of secular and ecclesiastical bodies, some official and some semi-official. The acclamation of citizens indicates that approval of legislation, as well as citizen involvement in communal administration, was relatively informal. Finally, the commune did not possess its own building for municipal administration. In this instance, the cathedral church of Santa Maria was the town hall. In other cases, the church of Sant' Andrea assumed this role. Count Otto's donation to the bishopric/city in 1137 took place in Sant' Andrea.[18] In sum, the formal regulation and distribution of powers was still rudimentary. It is only around 1200 that the commune begins to appear as something more substantial and autonomous.

That two consuls and two nobles serve as representatives raises other interesting questions about the composition of the ruling class. Is this a bipartite consulate of *maiores* and *minores*? While consulates of early Italian communes were typically composed of *maiores* representing the citizen class as a whole, there were cases, such as Viterbo, where divisions between *maiores* and *minores* were sufficiently sharp to become institutionalized in a bipartite magistracy.[19] This question is worth examining, as it will help clarify the fundamental issues that animated the city's political and religious life.

Before considering the status of Orvieto's consuls, it will be helpful to look more generally at the distinctions between *maiores* and *minores*. Twelfth-century sources generally use the terms *minores* or *pedites* to distinguish non-nobles from the nobility, who were commonly called *maiores* or *milites*. Only in the thirteenth century, when non-nobles began to develop their own political institutions, do the sources use the terms *nobiles* and *populares* to distinguish the two groups.[20] The terms *milites* and *pedites* bring to light one of the principal distinctions between *maiores* and *minores*. In the civic militia, nobles fought on horseback and the *popolo* supplied the contingent of foot soldiers, usually organized according to the regions of the city. There were important economic distinctions as well. The principal source of wealth for *maiores* was land in the *contado*, or surrounding countryside. *Minores* derived their wealth primarily from exercise of a profession or craft and secondarily from ownership of urban and rural property.[21]

Despite these differences, the relation between *maiores* and *minores* was not necessarily antagonistic. To begin with, the social boundary between the two groups was somewhat blurred. In Orvieto, there were few noble patrilineages with deep roots in the countryside. Most Orvietan noble families could be classified as petty nobles. This petty nobility consisted of landed proprietors, including some who made their fortunes as episcopal vassals, and the wealthiest and most successful members of the merchant and professional classes, including judges.[22] The boundary between the lowest levels of the nobility and the upper levels of the *minores* would be virtually impossible to distinguish. Moreover, the economic interests of the two groups were not as distinct as they might appear. Although land was concentrated in the hands of the nobility, *minores* still owned a considerable amount of land in the *contado*.[23] Furthermore, much of the economic activity of shopkeepers and artisans (e.g., butchers, fishmongers, tavern keepers, millers) involved the transformation of agrarian products into commodities.[24] *Maiores* and *minores* therefore shared a fundamental economic interest in pacifying the *contado*.

A closer look at Orvieto's two consuls—Pietro Alberici and Guilelmo di Giovanni Lupi—suggests that they were probably *maiores*. As noted earlier, Pietro's son was a cathedral canon. Guilelmo's brother was a judge, and his family appears in a series of episcopal documents that mention a cluster of notable landowners, including Cittadino Malabranca. To the extent that one can make a meaningful distinction between the two consuls and two noble representatives, the distinction between *capitanei* and *valvassores*, that is, between two groups of *maiores*, seems more appropriate than that between *maiores* and *minores*.

Distinctions between *maiores* and *minores* were important in Orvieto, but at this early stage of communal formation, they were not sufficiently sharp to become institutionalized into a bipartite magistracy. Only during the early thirteenth century do *minores* emerge as the *popolo*, building their own political institutions to protect their interests against the ruling elite. The most pressing issues of twelfth-century Orvietan society revolved around the bishopric, where the major disputes that defined the city's political and religious interests emerged. Territorial expansion was the first major issue shaping the city's political interests. The city rallied behind the bishopric in its dispute against the bishop of Sovanna and expanded Orvietan control to the west along the Via Francigena. Ildibrando's dispute with the cathedral chapter seems to have taken the momentum out of this expansion by the 1150s by shattering the unity of interests that made expansion possible. While the dispute emerged between two factions of *maiores* over control of episcopal property when the see was vacant,[25] it gradually merged with other disputes and became quite complicated. As a result, the common life was not only about clerical reform, but also about territorial expansion. Because Ildibrando allied with the urban clergy—a group of *minores*—issues concerning territorial expansion and the common life became closely connected with other issues, such as the ability of *minores* to invest their wealth and participate more actively and autonomously in their own parish instead of paying for the wealthy and privileged cathedral clergy. While one can identify distinctions between the political and economic interests of *maiores* and *minores*, such distinctions were not the defining features of the early commune. Rather they belonged to the complicated network of issues, such as territorial expansion, clerical reform, and lay spirituality, that intersected at the bishopric.

Pope Hadrian's treaty with Orvieto had far-reaching implications. Initially it seemed that his intervention in Orvieto restored harmony to Orvieto's tangled political and religious interests. He reinvigorated the city's territorial expansion, eased the bishopric's financial strains, and restored the cathedral chapter's commitment to clerical reform. The only cost for the Orvietans was an oath of fidelity. The oath of fidelity later proved to be a greater burden than the Orvietans had anticipated, as they were drawn into the papacy's battle against Frederick Barbarossa. Even more troubling, Innocent III expected Orvieto to subordinate its territorial ambitions to those of the papacy. As the hidden costs of Hadrian's treaty became apparent, the harmony between the city's political and religious interests disappeared. Because all of these issues converged at the bishopric, it was there that the tension was the greatest, and there that the tensions would have to be resolved.

THE SCHISM

Papal versus Imperial State Building

Relations between Frederick Barbarossa and Pope Hadrian IV grew increasingly bitter between 1155 and 1159. Two principal issues divided them. First, Frederick perceived Hadrian's treaty with William of Sicily as a betrayal of the Treaty of Constance and as a threat to his own Italian policy. Second, he had the same aspirations for northern Italy and Tuscany that Hadrian had for central Italy. He intended to restore order by creating a strong centralized state that exercised direct authority over feudal lords and nascent communes. He was, in effect, intent upon resurrecting the Italian kingdom.[26] In 1159 he sent imperial envoys into the patrimony to collect the *fodrum*, an exaction due from lands under imperial jurisdiction. This provocative act raised the tension between Frederick and Hadrian yet another notch.

The tumultuous politics of these years left the papacy divided between pro-imperial and pro-Norman parties. When Hadrian died in September 1159, the pro-imperial party elected Cardinal Octavian as Pope Victor IV. The pro-Norman party elected the papal chancellor, Cardinal Rolando Bandinelli, as Pope Alexander III. Alexander enjoyed general support throughout Europe. Nevertheless, by 1161 he had lost control over most of the patrimony. Boso recalled that in 1161, Alexander returned to Rome to dedicate the church of Santa Maria Nova. He was soon forced to depart for France, because imperial forces had taken over the entire patrimony from Acquapendente to Ceperano, with the exception of Orvieto, Terracino, Anagni, and various castles.[27] Before discussing developments in Orvieto during the schism, it is worth looking briefly at Barbarossa's efforts at state building in Italy, since these efforts profoundly influenced central Italian politics through the end of the century.

Royal authority had plummeted during the reigns of Lothar III and Conrad III. Frederick was intent upon rebuilding a strong state that could restore order in Germany and Italy. Control over northern Italy was a key to implementing his plans, for the communes had taken control of lucrative regalian rights, including administration of counties and castles; the right to choose consuls; and control of roads, tolls, and mints. Barbarossa's family possessions in Suabia and his marriage to Beatrice, who brought him Burgundy and Provence, strengthened the royal fisc. These resources, combined with regalian rights in northern Italy, would provide a firm financial basis for subduing rebellious German princes and rebuilding centralized power in Italy. In 1158 he appointed four Bolognese jurists and twenty-eight representatives of northern Italian cities to compile the Roncaglia decrees, a Domesday Book of sorts that recorded political and economic rights of the crown in northern Italy. After two decades of warfare, Frederick proved unable to overcome the resistance of the Lombard League, an alliance of northern Italian cities to defend their autonomy against Frederick's claims. The conflict was settled at the Peace of Constance in 1183, where Frederick renounced the Roncaglia decrees of 1158 and settled for a milder form of subjection.[28]

As resistance in northern Italy proved greater than Frederick expected, he began to shift the focus of his Italian policy toward central Italy, where imperial authority became a real and abiding reality during the schism and its aftermath. He issued numerous privileges and confirmations to bishoprics, monasteries, and churches in both northern and southern Tuscany. Imperial officials occupied and rendered justice in towns like Siena and Arezzo and in castle communities like Radicofani and Proceno—the very castles over which Popes Eugenius and Hadrian had endeavored to gain control. Despite these successes, he was unable to achieve his ultimate goal—to bring peace, stability, and prosperity to Italy. His Italian policy created a long and bitter dispute between two rival popes and a war that he waged against Pope Alexander III for control over the patrimony. Although the schism officially ended in 1177 with the Treaty of Venice, papal-imperial politics continued to trouble central Italy for the rest of the century.[29]

Déjà vu: The Revival of Episcopal Lordship

The battle for the patrimony polarized the region around Orvieto. Many local conflicts, which ultimately had little to do with each other or with the issues dividing Pope Alexander and Frederick Barbarossa, were swept into the currents of the papal-imperial conflict. On the one hand, the entrance of imperial troops into the region offered a powerful vehicle for resistance to those who were unhappy with the pro-papal politics of the Orvietan bishopric and commune. On the other hand, certain powerful families and smaller communities in the countryside, who felt threatened by the presence of imperial troops, looked to Orvieto for support. The most visible example of this process was the reawakening of the boundary dispute between the bishops of Orvieto and Sovana. Bishop Ranerio recalled, "During the time of Bishop Rustico [1168–1175] there was a schism between Pope Alexander and Emperor Frederick. Rustico was the catholic bishop and Pietro, of the family of Homodeo, was the schismatic. In this affair Rustico gave to his supporters many episcopal possessions in Mealla, Sant'Abundo, Valle Orvietano, and other places."[30] The schismatic Bishop Pietro di Homodeo was probably Bishop Pietro of Sovana. Several witnesses in 1194 remarked that Bishop Pietro of Sovana was, at least for a time, a schismatic along with Count Ildibrando Novello, an Aldobrandeschi.[31] Thus the region around Orvieto polarized around the "schismatics" Count Ildibrando Novello and Bishop Pietro of Sovana, on the one side, and the pro-papal bishopric and commune of Orvieto, on the other. With the papacy itself under siege, Orvietan control over its *contado* depended once again on the bishop's ability to exercise his diocesan authority.

During the early stages of the schism, it appeared that Orvieto's territorial gains during the early twelfth century would be reversed. With the help of Count Ildibrando and imperial troops, Bishop Pietro of Sovana took control over much of the western portion of the diocese that Orvietans had conquered in the 1140s. In 1194 Priest Stefano recalled that while Bishop Milo (1159–1161) collected tithes in Acquapendente, Bishop Rustico was prevented from doing so because of the schism.[32] The bishop of Sovana apparently regained control over Grotte as well. Priest Girardo recalled that Bishop Pietro of Sovana stopped in Grotte while on his way to Viterbo (probably in 1170) and confirmed children. Girardo made it clear that Bishop Pietro was able to do this only because Grotte was at war with Orvieto.[33] In 1194 Priest Giovanni, the syndic representing the bishop of Orvieto, was careful to point out that the bishops of Sovana had collected tithes in Grotte with the help of the *teutonici*, or Germans.[34]

The tide began to change in Orvieto's favor by the early 1170s, due in large part to the bishopric. While Acquapendente remained under imperial control for most of the remainder of the twelfth century, Bishop Rustico regained at least a measure of control over Grotte. Late in his episcopate he was able to remove several priests in Grotte from office.[35] Rustico excommunicated two other priests in Grotte because they had gone to the bishop of Sovana for ordination. Bishop Rustico restored them to their offices after they promised obedience to him.[36]

Territorial Expansion

Episcopal lordship and its ability to stabilize Orvietan territorial gains proved to be tremendously important for the commune, marking one of the most critical periods of growth and maturation. One of the goals of Frederick's Italian policy was to exercise direct authority over cities and rural counts. On the one hand, this was good news for the emerging communes, in that Frederick would not try to turn back the clock and subordinate them to comital authority. On the other hand, Frederick's determination to uphold the authority of rural lords meant that the potential for the cities to expand their control over the countryside was greatly limited.[37] He was, however, swimming against the tide. During the 1170s, as imperial policy became increasingly bogged down in the quagmire of the schism, central Italian cities like Arezzo, Siena, Perugia, and Florence experienced a period of tremendous territorial expansion. This was the period when the communes came into their own.

Orvieto was no different. During the late 1160s and 1170s, Orvietans made significant progress in subjugating powerful lords in the western *contado*. As was the case in the first half of the twelfth century, the bishopric was a conduit for this expansion. One of the best examples of the bishopric's role during these crucial years is found in the submission of Count Ranerio to the commune. Count Ranerio's submission was significant for several reasons. Most immediately, the territory that he controlled was quite extensive. In the longer term, it provided the foundation for Orvieto's most significant gains in the thirteenth century.

In 1168 Count Ranerio, acting on behalf of himself, his mother Teodora, and his brother Jacobo, submitted all of his territory to the Orvietan commune.[38] The path toward this submission apparently was prepared by Ranerio's earlier donations to the bishopric. While earlier donations to the bishopric provided the foundation for Ranerio's submission, the more immediate cause was a dispute with his kinsman. It appears that Count Ranerio, the head of a collateral branch of the Aldobrandeschi, was involved in a dispute over succession of his property with his cousin, Count Ildibrando Novello, the imperial partisan and supporter of Bishop Pietro of Sovana. Evidence for this dispute comes from a passing reference by one of the witnesses in 1194, who mentioned Count Ildibrando's sack of Latera, which belonged to Count Ranerio's brother, Jacobo.[39] Apparently, neither Jacobo nor Ranerio had any children in 1168. In the absence of heirs, their property could pass to the line of Count Ildibrando Novello. Ranerio's submission to Orvieto may have been one of several transactions intended to preclude Count Ildibrando from making a claim to his property.

Although the document recording Count Ranerio's submission to Orvieto does not mention the bishopric, other documents demonstrate that the bishopric played a pivotal role in the transaction. Apparently Ranerio had already donated much of his land to the Orvietan bishopric and received it back in fief. Although the document recording this transaction is no longer extant, witnesses in the Orvieto-Sovana dispute continually referred to the land of Count Ranerio as property of the bishopric.[40] In 1194 Roberto di Medico testified that the land of Count Ranerio belonged to the bishopric. This testimony is especially interesting because Roberto said that he had been present at the act of submission in 1168.[41] Arlotto di Berizo, one of the consuls of the Orvietan commune receiving the submission of Count Ranerio, corroborated Roberto's testimony.[42] The donation to the bishopric and submission to the commune were mutually reinforcing elements in the city's authority over Ranerio, as the submission added a military alliance to strengthen the bond that Ranerio had already established with Orvieto by his donation to the bishopric.

While the bishopric played a pivotal role in Ranerio's submission, it was the commune that benefited most from this territorial expansion, largely because the burdens of defending this property became too heavy for the bishopric to bear. The city's claim to Ranerio's land remained a point of conflict between Orvieto and Count Ildibrando Novello's successors well into the second decade of the thirteenth century. Maintaining and extending control over this critical territory dominated Orvietan politics during much of the thirteenth century.[43]

The Burden of Episcopal Lordship

The bishopric paid dearly for its role in Orvieto's territorial expansion during the schism. Its relation to a rural aristocrat named Tebalduccio and his family illustrates this point well. Tebalduccio appears in the sources as a member of the *lambardi*, or rural aristocracy of Flaiano, a small community near Acquapendente.[44] His enmity with the bishop of Sovana and Count Ildibrando Novello drove him into an alliance with the Orvietan bishopric. Ostensibly such an alliance with the rural aristocracy of a strategically important region would constitute a victory for the Orvietan bishopric. The cost of this alliance with Tebalduccio's family suggests otherwise. While many details concerning Tebalduccio's relation to the bishopric are lost, it appears that Bishop Rustico secured the military services of Tebalduccio's son, Stefano, by pledging episcopal property to him. In 1180 Bishop Riccardo, Rustico's successor, recovered episcopal property in Gervasio, held in pledge by Stefano.[45] Apparently Bishop Riccardo met with only limited success in recovering this property, for in 1212 Bishop Giovanni of Orvieto was still attempting to regain this land from Stefano's sons.[46] In other words, the cost of this alliance to the bishopric was the loss of control over episcopal property for almost forty years.

The burdens of territorial expansion plunged the bishopric headlong into an economic crisis. As the financial condition of the bishopric worsened, Bishop Rustico was forced to depend increasingly on the cathedral canons. This dependence led to the alienation of even more property, which Rustico had to use as security against loans. For example, he borrowed money from Rocco, the prior of the cathedral canons, and in return, pledged a baptismal church in Stiolo and episcopal revenues in Caio.[47] Rustico pledged another baptismal church and various revenues to the cathedral canon Tebaldo. As will become apparent, Rustico's reliance on the cathedral chapter would lead to new tensions between the chapter and his successor, Bishop Riccardo. Even more important, the bishop's economic dependence on the chapter would have disastrous consequences for the laity's perception of the bishopric.

THE CATHARS

In the midst of this economic crisis and Rustico's growing dependence on the cathedral chapter, episcopal authority plummeted. The *Passio Beati Petri Parentii Martiris*, or the *The Sufferings of the Blessed Martyr Pietro Parenzo*, which tells of the spread of heresy in Orvieto, dates the first appearance of Cathar heretics in Orvieto to Rustico's episcopate.[48] According to the *Passio*, Diotesalvi, a Florentine, and Gotardo, from Marzano, came to Orvieto sowing the seeds of Cathar dualism. They denied the presence of Christ in the Eucharist, the efficacy of baptism, and the value of prayers and alms for the dead. They preached that all popes after Pope Sylvester—the supposed recipient of the donation of Constantine—were condemned to eternal punishment. They believed that the devil created the visible world and ruled over it and that there was no gradation of rewards and punishments in the afterlife.[49]

Cathars were adherents to a dualist faith that ultimately derived from the Bogomils in Bulgaria. This heresy spread to Constantinople, where it was modified, and subsequently spread to western Europe. Cathars were most successful in southern France and northern and central Italy, where they organized a counterchurch with its own bishops and rudimentary hierarchy.[50] In northern Italy, there were Cathar bishops in Concorezzo, Desenzano, Bagnolo, and Vicenza, ruling over a host of communities in towns such as Como, Milan, Pavia, Cremona, Parma, Padua, Verona, Bologna, Treviso, and Venice. In central and north-central Italy, there were Cathar bishops in Florence and Spoleto, with communities in Pisa, Prato, Orvieto, Viterbo, and Rome.

The basic tenet of Cathar theology was dualism, or a belief in two fundamental principles: the God of light created all spiritual things, including the human soul; the devil created the material world. Some Cathars were radical dualists, believing that both Good and Evil were eternal principles. Others were moderate dualists, believing that Evil was a subordinate principle that originated with the fall of Lucifer.[51] Nevertheless, all agreed that matter was evil, from which several important beliefs followed. They rejected marriage and procreation as a perpetuation of the devil's reign over human souls. They held Catholic sacraments to be of no value, as they were grounded in material reality. They strongly denounced the papacy's claims to temporal authority, as seen in their condemnation of all popes after Sylvester, to whom the Emperor Constantine supposedly granted temporal authority over the west.

Salvation came through the practice of a rigorous asceticism to free the human soul from its imprisonment in the body. This brings us to the central figures of Catharism—the *perfecti*, or perfect. The perfect were a group distinct from the ordinary mass of Cathar believers. They were the small elite of traveling preachers who spread the faith and upon whom the success of the sect depended. Diotesalvi and Gotardo, who first brought Catharism to Orvieto, were no doubt *perfecti*. Those who chose such a life entered the ranks of the perfect through a ritual called the *consolamentum*, which was understood as the baptism by the Holy Spirit. The ritual involved placing a gospel or New Testament on the candidate's head and a laying on of hands.[52] Those who received the *consolamentum* committed themselves to a demanding life of voluntary poverty, fasting, prayer, and various ritual observances necessary for salvation.

There was an ethical gulf separating the perfect from common believers, who remained in the world, married, and lived ordinary lives. Their principal task was to support the perfect by providing food and shelter. In return they received instruction, the perfect's efficacious prayers, and hope of receiving the *consolamentum* on their deathbed. There probably was a significant gap in doctrinal knowledge as well. Catharism was a gnostic religion in the sense that its adherents were only gradually initiated into its mysteries. Although Cathars developed an elaborate theology, it is unlikely that it was systematically taught beyond the small group of the perfect. Since Cathar doctrine was based, at least in part, on a reading of the New Testament, people who listened to Cathar preachers found many of the biblical narratives, characters, and ethical exhortations that they would have heard in Catholic sermons. This is not to say that there were no differences. The perfect had two goals as they preached to the mass of ordinary believers.[53] First, they played upon the anticlerical sentiments of the laity by pointing out the many ways that the clergy fell short of the church's own evangelical ideals. Second, they introduced hearers to the concept of dualism. It was perhaps not overly difficult to sell the idea that the natural order was malevolent to an audience that was extremely vulnerable to disease, famine, and natural catastrophes. Neither was it difficult to apply the concept that matter was evil to the idea of ecclesiastical property. After all, was it not the desire to protect such property that diverted the clergy's attention away from the laity's spiritual needs?

As a result, the distinctions perceived by ordinary believers were most likely ethical ones. The ascetic rigor of the Cathar perfect seemed closer to the evangelical ideals of the gospel than the lifestyles of the local clergy. Theological distinctions between Catharism and Catholicism would not have been clear to most ordinary Cathar supporters, who received little or no instruction in the mysteries of Cathar theology and whose knowledge of Catholic theology would have been equally rudimentary.[54]

The Roof Is Leaking

There is little doubt that Catharism owed much of its appeal to the high ethical standards of the perfect. They evoked tremendous devotion and admiration from ordinary believers. The appeal of Catharism in Orvieto, however, cannot be fully understood apart from the context of the twelfth-century bishopric. The complicated network of interests tugging at the bishopric created a receptive audience for Cathar austerity by generating skepticism about the church's ability to address the laity's spiritual needs and aspirations.

The *Passio* offers little information concerning the early spread of heresy in Orvieto. There is, however, one vignette that is quite revealing. Apart from wandering preachers who brought the heresy to Orvieto, the *Passio* mentions several pious laypersons who were instrumental in the spread of heresy. Two women, Milita from Monte Amiata and Julitta from Florence, were well known in Orvieto for their piety. Milita, like a Martha, worked to repair the roof of the cathedral. Julitta, on the other hand, was devoted to the contemplative life. The majority of women in Orvieto regarded them as holy women. For a while they even fooled Bishop Riccardo, Rustico's successor, who received them into the confraternity of the clergy.[55] Their participation in the life of the Orvietan church reflects one of the most important trends in twelfth-century lay spirituality throughout Europe—the growing desire of laypersons to become actively involved alongside clergy in the spiritual life of the local church. The popularity of confraternities was one of the clearest manifestations of this trend.[56]

Milita is particularly interesting, for she illustrates how easily lay piety could move from Catholicism to Catharism, or even participate in both.[57] More important, she calls attention to the cathedral roof as a significant object in the religious imagination of Orvietan laypersons, pointing to the bishopric's role in creating and disappointing lay religious expectations. Apparently the cathedral was not receiving the maintenance it needed. Among the provisions in Bishop Ildibrando's agreement with the cathedral chapter in 1154 was his responsibility to repair the cathedral roof.[58] It still needed repair, or needed repair again, in the 1170s. The author of the *Passio* indicated that there was a large hole in the roof in 1200.[59] There are no records to indicate the extent to which bishops maintained the cathedral, but these passing comments suggest that on several occasions in the late twelfth century, bishops lacked either the will or the resources—most likely the latter—to give the cathedral the attention that it needed. The condition of the cathedral had important implications. The cathedral was the center of the city's religious life, and it is clear that Milita was dissatisfied with its state of disrepair.

The hole in the roof was a manifestation of deeper and more complicated problems. As noted earlier, episcopal lordship directed the bishop's attention and resources away from the spiritual needs of the laity. Revenues that could have been used for maintaining the cathedral were pledged to Orvietan knights and to cathedral canons. The pledge of episcopal resources to the cathedral chapter must have been especially disconcerting to laypersons like Milita, touching another likely tender spot concerning the laity's expectations of the bishopric. The organization of the canons into a cloistered body was an important aspect of eleventh-century reform traditions, raising expectations for the clergy's behavior and performance. The common life was supposed to have freed them from worldly concerns and allowed them to devote themselves more fully to God and to lay spiritual needs. Instead, it appears to have created a body of clergy that jealously defended its property at the expense of lay spiritual interests. Among other things, the chapter's economic rights in the city worked at cross-purposes with lay initiatives toward the development of urban parishes. Moreover, by holding the bishop economically captive, they implicated themselves in the deterioration of the city's spiritual center, the cathedral, for they were among the bishop's supporters to whom episcopal revenues had been diverted.

This is not to paint a picture of the cathedral canons as greedy and selfish. However much such human failings may have played a part, the problems were more structural and systemic. There were two fundamental problems. To begin with, episcopal lordship, which was imposed upon the bishopric by the political conditions of post-Carolingian Italy as much as it was chosen, was largely responsible for the bishop's economic dependence on the chapter. As for the chapter's jealous defense of its property, it was principled, at least in part, for it was rooted in the assumptions underlying the common life. These principles, however, created expectations for their behavior, which if not fulfilled, could have disastrous consequences.

These expectations were rooted in the work of eleventh-century reformers, who sought to protect the clergy from worldly pollution.[60] If those who distributed the sacraments were corrupt, then the entire church, the body of Christ, could be polluted. This Donatist strain in the writings and sermons of some eleventh-century reformers, while understandable in the context of the urgently felt need to improve the moral life of the clergy, ran the risk of unduly privileging the mystical contact between the clergy and the laity, as fellow members of the body of Christ, over the face-to-face dialogue of pastoral care. This association between the common life and purity accounts for the canons' jealous defense of their common property. Whether by pretense or by conviction, they could argue that by protecting the economic precondition of the common life, they were defending the church from pollution.

Things appeared different from the lay perspective. As demographic growth filled the regions of the city with people, the common life grew increasingly out of step with their spiritual aspirations. Economically, it created an obstacle to parish formation and the upkeep of the cathedral. Spiritually, the monastic ideal, upon which the common life was based, was ill suited to address the laity's growing hunger for active participation with the clergy in the spiritual life of the church. The Orvietan church was not entirely unresponsive to these developments, as Milita's participation in a confraternity suggests.[61] Nevertheless, the configuration of interests and traditions that shaped the bishopric during the previous decades placed it in an untenable position. It simply could not bear the burdens of episcopal lordship and still respond to the changing expectations and aspirations of the laity.

PATCHING THE HOLE

When Bishop Riccardo (1178–1202) entered Orvieto for the first time in 1178, the bishopric was dangerously weak, and it appears that a growing number of Orvietans were becoming weary of fighting the papacy's battles. Riccardo, who was from Gaeta, was probably the only twelfth-century Orvietan bishop not from Orvieto or its surrounding territory.[62] It is likely that Pope Alexander III either chose Riccardo or influenced his election as bishop of Orvieto to reinvigorate the bishopric and pro-papal sentiments in the city.[63]

On August 13, 1178, Riccardo received the following letter from Pope Alexander:

> As was proper, we readily received your messengers and letters, from which we understand that the clergy and people of your city received you in a fitting manner. Concerning this matter, we greatly rejoice, just as we have good reason to rejoice. Nevertheless, we caution your brothers [the cathedral chapter] and carefully exhort that you, with the help of heavenly grace and as a prudent man not unmindful of his office, diligently apply yourself to a good work with a view to the edification of your church with respect to both spiritualities and temporalities, and that you strive to instruct your subjects by word and example, so that accordingly you may be able to appear commendable before both God and men as you ought.[64]

The sense of relief in this letter suggests that before Riccardo went to Orvieto neither he nor Alexander were sure that the clergy and people of Orvieto would welcome his arrival.

Riccardo quickly set about restoring the economic base of the bishop's authority. Shortly after he arrived in Orvieto, he appealed to

Pope Alexander for assistance in a dispute with the cathedral canon, Tebaldo, who refused to relinquish property that he had received from Bishop Rustico. In response, Alexander wrote the following letter of August 13, 1178:

> To Priest Tebaldo. You should know that it has come to our attention that you presume to hold, without good reason, a certain baptismal church and tithes belonging to our venerable brother Riccardo, the Orvietan bishop, claiming that his predecessor left them to you in his last will. You also demand unjustly, as it is said, that certain payments from the *mensa* of the bishop be made to you. . . . If it is so, we command that you not delay in handing over the baptismal church with all of its possessions to the bishop and that you strive to render prompt obedience to your bishop as to a father, so that we will have no more reason to complain about you and we will not be forced to write concerning this matter again.[65]

The recovery of property from Tebaldo was only the first step in a massive recuperation of property and revenues. Riccardo recovered the baptismal church that Rustico had pledged to Rocco as well. In 1180 he redeemed property in Alfina held in pledge by Martinozzo, an Orvietan knight, and turned it into a source of revenue by leasing it. From the revenue generated by the lease, he redeemed other episcopal property in San Gervasio held by Stefano di Tebalduccio.[66] In 1182 he recovered several vineyards just outside of the city in Corsula from Blanco di Arcidosso and Tezalo di Rizuto, who had refused to recognize that they held the vineyards from the bishopric.[67] In that same year, he exacted a promise from Oderiscio di Gentile di Mancino not to attack San Vito, a well-endowed monastery and castle community that belonged to the episcopal *mensa*. In 1185 and 1189, he recovered episcopal property in Mealla.[68]

Bishop Riccardo attacked the problem of heresy with equal vigor. According to the *Passio*, he expelled Diotesalvi and Gotardo from Orvieto. As for the Orvietans who actively supported the heretics, some he killed, some he deprived of citizenship and drove into exile, and some he denied a Christian burial.[69] The *Passio*'s claim that Riccardo rid Orvieto of heresy until it erupted again in 1198 is probably exaggerated.[70] Nevertheless, it appears that Riccardo made real progress in addressing the problems that plagued the bishopric at the beginning of his episcopate.

Limited Success

Riccardo became bishop of Orvieto at an opportune time. Central Italy enjoyed a period of relative peace and stability following the papal-imperial agreements that brought an end to the schism. With the benefit of papal support and the end of the schism, it appears that Bishop Riccardo made progress in restoring episcopal authority in Orvieto by working within the framework of Hadrian's agreements. He restored a measure of balance between the bishop and chapter. As shown in the case of Milita, this economic balance had important implications for the bishop's spiritual authority. To the extent that he was able, he relied on the cooperation between Orvietan political and religious interests to bring the secular sword to bear upon the heretics.

This proved to be but a brief respite. Beginning in 1185, Henry VI, the son of Frederick Barbarossa, renewed an aggressive campaign to establish imperial authority in Italy. His efforts met with tremendous hostility from the newly elected pope, Urban III. Before becoming pope, Urban had been a bitter opponent of the emperor. His activity as pope was openly and intentionally hostile to Frederick and Henry VI.[71]

When Henry arrived in Italy in 1185, he could not simply pick up where his father left off. His father had met with considerable success in reconstructing an Italian kingdom until 1167, when his efforts lost momentum in face of the complicated politics of the schism. In the meantime, communes aggressively expanded into the countryside. If Henry intended to establish a strong centralized state that exercised direct authority over towns and feudatories, he would have to reverse these territorial gains. In 1186 Henry VI invaded central Italy and took control of Perugia, Viterbo, Narni, and other central Italian cities. As he entered Roman Tuscany, he reestablished imperial authority over castles along the Via Francigena, such as Radicofani and Proceno. Control of such an important trade route would facilitate his efforts to establish and maintain control over the cities.[72]

Henry also besieged Orvieto. While the siege was not successful, there was a group of Orvietans who supported Henry, as indicated

in an agreement of 1189 between him and Pope Clement III
(1187–1191) in which Henry promised to return "all the possessions
that Pope Lucius had in Orvieto, and if there are any who took an
oath to us who had previously sworn to Pope Lucius, we absolve
them of the oath."[73] Although his siege of Orvieto was ultimately
unsuccessful, his presence undoubtedly strengthened the position of
imperial partisans in the city.[74]

To sum up, Orvieto's alliance with the papacy proved more
costly than most Orvietans had anticipated. The city's political and
religious interests had become a tangled mess, as they were before
Hadrian's treaty of 1157, only now the bundle of issues had grown
more complicated with the addition of questions concerning the
city's subordination to the papacy. Was the papal alliance worth the
cost? Some Orvietans, like the jurist who argued on behalf of
the Orvietan bishop against the bishop of Sovana in 1194, believed
that the validity of the city's jurisdiction over the countryside
depended on a hierarchical chain of authority from the papacy,
through the bishopric, to the city. Moreover, while the papal alliance
drew Orvietans into a protracted and costly conflict, the city
emerged in the 1190s with significant territorial gains.

There were, however, serious questions that begged resolution.
Was the condominium between bishopric and commune still work-
able? Was it still possible to harmonize the city's territorial ambitions and religious interests through the bishopric? In the event of a
disagreement, whose interests would the bishopric represent—the
city's or the papacy's? There were some Orvietans—apparently a
minority in the 1190s—who felt that the bishopric represented the
papacy's interests and only a narrow slice of political and religious
interests in Orvieto. In the treaty of 1157, Hadrian seems to have
sacrificed the religious interests of *minores* by reaffirming the pre-
eminence of the cathedral clergy. This fostered an underlying disaffection with clerical hierarchy, as Orvietan receptivity to Cathars
suggests.

As a result, the bishopric entered the last decade of the twelfth
century in a precarious condition. It still had to protect and manage
its property in the countryside. Bishop Riccardo did not eradicate
heresy in Orvieto. The existence of both an antipapal faction and
heresy represented a potentially explosive mix, as the example of

Catharism in Languedoc clearly demonstrates. For almost a century, the Orvietan bishops had addressed these problems within the framework of episcopal lordship. A new crisis in 1198 will demonstrate that Bishop Riccardo's limited success was but the final glow of sunset on the intermediate period of episcopal lordship in Orvieto.

CHAPTER FIVE

LOOKING AT NEW THINGS
IN AN OLD WAY

*Pietro Parenzo and the Crisis
of Episcopal Authority*

BISHOP RICCARDO ATTEMPTED TO RELIEVE THE ECONOMIC
and religious problems created by the revival of episcopal lordship
during the schism by working within the parameters of Pope
Hadrian IV's agreements of 1156–1157. He met with only limited
success, for too much had changed in the political and religious landscape of central Italy during the schism and its aftermath. The extent
of these changes became painfully clear in the context of another
political and religious crisis that shook the bishopric and commune
in 1198. The crisis began when Pope Innocent III (1198–1216) capitalized on the power vacuum left by the death of Emperor Henry VI in
1197 and aggressively asserted the papacy's political jurisdiction in
central Italy. Among his first actions was to demand that Orvieto
hand over Acquapendente to the papacy. When the Orvietans resisted his efforts, Innocent placed Orvieto under interdict. Given the
core of antipapal feeling already in Orvieto and the openness of certain Orvietans to Catharism, the interdict ignited an explosive mix
of political and religious disaffection.

While Innocent's interdict provided the spark that caused the explosion, anticlerical and antipapal sentiments had been brewing for decades in Orvieto. There was a growing sense of frustration with the bishopric, which seemed too entangled in political struggles and increasingly out of step with lay religious expectations. It is worth considering the reasons behind this growing disconnection between the bishopric and the laity. From the perspective of at least some of the laity, the bishopric was too concerned with protecting its political and economic interests. From the perspective of the bishopric, its political influence was indispensable to its guardianship over the local church. The Orvietan bishops shared a widespread assumption within the ecclesiastical hierarchy that reform and the general well-being of the church was possible only if secular authorities subordinated their political interests to the church. This tradition, which was apparent by the time of Pope Gregory VII, continued to shape papal policy into the twelfth and thirteenth centuries. The experience of the Orvietan church seemed to confirm this tradition. When communal institutions were relatively immature and urban elites depended on episcopal and papal institutions, reform seemed to prosper. Pope Hadrian's reform of the cathedral chapter was part of a series of agreements that included the subjection of the commune to papal overlordship.

Neither the Orvietan bishops and cathedral canons nor the papacy realized that their assumptions about reform—that reform required the subordination of political interests to ecclesiastical authority—were grounded in historical conditions that were passing away. Their concept of reform reflected the conditions of a period characterized by relatively weak and rudimentary political institutions. These conditions caused secular rulers to rely more heavily on ecclesiastical institutions and resources. Under such conditions, reform was possible only if secular authorities bent their will to the church. While secular authorities were by no means pliant, their dependence on ecclesiastical institutions and resources gave ecclesiastical authorities a degree of leverage over their decisions. It was a different world by 1200. Communes like Orvieto had significantly expanded their territory, and their own institutions were becoming more sophisticated. As their dependence on episcopal and papal institutions decreased, the papacy and bishops lost a considerable degree of leverage over the city's political policies.

As the papacy and Orvietan bishops became increasingly frustrated in their efforts to marshal political interests behind their program of reform, they perceived communal autonomy as a threat to the church's spiritual well-being. In reality, these new historical conditions set in motion a process of reform that popes and bishops could influence, but not dictate. Just as older concepts of reform reflected historical conditions in which they emerged, new styles of reform emerged that reflected historical realities of the early thirteenth century. This new style of reform, which was largely bureaucratic in nature, evolved through a process of trial and error as a variety of political and religious actors, including popes, bishops, cathedral canons, laypersons of various wealth and status, and communal officials, struggled to adjust evangelical traditions and the increasingly sophisticated institutional and legal framework of the communes to each other.

Orvieto's dispute with Innocent III demonstrates the extent to which Innocent's and the Orvietan bishop's concept of reform was fast becoming an anachronism. Nowhere is this more clear than in the *Passio Beati Pietro Parentii Martiris*, written by the cathedral canon Maestro Giovanni in the midst of the crisis caused by the interdict.[1] The *Passio*, which recounts the murder of Pietro Parenzo, an Orvietan *podestà*, at the hands of heretics, was the first bold attempt by a representative of the bishopric to adjust to the new political and religious realities of the thirteenth-century communes. Because the *Passio* offered a vision of political and religious order that was essentially backward looking, recalling Pope Hadrian's arrangements of the 1150s, it proved to be an inadequate response to the changes that created the crisis in episcopal authority. The inadequacies of the *Passio*, however, are instructive. The *Passio* is like a water marker, measuring the extent to which the tides had changed.

PAPAL AUTHORITY AND THE CENTRAL
ITALIAN COMMUNES

Papal and Imperial Authority in Central Italy

Before examining Orvietan/papal relations during the first decade of the thirteenth century, it is necessary to look at the broader struggle between popes, kings/emperors, and communes for control in central Italy.[2] Henry VI, the son of Frederick Barbarossa, had taken control of central Italy by the late 1180s. He entrusted the duchy of Tuscany to his brother Philip, the duchy of Spoleto to Conrad of Urslingen, and the march of Ancona to Markward of Anweiler. Henry's control of central Italy gave him leverage to bargain for a more important goal—papal approval for his marriage to Constance, the daughter and heir of William II of Sicily. This marriage, which would allow Henry to add the crown of Sicily to the imperial crown, was a nightmare scenario for the papacy; for the key to papal politics in Italy since the eleventh century had been its ability to play German kings/emperors off of Norman kings. While Henry assumed the Sicilian crown in 1194, he never secured official recognition from the papacy.

When Henry died in 1197, imperial authority in Italy collapsed. Frederick II, his son by Constance, was only four years old. While Constance assumed the regency in Sicily, Otto of Brunswick and Philip, Henry's brother, battled for the German crown until Philip's death in 1208. Who would benefit from the disintegration of imperial power in central Italy? This was the central question for the papacy and central Italian communes in the late 1190s. When Henry VI died in September 1197, various towns in Tuscany formed the Tuscan League and proclaimed their independence from the empire. At the same time, Pope Celestine III began the process of reclaiming portions of the duchy of Spoleto, the march of Ancona, and Tuscany as possessions of the patrimony of St. Peter. After Celestine died in January 1198, Pope Innocent III continued the policy of recuperation, sending papal representatives throughout the patrimony to receive oaths of fidelity from towns and feudatories. He drove Conrad of Urslingen from Spoleto and came to terms with Markward of Anweiler in the march of Ancona. He wrested concessions from both Otto and Philip, who needed his support in their battle for the crown. Despite resistance from towns like Narni and Orvieto, it looked as though Innocent had consolidated his hold on the Tuscan patrimony as well as the duchy of Spoleto and the march of Ancona by 1202. In the years that followed, he worked hard to build an institutional structure for the papal state, appointing provincial rectors for Campagna-Marittima, the Tuscan patrimony, and the duchy of Spoleto. In 1207 he called a parliament at Viterbo, which issued legislation and organized a jurisdictional hierarchy of local and provincial courts.

Despite these seemingly impressive achievements, Pope Innocent's authority was precarious practically everywhere in central Italy. Markward of Anweiler rebelled in 1199, invaded Campagna, and made his way to Sicily, hoping to gain control over Frederick II and the regency of Sicily after the death of Constance. Innocent was forced to invest considerable resources fighting Markward. Innocent's efforts to secure control of the march of Ancona met with stiff resistance as well. A civil war in Rome erupted in 1202, as Roman aristocrats became increasingly disturbed at the aggrandizement of Innocent's family. After 1209, relations between Innocent and Otto became increasingly bitter, as Otto issued privileges to towns in the march of Ancona and the duchy of Spoleto in violation of previous agreements. In 1210 he took Radicofani, Acquapendente, and Montefiascone. Otto capitulated by 1213. Meanwhile, Innocent continued to battle towns like Narni, which refused to submit to papal authority.

Innocent's inability to bring the central Italian communes firmly under his control was a source of continual frustration. In a letter sent to the communes of Sutri, Orte, Amelia, Todi, Orvieto, and other communes in the patrimony, Innocent wrote, "To be sure, among our other engagements and worries, we do not discount the care and provision of the apostolic patrimony which belongs to our spiritual and temporal jurisdiction. . . . We know in fact what we recount with sadness and grief, that in it many disturb the peace, corrupt justice, commit violence on the road, attack the land . . . , seeking their own things and not those of Jesus Christ, abusing the patience of the apostolic seat."[3] The letter goes on to announce the arrival of a papal legate, accompanied by Pietro di Vico, the Roman prefect, to establish a measure of political order in the patrimony.[4]

Innocent dealt with this frustration by pushing harder; but the harder he pressed against the central Italian communes, the more obstinate they became. This sense of frustration is evident in the *Gesta Innocentii*, a contemporary account of Innocent's pontificate. After boasting of Innocent's accomplishments in subduing the patrimony, the author of the *Gesta* wrote, "Albeit he would have this detestable worry (for which reason he often used to say, 'He who touches pitch will be polluted by it') especially because the labor was great and the fruit small and, because of ever increasing evil, men were not able to be easily coerced. Besides, the more he desired to be free of secular affairs, the more he was entangled in worldly cares."[5] There is an element of truth in this description. By launching interdicts, excommunications, and armies in an effort to enforce papal sovereignty in central Italy, Innocent appeared increasingly weak, because his actions motivated a number of communes to create a united front against papal authority. This was certainly the case in his dispute with Orvieto for control over Acquapendente. It was during Innocent's pontificate that the Orvietans learned just how costly their submission to the papacy could become.

Orvieto, Acquapendente, and Pope Innocent III

Orvietan efforts to control Acquapendente began as early as the 1140s, when Bishop Ildibrando directed the aggressive expansion of Orvieto along the western border of the diocese. From the time of Orvieto's treaty with Pope Hadrian in 1157, Orvietans enjoyed papal approval of their attempts to subdue Acquapendente. This understanding between Orvieto and the papacy, however, was of little practical value. For most of the period between 1161 and the mid-1190s, Acquapendente managed to escape the yoke of Orvieto by submitting to imperial troops. Although there was ultimately little that the Orvietans could do, they resisted the imperial takeover of the town. Orvieto probably fought two wars against Acquapendente between 1170 and 1190. Although it is difficult to date these wars, it is likely that one of them occurred in the early 1170s.[6] There is no information concerning the date of the second war. In 1196, as imperial control in central Italy was unraveling, Orvieto went to war against Acquapendente a third time. Orvieto was successful and forced Acquapendente to pay an annual tribute, to tear down a portion of the city wall, and to relinquish its claims in Monte Rofeno, an important region in Orvieto's northwestern *contado*.[7] It appeared that Orvietans finally gained the prize that had eluded them for so long.

The victory was short-lived. In 1198 Innocent claimed that Acquapendente was directly subject to the papacy and demanded that Orvieto relinquish its claims. He placed Orvieto under interdict until it obeyed papal orders. The *Gesta* mentioned the recovery of

Acquapendente as one of Innocent's early successes in reestablishing papal control over the patrimony. "After these things [the recovery of Tuscia and the duchy of Spoleto] he worked to recapture Radicofani, Acquapendente, Montefiascone, and Tusculum, which he recovered not without effort and expense, liberating Acquapendente from the Orvietans, against whom the Acquapendentans fought bitterly."[8] From the viewpoint of Innocent's biographer, Innocent had to liberate Acquapendente from the Orvietans just as he had to liberate other towns in the patrimony from the Germans. The portrayal of Orvieto in the *Gesta Innocentii* is hardly flattering, indicating the degree of tension between Innocent and Orvieto.

The mention of Tuscia along with small towns and communities in the region makes it clear that the clash between Innocent and the Orvietans was closely connected to a complicated network of conflicts involving Innocent and other central Italian communes. Orvieto responded to the papal interdict by allying with Viterbo and the Tuscan League, which was engaged in a war against Pope Innocent and the Romans. The alliances that formed around the war between Viterbo and Rome illustrate the tangled network of interests in central Italy that Innocent sought in vain to control. The Viterbese were attempting to subdue the neighboring town of Vitorchiano, which appealed to the Romans for help. Viterbo asked for support from Orvieto and the Tuscan League when they learned that Vitorchiano had secured Roman military support. Orvieto, apart from having already been alienated by Innocent's interdict, supported Viterbo in return for Viterbo's earlier assistance in Orvieto's conquest of Acquapendente.

Innocent was drawn into the conflict between Viterbo and Rome largely against his will, as an unintended consequence of his efforts to reestablish papal authority in Rome. During the first two years of his pontificate—before the war with Viterbo—Innocent faced considerable opposition within Rome.[9] By using factional divisions within the senatorial aristocracy to his own advantage, he gained support from at least some powerful senatorial families, which traditionally had been hostile to the papacy.[10] In this way, Innocent was able to establish a measure of control over the city. The Roman-Viterbese war, however, placed Innocent in a difficult position. If he supported the interests of the Roman aristocracy, with whom he had only recently reached a rapprochement, he would alienate Viterbo, another important city in his policy of recuperation. Innocent had already warned Viterbo about their aggression against Vitorchiano, but the Viterbese turned a deaf ear and even helped Narni in its rebellion against the papacy. Given the recalcitrance of the Viterbese, Innocent threw in his lot with the Romans and placed Viterbo under interdict. Innocent then commanded rectors of Tuscany, who by that time had arrived in Orvieto, to withdraw their support from Viterbo.[11] The rectors responded that they had sworn to help Viterbo and therefore could not withdraw without breaking an oath. Innocent reminded them that the Tuscan League had also sworn an oath to the church. According to the *Gesta Innocentii*, the Tuscan League withdrew. The Romans provisioned Vitorchiano and then defeated Viterbo. The author of the *Gesta* leaves the impression that the troops from the Tuscan League came to Orvieto but went no further after Innocent ordered them to refrain from helping Viterbo. While the Tuscan League may have obeyed Innocent, it is clear that Orvieto fought on behalf of Viterbo against Rome.[12]

Ultimately, the advantages of reconciliation between Innocent and Orvieto outweighed the importance of issues that separated them. Orvieto's assistance to Viterbo impressed upon Innocent the importance of settling his dispute with the Orvietans. Neither Innocent nor Rome could afford to drive them into the Tuscan League. So long as Orvieto was estranged from the papacy, Innocent would find it more difficult to enforce his claims to Acquapendente and the strategically important region along the Via Francigena. An alliance with Innocent and Rome had much to offer Orvietans as well. The city was dangerously divided and needed an outsider to calm factional strife.

In 1199 Pietro Parenzo, a Roman aristocrat, came to Orvieto to serve as rector, or *podestà*.[13] Pietro's arrival marks a fundamental transition in Orvietan politics in two respects. The commune had outgrown its original institutional structure by 1200. Between 1200 and 1220, the office of *podestà* gradually replaced the consulate. As the city and its politics grew more complicated, the consulate proved unable to eliminate violent struggles for political control among the urban aristocracy.[14] Unlike a consul, the *podestà* was usually a foreign nobleman, who brought with him his own staff of judges and knights for the administration of justice. He ruled as a stranger to the individual interests that threatened to divide the commune. His staff of judges advised him in the application of a theoretically impersonal law to settle disputes among parties who might otherwise resort to violence.

Pietro's arrival represents a realignment of Orvietan politics as well as a change in the city's governing institutions. Jean-Claude Maire Vigueur remarked that 1200–1250 was the golden age of Roman *podestà* in central Italy. This was certainly true of Orvieto. During this period, fourteen Roman *podestà* ruled Orvieto—seven of them members of Pietro's family. It is important to note that recruitment of Roman *podestà* indicates a realignment of Orvietan politics toward Rome, but not necessarily toward the papacy. Roman *podestà* came from the senatorial class, whose relations with the papacy were often strained. This was the class that led the rebellion against the papacy in 1143; therefore, they had considerable experience in fighting against papal control. While some Roman *podestà* that ruled Orvieto were strong papal allies, others were openly hostile.[15] Pietro is a fascinating figure because his relation to Pope Innocent is ambiguous. This made him a useful compromise candidate for Orvietan factions, for some could accept him as a Roman representative, while others could accept him as a papal representative. Maestro Giovanni's unambiguous image of Pietro stands in sharp relief against this complicated relation between Pietro, the papacy, and the tangled web of central Italian politics.

PIETRO PARENZO AND THE *PASSIO*

What would be the role of the bishopric in this new world of self-confident communes? In the heat of the crisis in episcopal authority caused by the interdict, Maestro Giovanni, a cathedral canon, wrote the *Passio*, which tells the story of Pietro Parenzo's efforts to quell the political and religious dissent that exploded after the interdict. Pietro aggressively persecuted both political and religious dissenters as Cathar heretics. The dissenters were equally aggressive and murdered Pietro less than three months after his arrival. Shortly after his death there were reports of miracles at his tomb, leading Giovanni and other pro-papal Orvietans to proclaim him a martyr.

The *Passio* is the first bold attempt by a representative of the bishopric to define the bishopric's place in the new world of the maturing commune. Giovanni offered the image of Pietro the martyr to Innocent and the commune, hoping to convince them that their differences were less important than their common interests. By portraying Pietro as the embodiment of harmony between papal, communal, and episcopal interests, Giovanni hoped to turn back the clock to Pope Hadrian's Orvieto, the blueprint embedded in episcopal consciousness for political and ecclesiastical order.

Pietro the Podestà

According to the *Passio*, Bishop Riccardo drove heretics from the city and faced no more challenges to his spiritual authority until 1198, when Innocent's interdict reignited religious dissent and antipapal sentiments. Innocent forced Riccardo to leave the city and reside in Rome until the Orvietans relinquished their claim to Acquapendente. Heretics returned during his absence and took control of Orvieto.[16] It is at this point that Pietro came to Orvieto to rescue its faithful catholic citizens from heretics.

Although the *Passio* refers to all who opposed Pietro and the papacy as heretics, it is clear that Pietro faced a battle on two related fronts, one political and one religious. On the first front, there was an antipapal faction led by certain powerful Orvietan aristocratic families, presumably the same group that pledged oaths of loyalty to Henry VI in 1186. On the second front, there were those who were religiously inclined to support Cathars. As Carol Lansing has shown, this second group came largely from the *popolo*, who would play an increasingly influential role in the city's political development during the early decades of the thirteenth century.[17]

These two fronts are evident in Pietro's first heroic exploit. According to the *Passio*, on the first day of Lent, heretics, begrudging the unity of the Catholics, broke the peace and started a tremendous battle in the public square. Pietro rode into battle and, at the risk of his own life, separated the combatants. By divine grace he was unharmed. He punished all who participated in the battle and tore down the palaces and towers from which they fought.[18] In addition to those who fought from their towers and palaces, many more people fought on the ground, presumably *pedites*, or non-nobles. Giovanni mentions that Pietro instituted lighter punishments for these foot soldiers because many of them were wounded in the fighting.[19]

The lack of distinction between these two groups in Giovanni's account is credible to a certain extent. There is no reason to doubt that antipapal nobles and Cathars united against a common enemy, or even that there were Cathar sympathizers among the antipapal faction. At the same time, Giovanni had an interest in blurring the distinctions. As he told the story of Pietro, he was, in effect, trying to kill two birds with one stone. On the one hand, it is clear from the description of nobles fighting from towers that Pietro was attempting to suppress factional strife more than heresy. More specifically, he was attempting to suppress a faction of noble families who rose to prominence in the midst of the interdict and tried to steer Orvieto into an alliance with the Tuscan League. On the other hand, he attempted to suppress heresy. His role here was less prominent. Pietro addressed challenges to the bishopric's spiritual authority by cooperating with Bishop Riccardo in an inquisition.[20] He was the secular arm ready to wield the sword at the bishop's request. There is reason to believe that Pietro's efforts on both fronts met with only limited success. An inquisition was not likely to convince Cathar sympathizers that the bishop was more concerned than Cathar perfect for the spiritual well-being of the laity. Pietro's heroic exploits in the public square did not effectively suppress the antipapal faction, as indicated by his murder just three months later.

Pietro the Martyr

When Pietro was murdered, Maestro Giovanni hoped that Pietro the martyr could accomplish what Pietro the rector could not, that is, restore the ailing bishopric to health by reestablishing the harmony between episcopal, communal, and papal interests that Pope Hadrian created in 1157. By virtue of his death at the hands of papal opponents, Pietro had tremendous potential as a religious symbol. In the *Passio*, Maestro Giovanni attempted to channel religious enthusiasm aroused by Pietro's martyrdom to reestablish the centrality of episcopal and papal interests in communal politics. With this aim, Giovanni crafted the image of Pietro for two audiences. First, he wanted to remind the commune of the importance of episcopal and papal authority. Second, he sought to warn Pope Innocent that he could not afford to alienate Orvieto, a traditionally loyal papal ally.

In the *Passio*, Pietro sanctified the unity of communal and epis-copal interests. The cathedral is the focus of a subnarrative that teaches with unmistakable clarity that God sent Pietro to call Orvietans back to their bishop. In this respect, Maestro Giovanni's account of Pietro's burial is one of the most telling passages in the *Passio*.

> Concerning his burial, there was considerable disagreement among the citizens, some wanting to bury him in the aforemen-tioned church [Sant' Andrea] and others who agreed with Enrico, the judge, demanding rightly to bury him in the major church. . . . For it was both fitting and reasonable that the one who had been murdered by the blasphemers of Jesus Christ and his glorious vir-gin mother, should be buried in their church and that the same church should receive an increase in honor and respect. For the major church had come to such a lowly state that, at all times, with the exception of the feast of the Assumption of the Blessed Virgin, Christmas, and Easter, the church was deprived of atten-dance and respect and there were scarcely three lamps inside to provide light. And so, the patron of the Orvietans deserved to be buried in that tomb located in the very place where he was so often present, discussing with Bishop Riccardo how to remove the fetid heresy from the field of the church. And the place where his tomb rests had almost no protection from the rain, given the poor condition of the roof above it. As a result, that deserted place, with the rain irrigating it and the grass growing, appeared like a meadow.[21]

The cathedral, the symbol of episcopal authority in Orvieto, was practically an abandoned building, a religious center without charisma. Apart from grass growing on the floor, there was scarcely any sign of life in the dimly lit structure except on major feast days.

The dilapidated cathedral seemed ill suited for the burial of a martyr. According to Maestro Giovanni, however, it was fitting that Pietro should be buried there. In the cathedral he would call Orvietans' attention back to the city's religious center and remind the commune that its politics needed to be subject to the church's spiritual guidance. Within the logic of the *Passio*, progress from chaos to order was, in effect, a pilgrimage to the cathedral. In the first half of the narrative, the cathedral played only a minor role. It was a place of quiet where Pietro and Bishop Riccardo withdrew to discuss plans for reordering the political and religious space beyond the cathedral walls, where chaos reigned. When Pietro's martyrdom miraculously restored a sense of order to the city, the cathedral became, as it was supposed to be, a center of religious charisma. Giovanni writes,

> Among all of the miracles that God exhibited in Orvieto through his martyr, one particularly wonderful miracle often occurred like a flash in the presence of a multitude of people. Countless times, while a large crowd of believers and unbelievers were standing by and watching, a fire from heaven, burning scarlet and gold, came down and miraculously lit the lamps, candles, and lanterns when- ever their own flames had burnt out. By this miracle the hearts of the faithful were set ablaze for the church of the mother of God, which used to be practically abandoned, compelling them to visit the tomb of the martyr. Even the false accusers who used to call that church a den of thieves hearkened to their conscience and were visiting the church with devotion. Truly it was expedient that one died for the people so that the heretics, who previously were preaching in the plazas and public places, would then be silent and our entire city would not perish.[22]

Graced by Pietro's tomb, the cathedral became a place crowded with people and light. It was the living symbol of a city rescued from destruction.

Similarly, Pietro reminded Orvietans that the commune could not survive outside of the framework of papal authority. After casti- gating those who refused to acknowledge the miraculous lighting of the cathedral and many other wonders that God worked through Pietro, Giovanni writes, "Let the vassals and fief-holders of Jesus Christ, who live not from their own patrimony but from that of Jesus Christ, consider that light . . . and let them call back that which strays, heal that which is sick, and bind together that which is shat- tered, not fearing the threats of men, because God wanted to estab- lish this martyr to be an armed warrior of the church, placing him as an example for all *fideles*. Indeed the ones who will have refused to imitate the example of this one in the battle of his Lord, whether from fear or love of men, let them know that they will lose their fief for their ungratefulness and will be cast away from the court of their heavenly Lord."[23] This passage recalls the treaty of 1157 between Pope Hadrian and Orvieto in which Orvietans swore fidelity to the pope and recognized that they held their city from the papacy.[24] This image of Orvieto as a papal vassal apparently was an important symbol for the Orvietan political community. It is the same image expressed by the Orvietan jurist who recalled that the counts of Orvieto held the city from the papacy.[25]

In addition to reminding Orvietans of their political roots, Giovanni argued that Pietro's miracles were a testimony to papal authority. In reference to a miracle in which Pietro's blood revived a barren tree, Giovanni writes, "Therefore our tree [i.e., Pietro], established and rooted on the firm rock, was bound to produce commendable fruit, because Pietro Parenzo exercised just vengeance against the heretics, not by his own authority but by the authority of the papacy, being established upon the firm rock, the mainstay of faith."[26] Giovanni reminded Orvietans that God's mercy and power had come to them through the papacy.

There are lessons in the *Passio* for Pope Innocent as well. Maestro Giovanni reminded Innocent that Orvieto was a loyal subject of the papacy. Indeed, the *Passio* is as much a declaration of Orvieto's loyalty to papal authority as it is an appeal to Orvietans not to reject their political and religious roots. Throughout the *Passio*, Orvietans did all in their power to obey the church. When heresy spread after Rustico's episcopate, Bishop Riccardo aggressively rooted out heretics.[27] After the interdict, when heretics were close to taking control of the city, it was Orvietan Catholics who initiated the call of Pietro from Rome. When they requested help in rooting out heretics, they specifically requested one who could restore Orvieto to papal favor and to peace with the Romans.[28] Orvietans received Pietro with tremendous enthusiasm.[29] After Pietro's martyrdom, they drove heretics from the city.[30]

In addition to proclaiming Orvietan loyalty, Giovanni subtly reprimands the pope. By placing Orvieto under interdict, Innocent not only risked alienating his political allies, he endangered souls of good Catholics. Concerning the dispute over Acquapendente, Maestro Giovanni recalled, "After these events [Riccardo's expulsion of heretics], when there arose a serious dispute between Pope Innocent III and the Orvietans over the city of Acquapendente, which the pope claimed belonged to him, Innocent bound the Orvietans with the punishment of anathema, while the bishop of the city was held against his will in Rome for almost nine months, censured by the pope. With the shepherd absent, the sheep, wandering from the flock, were exposed to the teeth of devouring wolves, because where there is not a governor constantly present, the people readily run to sin."[31] Although Giovanni does not explicitly blame Innocent, the chain of cause and effect is clear enough. The problem of heresy was under control until Innocent detained Riccardo in Rome. In the absence of its shepherd, the Orvietan flock was left defenseless. In this passage Giovanni mentions the cause of the dispute in passing, as if it were too insignificant to mention. Innocent interdicted Orvieto over a territorial dispute. As a result, heretics took control of Orvieto and faithful Orvietan Catholics were treated as if they were heretics. This is hardly a flattering description of papal politics.

The *Passio* thus called Orvietans and Innocent to meet halfway. According to Giovanni, Orvietans were too quick to abandon their religious responsibilities in pursuit of their political interests. Likewise, Innocent failed to weigh the political and spiritual consequences of his actions. Direct control over Acquapendente would be of little benefit to him if Orvieto became an enemy. More important, if the ultimate goal of his politics was the well-being of the church, then his policy regarding Orvieto and Acquapendente was a failure.

SUCCESS AND FAILURE

What Pietro the *podestà* could not accomplish, Pietro the martyr could not accomplish either. This is not to say that the *podestà* and the martyr achieved nothing. He temporarily restored a measure of stability in Orvieto. Ultimately, however, Pietro failed, at least when measured by Giovanni's expectations. Giovanni looked to Pietro to effect a fundamental realignment of papal and communal interests as a framework for restoring the bishop's spiritual authority. In other words, Giovanni hoped that Pietro could erase changes in the political and religious landscape, not simply work within them.

Success

Given the tangled mess of central Italian politics that brought Pietro to Orvieto, his achievement was more than negligible, at least in the short term. According to the *Passio,* his posthumous miracles generated considerable religious excitement in Orvieto. Giovanni's account of enthusiasm generated by Pietro probably is not too exaggerated. By 1200, Orvietans had set aside a special feast day for their saint. In that year Chiusi submitted to Orvieto and promised to pay a tribute of twenty pounds of wax to the cathedral each year on the feast of the Assumption or on the feast of Pietro the martyr.[32] According to Giovanni, Pietro's posthumous miracles inspired Orvietans to drive heretics out of Orvieto. Apparently there is some truth in this as well. In the years following Pietro's death, when a *podestà* or consul took office in Orvieto, he had to promise, among other things, not to alienate property that the commune confiscated from those who were exiled on account of Pietro's death.[33] Finally, the image of Pietro as the ideal Christian knight, who wielded the secular sword in defense of the church, left a lasting impression on Orvietan political consciousness. The Orvietan ruling elite took their duty to protect the local church seriously.

The relationship between Orvieto and Innocent in the years following Pietro's death was sometimes amicable. Innocent and Orvieto seem to have reached an understanding concerning Acquapendente.[34] The Orvietan bishop and cathedral chapter remained faithful servants of the papacy. In 1205 Innocent sent Capitano, the archdeacon of Orvieto, along with Bishop Matteo, Riccardo's successor, to help root out heretics from Viterbo.[35] He also sent them to investigate other disputes that had been submitted to the papacy for resolution.[36] In a privilege granted to the Orvietans in 1208, Innocent referred to the Orvietans as "our beloved sons and vassals of the Orvietan commune who, persisting firm and immovable in their faith and devotion to the mother church of Rome, are not able to be torn away in a time of tempest by any persuasion or temptation."[37] It is tempting to add these words to the list of Pietro's posthumous miracles.

Failure

Pietro's success in reestablishing Orvietan-papal relations on a firm footing was more illusory than real. Only one year after Innocent issued this privilege, he wrote a scathing letter to the Orvietans, who were at war with Acquapendente once again.

> Long and often we have endured, waiting if by chance our kindness would call you to repentance. But behold what we report with grief, that our patience has only made you more insolent so that your latest deeds are worse than your prior ones. . . . Because often we have tried to cure your affliction with various remedies, which you always abuse, there remains no alternative but to apply the sword or fire. Indeed, it was not sufficient that we have, till now, been provoked by your many offenses (which would be long in enumerating individually even if you did not presume to add this to the total of your offenses) so that recently, before our very eyes, you have plundered Acquapendente without presenting or offering any just cause to us. Not wishing to bear your insolence with goodwill any further, we command, by the apostolic letters sent to you, that it will be satisfactory to us if, within fifteen days, you give back in its entirety that which you took and that you cease your attacks against Acquapendente as well as the land in Val di Lago.[38]

After this condemnation of Orvieto's actions, Innocent threatened to excommunicate communal officials and to place Orvieto under interdict.[39]

In reality, Maestro Giovanni's Pietro, the image of harmony between communal, episcopal, and papal interests, had little effect on relations between Orvieto and Innocent. While Orvietans wanted to be faithful to the papacy, desire to solidify control over the *contado* was the guiding principle of their politics. When this required the Orvietans to defy the papacy, they did so. In 1211 even Bishop Giovanni, the same Giovanni who wrote the *Passio*, acted in defiance of the papacy by renewing a feudal contract between the bishopric and Count Bulgarello of Parrano. At the time, Bulgarello was under a sentence of excommunication for his allegiance to Otto IV. The sentence of excommunication made his oath of no value, at least in theory.[40] In 1214 Orvieto again defied the papacy and allied with Narni, as both Orvieto and Narni were fighting against Todi and Amelia. Narni was under interdict at that time for its rebellion against the papacy. Nevertheless, Orvieto needed an ally in its conflict with Todi and Amelia over territory in the southeastern portion of the Orvietan *contado*.[41] Apparently, Innocent placed Orvieto under interdict once again, this time for its support of Narni.

This is not to say that Orvieto was defiant against the papacy in principle. The problem was that Orvietans drew a boundary between papal authority and their own political interests, a boundary that did not exist in Innocent's political and religious vision of the patrimony. It was a boundary that Maestro Giovanni hoped that Pietro the martyr could eliminate, or at least straddle, for Giovanni could conceive of no other foundation for episcopal authority apart from a harmony of Orvietan and papal political interests. Unfortunately, it would take a more powerful saint than Pietro to cause Orvietans to sacrifice their autonomy and territorial ambitions to the papacy.

Pietro's success against heretics was limited as well. While communal officials punished some heretics with exile and confiscation of property, Cathars maintained a strong presence in Orvieto from the 1190s to 1260.[42] This enduring presence of Cathars is not surprising. Pietro was first and foremost a centerpiece in a complicated political deal between Orvieto, Innocent III, and the Roman commune. There is no reason to expect that an image of a Christian knight, who wielded the secular sword for the papacy and who confiscated the property of dissenters, would have an appeal to Cathar sympathizers and laypersons looking for a bishop that was more responsive to their spiritual concerns. Pietro did nothing to repair the hole in the cathedral roof; and try as it might, the *Passio* could neither overlook nor overcome the cathedral's embarrassing state of disrepair.

Pietro was, in reality, an anachronism. As a saint, he belonged to the middle years of the twelfth century when there was a close connection between the religious and political interests of the papacy, bishopric, and commune. Giovanni hoped that this order would reemerge as central Italy began to quiet down in the late 1190s. When Giovanni wrote the *Passio*, a return to the order of the middle years of the twelfth century was no longer possible. Development of the central Italian communes and the papacy's determination to transform the patrimony of St. Peter into a territorial state left no room for the types of compromises that Hadrian was able to make with Orvieto in the 1150s.

THE REJECTION OF PIETRO

Innocent came to Orvieto on April 28, 1216, in the midst of a preaching tour intended to launch a new crusade.[43] On the first of May he celebrated mass in the cathedral, having relaxed the interdict the previous day. After celebrating mass, he began to preach the crusade. The crowd grew too large for either the cathedral or the *palazzo comunale*, so they moved to an open field near the edge of the city. Because it was raining, Orvietans built a temporary portico where Innocent could stand. Although he was exhausted, he continued to preach, inspired by the devotion of the Orvietans who stood in the pouring rain to hear him. Over two thousand Orvietans received the sign of the cross that day, promising to support the crusade, as they were able.

There is a more somber reference to Innocent's visit in an addendum to the *Passio*, probably written shortly after Innocent left Orvieto. While Innocent was in Orvieto, the author of the addendum gathered over fifty witnesses who wanted to appear before Innocent to testify to a miracle of Pietro Parenzo. Innocent refused them audience.[44] There was, in fact, little chance that Innocent would canonize Pietro. To begin with, Pietro was an unusual saint, even for the twelfth century. The majority of twelfth-century Umbrian saints were bishops and monks.[45] The wave of the future was St. Francis, whose radical vow of poverty had more in common with the Orvietan heretics than with Pietro's knightly spirituality. Without denying the importance of this sea change in religious ideals and the increasingly stringent criteria that Innocent demanded of local communities seeking canonization for their saints, one must not ignore local political dynamics in explaining Innocent's rejection of Pietro. The relationship between Pietro's family and the papacy was enough to preclude his canonization. The Parentii belonged to the same Roman senatorial aristocracy that had been a thorn in the side of the papacy since the formation of the Roman commune in 1143. Although his family probably was part of a faction of senatorial families that allied with Innocent in 1198, there is good reason to believe that their loyalty was not deep. In 1219 Parenzo di Parenzo, Pietro's brother, wrote on behalf of the Roman senate, offering an imperial coronation to Frederick II in defiance of Pope Honorius III. In 1221 he was once again at odds with the pope and was excommunicated.[46]

This same Parenzo served as *podestà* of Orvieto during the three years following the death of his brother Pietro.

Pietro's family was a living symbol of all that stood in the way of Innocent's vision of political and religious order for central Italy. Innocent's refusal to canonize Pietro closed the door on this first attempt by representatives of the bishopric to adjust to the new world of the communes. The bishopric would have to look for another foundation on which to rebuild its authority.

CHAPTER SIX

LOOKING AT OLD THINGS
IN A NEW WAY

The Making of an Episcopal Register

THERE IS AN INTERESTING AMBIGUITY TO ELEVENTH- AND TWELFTH-century Italy. This was the period and region where the study of Roman law was reborn. The field of law was marked by tremendous experimentation and creativity, both in the schools and in the daily practice of notaries and lawyers. Indeed, the two drew momentum from each other. At the same time, it seemed to be a period of lawlessness. As notaries and lawyers elaborated an increasingly sophisticated terminology for defining property and rights, there remained a lack of public authority to implement many of these developments.[1] As noted earlier, the problem was not so much an absence of public authority as a superabundance. Signorial lords and rural communes attempted to carve out independent jurisdictions in the countryside. Bishops, in conjunction with urban elites, used their dioceses as frameworks for drawing these rural lordships under the jurisdiction of cities. Finally, popes and emperors sought to build territorial states out of this patchwork of urban and rural jurisdictions. The result was endemic warfare for much of the eleventh and twelfth centuries. By the late twelfth and early thirteenth centuries, communes emerged as the defining features of the Italian political landscape. Communes and law were, in effect, siblings in the quest for order. The commune proved to be the public authority that could most effectively employ the skills of its precocious sibling to provide a more lasting foundation for order and stability.

The bishopric played a fundamental role in this aspect of communal development as well, by schooling the commune in the art of administration. By the eleventh and twelfth centuries, a coalition of urban elites, consisting of knights and legal professionals, formed around the bishopric to expand the city's control over its *contado*. The commune outgrew this type of dependence on the bishopric by the late twelfth century. Not even Pietro Parenzo could convince Orvietans to subordinate their territorial policy to the bishopric. Even worse, the bishopric seemed defenseless against laypersons, whose frustration with the progress of reform caused them to throw in their lot with Cathars. In an attempt to adjust to these new political realities, bishops increasingly looked to legal professionals to craft bureaucratic solutions that would reduce tensions between the city's political and religious interests to a tolerable level. In doing so, they developed administrative methods that were readily applicable to the commune in its efforts to manage factional strife and tensions between nobles and *popolani*. In examining these processes, it is worth recalling Robert Brentano's description of similar changes in Rieti, albeit at a later stage, as "a normalization, perhaps even civilization, certainly bureaucratization."[2] The development of bureaucratic solutions was an integral part of the development of civil society.

Historians have highlighted the importance of written documentation in the development of political institutions and, more particularly, the importance of notaries and lawyers in the political culture of the Italian communes.[3] The fascinating role of notaries and lawyers in ecclesiastical administration and reform has received considerably less attention.[4] This neglect is due in part to a tendency to overdetermine certain tensions that were enduring features of life in the Italian city-states. The communes, the *popolo*, and especially legal professionals are rightly seen as progressive forces and somewhat misleadingly portrayed as precociously secular. As Maureen

Miller has shown in her study of Verona, religious sentiments of notaries and judges often were conservative.[5]

In the remaining chapters I examine the pivotal role of notaries and legal professionals in facilitating the bishopric's adjustment to the new world of the communes and in helping the Orvietan bishops to make the local church more responsive to the laity's spiritual expectations and aspirations. These developments begin with Bishop Giovanni, who used notaries and notarial technologies of record keeping to transform episcopal administration.

BISHOP GIOVANNI: CAPTURING THE BISHOPRIC
IN A REGISTER

As already indicated, the use of notaries in episcopal administration was widespread in Italy and dates back to the early Middle Ages.[6] Still, the role of notaries in thirteenth-century episcopal administration was something new. As notaries established a foot in both communal and episcopal administration, they provided a means for the commune's political and religious cultures to adjust to each other. In Orvieto, the pioneer in this process was Bishop Giovanni.

On September 26, 1211, a little more than ten years after Maestro Giovanni wrote the *Passio*, he was elected bishop of Orvieto. Giovanni offers a fascinating glimpse into the process of trial and error whereby the Orvietan church adjusted to the new political realities of central Italy. As a cathedral canon, he wrote the *Passio* in an attempt to reconstruct the political and religious bonds that united the twelfth-century bishopric, commune, and papacy. In the *Passio*, Giovanni argued that the best way to respond to antipapal politics and challenges to episcopal authority was to convince communal officials to forcefully suppress dissent. This trial was a failure.

During his short episcopate of one year and three months, he laid a foundation for rebuilding episcopal authority in Orvieto. The key to his success was the incorporation of notaries and notarial technologies of record keeping into episcopal administration. In so doing, Bishop Giovanni incorporated the religious and political interests of *minores* like Milita, the early Cathar sympathizer, whose concern for the cathedral's state of disrepair reflected widespread disaffection with the diversion of episcopal property to urban nobles. He called upon these legal professionals to spin an increasingly dense web of documents and administrative techniques to more carefully guard the integrity of ecclesiastical property.

Notarial Registers

Notaries, who had obtained a new level of autonomy as royal authority collapsed in Italy, became the source of *publica fides*. Along with these changes, notaries began to develop new procedures for redacting and storing documents. In the early Middle Ages, notaries began the process of making a document by taking notes of the transaction, often on the back of the same parchment that the final document was written. From these notes he drew up the final document, or *mundum*. Once the notary delivered the *mundum* to the interested parties, he was no longer responsible for preserving memory of the transaction. During the eleventh and twelfth centuries, a new step in the process emerged. After taking notes, notaries began to redact rough drafts, of sorts, called *dicta* (later called *imbreviature*). *Dicta* were very similar to *mundi*, only they had a few abbreviated sections. By the twelfth century, *dicta* were accorded probative value, prompting notaries to preserve them in registers. By the thirteenth century, many communal statutes required notaries to preserve their *imbreviature*. The oldest extant Italian notarial registers were compiled in Genoa in the 1150s. Although no longer extant, there apparently were notarial registers in Orvieto by the late twelfth century.[7]

Use of notarial registers allowed notaries to streamline production of documents. By the twelfth century, notaries followed three steps in redacting documents: taking notes, making an *imbreviatura* and recording it in a register, and finally, producing the *mundum* on a parchment. Notaries gradually simplified the process to writing notes directly into the register and redacting the *mundum*. If clients wished to save money, they could request the notary to enregister notes and not redact the *mundum*. If a dispute arose and a client needed a document, he or she could ask the notary to redact the *mundum* from the entry in the register.[8]

The formation of notarial registers belongs to an important transition in the uses of literacy between the twelfth and thirteenth centuries. As M. T. Clanchy commented in his study of record keeping and the uses of literacy in England, "the twelfth century had been a great period of making documents, [and] the thirteenth was the century of keeping them."[9] The same is true of France, where Philip II's chancery began to experiment with registers and new forms of record retention during the first decade of the thirteenth century.[10] In this sense, Italy provides an interesting parallel to the experiences of England and France. The contrast between Italy and England is equally striking. In England, innovations in making and keeping documents came largely from the royal chancery and filtered down to the local level.[11] As a result, changes in the uses of literacy often leveraged royal power—Edward's *quo warranto* proceedings providing one of the best examples. In Italy, innovations came not from a centralized authority, but from notaries. Just as innovations that originated from the royal chancery leveraged royal power, innovations emanating from the class of legal professionals in Italy leveraged their power in the emerging world of the communes.

Innovations in record keeping made notaries the principal deposits of juridical memory.[12] They were largely responsible for defining the shape of this memory as well. Most notaries possessed at least a degree of legal training, and beginning in the ninth century, it was increasingly common for notaries to become judges.[13] Between the tenth and thirteenth centuries, the demand for their legal expertise increased dramatically. Demographic expansion, a growth in trade, increased circulation of currency, a change of family structures, and the parceling of landed estates created a more liquid land market, a more sophisticated structure of rents, and an increased potential for conflict over inheritance and divided estates. Consequently, recourse to notaries for written documents increased as a rapidly changing society called upon them to lend a measure of definition and constraint to these unsettling changes.[14] Developments in notarial technology thus represent efforts by notaries to adapt legal structures to rapidly changing social and economic conditions.

In discussing the role of notaries in episcopal and communal administration, it is important to recall their professional and social status. Judges enjoyed a higher status within the profession than notaries. This professional *cursus honorum* often translated into a distinction in social status. Most notaries belonged to the upper ranks of *minores*; many judges belonged to the urban ruling elite. Thus the class of legal professionals straddled the boundary between *maiores* and *minores*, making them well suited to renegotiate relations between political and religious interests of *minores* and *maiores*, which were growing increasingly strained by the end of the twelfth century.

Bishop Giovanni's Register

Bishop Giovanni's administrative innovations, like the *Passio*, were part of a process of trial and error. He was not a visionary preparing the church for the coming of a new social order. Rather, the new order came to him in bits and pieces, disguised as the daily task of ecclesiastical administration. Unlike the *Passio*, Giovanni's administrative reforms were remarkably successful. Register B, one of three episcopal registers housed in the Orvietan episcopal archive, contains sufficient evidence to retrace Giovanni's steps as he groped toward his innovative solution.

The entries in the register dating between 1211 and the 1240s—during the episcopates of Bishops Giovanni and Ranerio—are characterized by tremendous variety in form, structure, and content, reminding us of the experimental nature of the process. Clanchy commented that from the perspective of the modern observer, the medieval archive "looked more like a magpie's nest than a filing system for documents."[15] This certainly applies to the early entries in Register B, especially when one compares them with entries from the second half of the thirteenth century. By the 1250s the apparent lack of systematization increasingly gives way to a monotonous regularity. By this time, recording and using documents had become a comfortable routine for the Orvietan bishops. The appearance of an index for the register by the fourteenth century represents the culmination of this routinization of record keeping. The remainder of this book is interested primarily in the "magpie's nest"—that part of the register that marks the fascinating transition from memory to written record, to use Clanchy's felicitous phrase. It is in the effort to order the magpie's nest that Orvietan bishops adjusted the local church to the new world of the commune.

With the exception of a few entries in Registers A and C, all episcopal records dating before the mid-twelfth century are contained in *quaterni* 7–16 of Register B.[16] The entries in these *quaterni* span the years 1024 to 1255.[17] *Quaterni* 7–16 seem to have constituted a register of sorts by 1248. Although it is impossible to determine if these ten *quaterni* were actually bound together, the numbering of the folios and other internal evidence indicate that they comprised a single collection, compiled over the course of almost forty years. The process of compilation probably began with Bishop Giovanni (1211–1212), during whose episcopate the five earliest *quaterni* (8, 9, 10, 12, and 13) were redacted. The remaining *quaterni* (7, 11, 14, 15, and 16) were redacted during the episcopate of Ranerio (1228–1248).

The structure and content of these early *quaterni* shed considerable light on Giovanni's innovations and on the use of episcopal documentation by his predecessors. Most entries in the eighth *quaternus* date from Giovanni's episcopate and follow standard notarial protocol, assuring their value as proof in a legal proceeding. Giovanni apparently intended to use the four remaining *quaterni* for internal administration, for they do not follow standard notarial protocol. The ninth *quaternus* contains an inventory of episcopal possessions. The tenth is a copy of a dispute between the bishops of Orvieto and Sovana over diocesan boundaries. The twelfth contains copies of eleventh- and twelfth-century documents. The thirteenth contains various disputes brought before Bishop Giovanni for judgment.[18]

These diverse collections apparently belong to a common process and represent stages in Giovanni's efforts to compile an inventory of episcopal possessions and revenues. Giovanni's methods and intentions in compiling these *quaterni*, especially *quaterni* 8, 9, and 12, become visible in a series of documents related to the castle community of Parrano, over which Orvietan bishops exercised overlordship. The first entry in the twelfth *quaternus* is a copy of a document executed in 1172 in which Count Ranerio of Parrano swore fidelity to Bishop Rustico (1168–1175) and recognized that he held the castle of Parrano in fief from the bishopric.[19] Another entry in the same *quaternus*, dated 1118, records the promise of Count Ranerio's ancestor, Count Bernardo of Parrano, to protect episcopal claims to the same castle.[20] The 1172 agreement between Bishop Rustico and Count Ranerio also appears in the eighth *quaternus*.[21] Here, the document constitutes only the first part of a fascinating and much longer entry, dated April 9, 1212, in which Bishop Giovanni renegotiated the 1172 agreement. Between the copy of the 1172 agreement at the beginning of this document and the new agreement in 1212 is a short narrative connecting the two. The narrative recounts that in 1211, Bishop Giovanni asked Count

Bulgarello of Parrano by what right he held the castle of Parrano. Count Bulgarello showed Bishop Giovanni the document executed in 1172. After inspecting it, Bishop Giovanni declared that it was not valid. It did not indicate that the cathedral canons had given their consent to the agreement, nor had a notary executed it. Giovanni argued that because the document was carelessly executed, it contained certain provisions that were not true, while omitting other provisions that it should have contained. Following this brief narrative is the contract that Bishop Giovanni renegotiated.

Although the narrative does not specify why Bishop Giovanni asked Count Bulgarello about his rights to Parrano, the compilation of Giovanni's inventory in the ninth *quaternus* provides the most likely occasion for the inquiry.[22] Thus the documents concerning Parrano point to a series of events linking the twelfth, eighth, and ninth *quaterni*. Count Bulgarello, when asked about his rights to the castle of Parrano, showed Bishop Giovanni a copy of the 1172 agreement. Giovanni then copied it into the twelfth *quaternus*. Based on this copy, he renegotiated the agreement and copied both the old and the new agreement into the eighth *quaternus*, this one according to standard notarial protocol. He then used the renegotiated agreement as a source for his inventory in the ninth *quaternus*.

A similar process is evident in a series of documents concerning episcopal possessions in Mealla. In 1212 Bishop Giovanni sought to recover episcopal property in Mealla and San Gervasio from the sons of Stefano di Tebalduccio, who held the property in pledge during the Alexandrian schism (1159–1178). Bishop Giovanni submitted the dispute to arbitration on October 24, 1212. The document recording the decision is copied into the eighth *quaternus*, according to standard notarial protocol.[23] It begins by noting that the dispute first arose when Priest Bernardo, a representative of the bishop, inquired into the rights of Stefano's sons in this property. Once again, the inventory in the ninth *quaternus* provides the most likely occasion for the inquiry.[24] The dispute came to the attention of Pope Innocent III, perhaps through an appeal by Bishop Giovanni. Innocent wrote a letter to the *podestà* and consuls of Orvieto on October 3, 1212, exhorting them to defend the church's property against Stefano's sons.[25] Three weeks later, Bishop Giovanni and the sons of Stefano submitted the dispute for arbitration. This dispute probably accounts for the presence of two more twelfth-century documents copied into the twelfth *quaternus*.[26]

Documents concerning episcopal rights in Corsula follow the same pattern. The eighth *quaternus* contains a document dated June 1212 in which Bishop Giovanni confirmed Ranerio Valentini as *castaldus* of Corsula, a position that Ranerio held under Bishops Riccardo and Matteo (1202–1211).[27] After confirming him in office, Giovanni specified property and revenues in Corsula to which Ranerio was entitled. The definition of Ranerio's salary is the most likely reason for four copies of twelfth-century documents concerning Corsula found in the twelfth *quaternus*.[28] In light of the examples of Parrano and Mealla, it is likely that the occasion for confirming Ranerio as *castaldus* and defining his rights in the region arose from Giovanni's efforts to compile an inventory of episcopal revenues in Corsula.

In sum, it appears that the twelfth *quaternus* was a preliminary stage in the compilation of the inventory found in the ninth *quaternus*. Giovanni would begin by making an inquiry into episcopal rights in a given region. In some cases, the inquiry involved gathering and copying twelfth-century documents, especially when the inquiry led to a question concerning episcopal rights. Giovanni gathered the documents in the twelfth *quaternus* for internal administration, that is, for compilation of an inventory, as evidenced by their lack of standard notarial protocol for authenticating copies, which would have been necessary if he intended to use them as evidence in a legal dispute. The settlement of disputes and other activities whereby Bishop Giovanni affirmed episcopal rights were copied into the eighth *quaternus* and, in a few instances, the first half of the thirteenth. These documents follow standard notarial protocol. The inventory in the ninth *quaternus* reflects the results of this process. This is not to say that all of the entries in the eighth, twelfth, and thirteenth *quaterni* are directly related to the inventory. Nevertheless, the compilation of the inventory appears to have been the principal force in the production of these *quaterni*.

The tenth *quaternus*, which contains a copy of the dispute between the bishops of Orvieto and Sovana over diocesan boundaries, is an interesting departure from the other four. Although there are a few entries in Giovanni's inventory concerning property in the disputed region, his interest in the dispute reaches beyond the inventory of episcopal property to broader questions of diocesan authority. In June 1212, Bishop Giovanni made a detailed inquiry into the condition of churches in Acquapendente. The results of this inquiry are recorded in the twelfth *quaternus*.[29] Perhaps this inquiry was the occasion for preserving the dispute between the bishops of Orvieto and Sovana, seeing that Acquapendente was one of the principal areas of conflict. The northwestern portion of the diocese around Acquapendente was an especially troublesome region for Orvietan bishops. The monastery of San Sepolcro in Acquapendente offered stubborn resistance to episcopal authority. The abbot argued that neither the monastery nor most of its subject churches were under the Orvietan bishop's diocesan authority because Acquapendente was not in the diocese of Orvieto. This particular conflict began as early as the episcopate of Matteo (1202–1211) and continued well into the episcopate of Ranerio (1228–1248).[30] Giovanni's attempt to assert his authority over churches in the region is, perhaps, the occasion for the compilation of the tenth *quaternus*.

Episcopal Administration before Registers

In his study of cathedral schools in the eleventh century, C. Stephen Jaeger warned that progressive models of historical development are prone to the fallacy that "growing literacy represents improvement, increasing sophistication, a move from an archaic and primitive to an advanced culture."[31] This warning is worth heeding when thinking about the growing use of documentation in Orvieto. While Giovanni's predecessors had a different understanding of the use of documentation, their system of administration did not necessarily lack sophistication. As will soon become apparent, Giovanni's ability to construct his inventory and early *quaterni* depended on a relatively sophisticated administrative structure that could function reasonably well without relying heavily on documents. The transition to a greater reliance on written documentation in Orvieto is analogous to the transition from Anglo-Saxon to Norman administration described by Clanchy. Following earlier studies of Anglo-Saxon and Norman administration, Clanchy argued, "the Anglo-Saxon kingdom was managed through elaborate customary mechanisms, which did not depend on masses of record-keeping." The Normans began to standardize and depersonalize this system through the use of written documentation.[32]

Does Jaeger's warning about models of historical progress mean that the use of written documentation to fortify a customary system of administration was a matter of indifference? Developments in Orvietan episcopal administration would suggest that a concept of progress, if properly understood, does not do injustice to the past. While it makes little sense to think of customary modes of administration as intrinsically inferior to literate modes of administration, it is certainly possible for one to be superior to the other relative to a specific historical context. One of the principal arguments I will make is that the Orvietan bishopric could not have adjusted to the new political realities of the commune without adopting notarial technologies of record keeping.

Bishop Giovanni initiated the transition in episcopal administration from a reliance on customary mechanism to a growing reliance on written documentation. On the one hand, Giovanni's efforts to restore episcopal authority by regathering the fragments of the *mensa* are similar to efforts of twelfth-century bishops such as Riccardo. On the other hand, Giovanni developed a remarkably innovative way of going about it. Compiling documents in an episcopal register apparently was a new form of record keeping for the Orvietan bishops. Various complaints concerning episcopal documentation scattered throughout these *quaterni* tend to confirm that Orvietan bishops were not accustomed to preserving and using written documentation in any systematic fashion. In the ninth *quaternus*, Seraphyno, the notary who copied the inventory, wrote that when Bishop Giovanni entered office, there was no description of episcopal possessions.[33] According to Bishop Ranerio, the episcopal archive had been in lamentable condition since the mid-twelfth century. Most episcopal documents from the first half of the twelfth century were lost to fire.[34] Episcopal documents fared no better in the second half of the twelfth century. Ranerio wrote that most instruments documenting property in Giovanni's inventory had been lost.[35] Finally, Ranerio complained that most documents executed during the episcopate of his predecessor, Capitano (1213–1228), had disappeared.[36] The inventory compiled by Bishop Giovanni survived, but according to Ranerio, Bishop Capitano found little use for it. As a result, the inventory was forgotten for the most part, and the bishopric suffered a considerable loss of property and revenues.

Although Ranerio attributed the poor condition of the episcopal archive to carelessness, the tendency of documents to flee the confines of the archive probably is attributable to a different understanding of the use of documents by Giovanni's predecessors. From the little information that can be gathered about twelfth-century episcopal administration in Orvieto, it seems to have been based primarily upon the oral memory of locals familiar with their surroundings. The vast majority of Orvieto's twelfth- and early thirteenth-century bishops were from Orvieto. Before becoming bishops, they had spent several decades as members of the Orvietan clergy, usually as cathedral canons, and were therefore familiar with the local ecclesiastical landscape. In a system of administration based primarily on oral memory, documents were useful only as proof in the case of disputes. This "inconsistent but coherent oral church," to use Robert Brentano's words, was typical for the eleventh- and twelfth-century Italian church.[37]

The bishop's familiarity with the complicated network of episcopal rights and property was reinforced by continual personal contact with his spiritual and temporal subjects. Many witnesses in the Orvieto-Sovana dispute recalled bishops perambulating throughout the diocese. Dominico of Ripazurla testified that he had personally accompanied Bishops Gualfredo, Ildibrando, Guiscardo, and Milo to collect tithes in Bisenzio, San Lorenzo, Gradulis, Sant' Hyppolyto, Acquapendente, and Proceno.[38] Dono, the archdeacon of Orvieto, testified that bishops of Orvieto had established their authority in Acquapendente, Grotte, Gradulis, San Lorenzo and the church of Sant' Hippolyto by consecrating churches, ordaining clergy, calling councils, interdicting and restoring offices, and offering penance to public criminals.[39]

The contact between the bishop and his diocese, however, was occasional, for the bishop, like other mortals, was limited by space and time. Nevertheless, the administrative structure of the bishopric allowed bishops to maintain continual contact with the diocese through their representatives. The bishop's diocesan authority was felt at the level of the local parish through the clergy. Apart from exercising their normal parish duties, local clergy were sometimes called upon to perform various tasks for the bishop. Priest Tebaldo testified that he collected tithes for the bishop of Orvieto from San Sepolcro. He also collected tithes in Grotte and San Lorenzo for the provost of Santa Cristina in Bolsena, which tithes the provost held in fief from the Orvietan bishop.[40]

Bishops asserted their temporal authority over the episcopal *mensa* through local officials appointed to manage and protect episcopal property. Bishops relied on *castaldi* and *fideles* to protect and administer property in various small communities over which the bishopric exercised temporal authority. Bishop Giovanni's confirmation of Ranerio Valentini as a *castaldus* in Corsula offers a glimpse into episcopal administration over portions of the *mensa* located in the countryside. The *castaldus* was a familiar official in twelfth-century episcopal administration, acting as the bishop's agent in rural communes and castle communities.[41] In some cases, local communities belonged to wealthy churches or monasteries, which, in turn, belonged to the episcopal *mensa*. In these instances, *castaldi* were directly appointed by and answerable to the church or monastery. Nevertheless, these officials ultimately answered to the bishop.[42] Thus a bishop's spiritual and temporal authority extended to thousands of people scattered throughout the diocese and *contado*, sometimes through direct personal contact, but more often through a capillary network of clergy, *castaldi*, *fideles*, and other local representatives. Memory of episcopal rights found constant reinforcement in such personal contacts.

From all indications, compilation of the inventory was primarily an oral process. Comments of Seraphyno and Bishop Ranerio concerning the lamentable condition of the episcopal archive suggest that Giovanni had to compile much of his inventory without benefit of written documentation. Several entries in the inventory were clearly based on oral testimony.[43] Moreover, the simplicity of most entries suggests that the inquisition into episcopal property was an oral process. Most entries contain only a personal name, the amount of rent owed, and the type of property for which a person owed rent. Finally, the size of the inventory suggests the same. The inventory contains almost five hundred entries. Bishop Ranerio's comments make it abundantly clear that no such collection of documents existed in the episcopal archive during the early decades of the thirteenth century.

While Giovanni's inventory measures the strength of a system of administration based on personal contact, he compiled the inventory because he realized that there was an inescapably fragile quality to this system. The very institutional links that sustained memory of episcopal rights could also promote forgetfulness. There were always centrifugal forces working against institutional links that connected scattered local communities to episcopal authority. The Orvieto-Sovana dispute is replete with examples of priests using the dispute as an opportunity to escape episcopal authority. For example, Girardo, a priest from Grotte, recalled that the bishop of Sovana ordained him. Shortly thereafter, the bishop of Orvieto removed him from office. Only after trying unsuccessfully to be reinstated by the bishop of Sovana did he return to the obedience of the Orvietan bishop.[44] The same centrifugal forces threatened episcopal authority over officials managing the *mensa*. The *castaldus* in Corsula confirmed by Bishop Giovanni was already deeply entrenched, having held the position for over ten years. It is easy to imagine that over the course of ten years, memory of episcopal revenues to which the *castaldus* was entitled could become quite flexible, especially as the *castaldus* himself was one of the principal custodians of this memory.

When memory is too flexible, it becomes forgetfulness. Only at this point did twelfth-century bishops use written documents. Use of documents solely as proof in disputes accounts for their loss as well as their preservation. As the example of Bishop Giovanni indicates, disputes over episcopal rights tended to single out which among countless old documents were worth collecting. For the many more cases in which episcopal memory was not contested, relegation of documents to the function of backup memory meant that management of episcopal documentation was not as careful as it could have been. This is one reason why Bishop Ranerio complained so persistently that episcopal property and rights were poorly documented.

There is still another reason for inattention to documentation. By the 1180s, Orvietan bishops entrusted management of episcopal documents to public notaries who executed them. Bishop Ranerio knew where to find documents when he needed them. After one of his complaints about loss of documents, he wrote that he was going to recover as many of Capitano's documents as possible from public notaries and carefully preserve them in the episcopal archive.[45] Likewise, Giovanni probably gathered most of the twelfth-century documents in Register B from public notaries. Otherwise it would be difficult to account for the chance survival of only those eleventh-

and twelfth-century documents that the early-thirteenth-century bishops needed for their disputes.

Episcopal documents were scattered among offices of notaries who executed them, or, in the case of notaries who had died, instruments were passed along to their heirs and sometimes lost.[46] This meant that episcopal documents were usually available, although not always immediately accessible. Nevertheless, twelfth-century bishops were satisfied with this arrangement since there was no perceived need for these documents in daily administration of the bishopric. Bishop Giovanni's innovation was to add a new dimension to the use of written documentation for episcopal administration. For twelfth-century bishops, offices of notaries were graveyards where fragments of episcopal administration were buried and lost to memory. Twelfth-century bishops seemed content to allow memory of episcopal administration to decay. Bishop Giovanni realized that he could keep a more vigilant eye on the diocese by incorporating documents into daily administration.

Notaries and the Bishopric: Breaking the Cycle of Reform

Because discovery of an effective way to regulate this problem largely eluded Giovanni's predecessors, ecclesiastical reform in twelfth-century Orvieto followed a cyclical pattern. The bishopric depended on military services of urban and rural aristocratic families to protect ecclesiastical property and rights in the countryside. These families often received pledges of episcopal property in payment for their services. Given the bishopric's prominent role in the conquest of the *contado*, there was a natural tendency for episcopal revenues to flow out to powerful families on whom the bishopric depended for military support. In periods of aggressive expansion or political unrest, the rate of outflow increased significantly. Ultimately there came a point when the dislocation of episcopal property created sufficient disorder in the local church to spark reform. In the mid-1150s, Pope Hadrian IV, the cathedral chapter, and Bishop Guiscardo (1157–1159) joined together to gather episcopal property held in pledge by several powerful Orvietan families. This reforming activity followed more than a decade of conflict in which the papacy, bishopric, and commune sought to establish their religious and political authority to the west of the city. The next period of reform followed the tumultuous years of the papal schism when Frederick Barbarossa took control of much of central Italy. Bishop Riccardo (1178–1202) devoted the early years of his episcopate to recovering episcopal property. Although the schism ended in 1178, there was still considerable political and religious unrest during the 1180s and 1190s. By the latter years of Riccardo's episcopate, the Orvietan bishopric once again was in tremendous disorder, as indicated by Giovanni's account of events surrounding the death of Pietro Parenzo in 1199. Bishop Matteo (1202–1211) does not seem to have taken any significant steps toward reform. Therefore, when Giovanni became bishop in September 1211, he faced the task of gathering episcopal property once again. His reforms, however, were qualitatively different from those of his predecessors. He set the bishopric on a path that would eventually break the cycle of reform and decadence by incorporating a more efficient administrative technology. The relationship between the bishopric and powerful families during the twelfth century created a natural tendency for episcopal property to float between the two. By incorporating notarial technology into episcopal administration, Bishop Giovanni introduced a method for securing the bond between the bishopric and its property, reducing the opportunity for powerful families to exploit episcopal wealth.

While Giovanni's experiments in administration were innovative with respect to his predecessors, they were typical for the thirteenth-century Italian church.[47] It was no coincidence that experimentation with registers became widespread during the thirteenth century, for it was during this period that communes began to express their independence more stridently. Città di Castello offers an interesting parallel. As was the case in Orvieto, its bishops began compiling episcopal registers in the midst of intense conflict between the bishopric and commune.[48] The example of Orvieto suggests that this period of conflict does not necessarily mark the beginning of the bishop's marginalization and a corresponding secularization of communal culture. It simply marks a renegotiation of political and religious interests.

THE SOCIAL AND INSTITUTIONAL DEVELOPMENT
OF THE COMMUNES

Just as notaries developed new technologies for renegotiating the relation between religious interests of aristocrats and *minores/*

popolani that tugged at the bishopric, they influenced competing political interests in the commune. The emergence of legal professionals in communal politics coincided with a period of tremendous growth. Following territorial gains of the late twelfth century, Orvieto experienced yet another wave of expansion in the early thirteenth century. Between 1198 and 1216, territory subject to Orvieto nearly tripled in size.[49] This rapid growth placed considerable strain on communal institutions. Not only was there an increased administrative burden, there was the equally difficult task of restraining competition among powerful families for the fruits of these conquests. *Podestà* began to replace consuls, as factional conflict for control of the consulate proved too great for Orvietans to resolve. This was also the period that saw the transformation of *minores* into the *popolo*. In the midst of strains caused by rapid growth, political differences between *maiores* and *minores* became sufficiently large for *minores* to organize as a political class.

The Rise of the Popolo

Along with the transition from consuls to *podestà*, the rise of the *popolo* represents one of the most important developments in the political life of thirteenth-century Italian communes. Interests of *maiores* and *minores* were divided on some issues and united on others during the twelfth century. While *minores* benefited from territorial expansion, they became increasingly wary of aristocratic power during the early decades of the thirteenth century. Nobles did not always exercise their military skills for the general interest of the commune. Because they possessed sufficient wealth and military power to act independently, their interests naturally gravitated more narrowly around family and lineage. In such cases, they became a threat to the commune's economic and political stability. For example, when knights fought for the commune, they often received communal property in pledge for their services. In theory, communal officials would redeem this property with a cash payment. In practice, communal property tended to gravitate toward the nobility and remain under their control, because many of the same nobles who held property in pledge also filled the highest political offices. Just as the pledge of ecclesiastical property to episcopal vassals caused widespread religious disaffection among *minores*, pledges of communal property created political problems.

Equally problematic was the tendency for aristocratic factional strife to turn violent, endangering the commune's political stability.[50] Although Orvieto did not have large and violent patrilineages like the ones in Siena and Florence, the city was by no means immune from violent clashes between noble factions, as indicated by the battles in the public square recounted in the *Passio*. Almost inevitably, this violence spilled over to *minores*, who were less capable of defending themselves and often unable to bear the economic burden of damaged property and interrupted commerce. Thus efforts to prevent appropriation of communal property and to restrain factional violence account for the transformation of *minores* into the *popolo*. *Popolani* worked to protect their interests in two ways. They developed their own broadly based institutions to counterbalance the military might of the nobility, and they developed administrative techniques to protect communal property and interests.

The structure of *popolani* institutions in Orvieto is most evident in their participation in the General Assembly, which was the city's legislative body.[51] The assembly, called the General and Special Council, consisted of a Council of Two Hundred, a Council of One Hundred, rectors of the guilds, chiefs of the city's regions, and a few other officers whose participation in the council varied.[52] While there were individual *popolani* who sat on the Council of One Hundred or Council of Two Hundred, rectors of guilds and chiefs of the city's regions represented the *popolo* as an institution. Chiefs of the city's regions represented the military organization of the *popolo*, recalling the designation of non-nobles as *pedites* in the twelfth-century sources. Rectors of guilds represented the economic interests of the *popolo*. These *popolani* institutions began to play a visible role in communal politics by the first two decades of the thirteenth century. There are hints of an institutional organization of the *popolo* by district as early as 1207.[53] In 1214 leaders of the guild community represented the commune in treaties with other cities.[54] Development of *popolani* institutions culminated in 1250, when the *popolo* chose their own captain, who sometimes replaced the *podestà* as the city's supreme executive official. Thus when the need arose and when the *popolo* were united, the topographical and economic structure of *popolani* institutions allowed the *popolo* to compete with the ruling elite in cases where the interests of the two clashed.

Renegotiating Political Interests

While the *popolo* organized as a political body in opposition to the nobility, they still cooperated with the nobility in the formation of a broader Orvietan political community. It is here that the role of legal professionals is so important. They constructed an administrative framework that respected important leadership roles of the nobility, while carefully safeguarding *popolani* rights and interests. In this respect, Giovanni's innovations in episcopal administration seem to have offered a model for the commune. By the 1220s, about a decade after Giovanni compiled his *quaterni*, Orvietan *podestà* were commissioning notaries to compile communal registers, known as *libri iurium* or *libri memoriales*.[55] The oldest of these registers in Orvieto, ASO Titolario Cod A, contains mostly acts of submission, treaties, and disputes that defined the rights of the commune over towns, communities, and feudatories in the countryside. The remaining entries record matters of internal administration, such as public works, communal justice, payment of officials' salaries, and payment of debt by creditors of the commune.

Communal constitutions are yet another monument to the work of legal professionals. They too begin to appear during the period when *podestà* were replacing consuls.[56] Redaction of a constitution and statutes guided the *podestà* in his task to restrain aristocratic violence. The first reference to Orvietan statutes appears in relation to measures passed in 1221 against the Bovacciani, one of Orvieto's few patrilineages that exercised tremendous power in and around Orvieto.[57] More generally, the constitution provided a tool for the *podestà* and his staff to rule the commune according to its own customs. For example, in 1222 Tommaso, the *podestà* of Orvieto, decided a case brought to him concerning a creditor of the commune *iuxta tenorem capituli constituti*.[58] Other forms of documentation helped the *podestà* to enforce the city's jurisdiction over the countryside and to protect communal property. Reminiscent of Giovanni's inventory of 1211–1212, a survey of *comunalie*, or communal property, ordered by the *popolo* in 1244, represents an attempt to exercise tighter control over communal property and to prevent its appropriation by powerful urban nobles.[59] In this way, legal professionals were busy constructing a social map of carefully documented rights and boundaries that would greatly reduce the room for violent and egoistic impulses that threatened social stability.

Episcopal and communal administration developed according to a common logic during the early decades of the thirteenth century. The role of notaries in episcopal and communal administration is striking. Not only did the bishopric and commune incorporate the same technology, in many cases they used the same notaries. Approximately fifty different notaries appear in AVO Cod B and ASO Titolario Cod A. Ten of these fifty notaries redacted documents in both registers. Just as Bishop Giovanni incorporated notarial technology into episcopal administration to protect episcopal property, notaries supplemented *popolani* institutions with a map of documented rights to prevent the appropriation of communal property and rights in the countryside from the same group of powerful families. The commune learned from experiences in episcopal administration. As will become apparent, the significance of these developments goes far beyond the mundane tasks of administration. By shaping episcopal and communal administration, notaries played a fundamental role in fashioning the political and religious values that defined Orvietans—nobles, *popolani*, and their church—as a community.

CHAPTER SEVEN

HOW THE PAST BECOMES A RUMOR

The Notarialization of Historical Consciousness

THE INFLUENCE OF LEGAL PROFESSIONALS IN COMMUNAL AND episcopal administration had implications that transcended the development of the institutions themselves. A witness in the canonization process of Ambrogio of Massa provides a fascinating example of this. In 1240 Palmeria, a woman from Viterbo, testified before Bishop Ranerio of Orvieto that Ambrogio of Massa, a local Franciscan, had delivered her from several particularly ferocious demons. One of the witnesses confirming Palmeria's testimony added a small but remarkably telling detail. Blasio, a herdsman from Viterbo, said that one of the demons was a judge; therefore, there was nothing Palmeria could do to resist his wisdom.[1] Blasio's attribution of an irresistible wisdom to the demon-judge is a wonderful illustration of the power that contemporaries accorded to judges and notaries in thirteenth-century Italian communes. Although legal professionals rarely held the highest and most visible offices in the commune, their influence was pervasive.[2]

As notaries refashioned the institutional and administrative structures of the bishopric and commune, they created conditions for the bishopric to adjust to the new world of the commune, and to define a new balance between lordship and reform. Before examining the readjustment between lordship and reform in detail in chapter 8, I will examine a more subtle aspect of notarial influence on the bishopric and commune. Notaries changed the way Orvietans thought about their past.[3] This new understanding of the past brought bishopric and commune closer together in their approach to the pressing issues of the present. Bishop Ranerio provides a unique source for exploring the development of historical consciousness in Orvieto. Shortly after his election as bishop in 1228, he scribbled some historical reflections on the bishopric in the margins of the episcopal register that Giovanni had compiled.[4] These margin comments, along with other Orvietan historical and hagiographical texts, reflect the pervasive influence of notaries on the Orvietans' sense of their past.

HISTORICAL WRITING IN ITALY BETWEEN THE ELEVENTH AND THIRTEENTH CENTURIES

The role of notaries in the development of civic historical consciousness was not peculiar to Orvieto. Indeed, Orvietan texts must be understood in the context of a broader revival of historical writing in Italy between the eleventh and thirteenth centuries. This renaissance went through three overlapping phases. Institutional histories of monasteries dominated the first phase. The growing prominence of episcopal biographies marks the transition to the second phase. Finally, by the thirteenth century, communal chronicles, largely written by notaries and compiled from notarial registers, became the dominant mode of historical writing. These three phases correspond to stages in the political reconfiguration of Italy. Monastic histories looked back to the old Carolingian political order. They were based on collections of charters, the most important of which were issued by emperors and counts and executed by imperial and comital notaries. Episcopal biographies, which largely ignored charter collections and the old political order from which they came, belong to the transitional period of episcopal lordship. Finally, the formation of autonomous communes provides the context for communal chronicles, mostly written by notaries from the registers that they compiled for their cities.

Monastic Histories

Monastic histories that dominated the early stages of the revival in Italian historical writing emerged from a clearly defined tradition with roots in the Carolingian world. These institutional histories were essentially narratives of cartularies. Collections of documents recording sales, purchases, donations, privileges, disputes, rental contracts, treaties, and inventories over a long period of time naturally lent themselves to institutional history. Cartularies and registers thus functioned as seeds of historical consciousness. Among the purest examples of this relation between cartulary and narrative are episcopal and monastic histories, commonly called *gesta episcoporum* and *gesta abbatum*. While the ultimate model for these histories is the *Liber Pontificalis*, the genre is more directly a product of the Carolingian and Ottonian worlds. During the eighth century, as the relationship between the Carolingians and the papacy developed, imitations of the *Liber Pontificalis* began to appear in Austrasia, the core of Carolingian power.[5] The ideal type of these histories is a catalog of prelates, supplemented with such information as dates of tenure, construction projects, gifts, and acquisitions.[6] While the authors used chronicles, hagiography, and oral tradition, the most important sources were cartularies. Because the authors often inserted documents into the narrative, these histories sometimes functioned as cartularies by preserving the contents of documents subsequently lost.[7]

Authors of episcopal and monastic histories looked to a deep and sacred past to make their narratives more compelling. A great saint often stood at the beginning of the list of prelates. For example, Paul the Deacon traced the origin of the church of Metz to Clement, a disciple of the Apostle Peter. The authors thus sought to construct a sacred history of a place and make the present bishop or abbot the heir of that sacred history.[8]

One of the most striking characteristics of these histories is their conservative disposition toward the past. No doubt there was a theological aspect to this conservatism. The past revealed God's activity in the world through Jesus, the apostles, and the host of martyrs and saints. Nevertheless, God was not the only figure entering into and shaping the history of the church. Emperors, kings, and counts granted property, privileges, and immunities to ecclesiastical institutions. Beyond the religious sentiments motivating these gifts, such acts of patronage served to draw local institutions and their corresponding networks of public and private relations into the apparatus of the comital, royal, or imperial patron. The *gesta* were tools both for negotiating the inevitable tensions that arose in the construction of such political networks, and for depositing these networks into collective memory (hence their conservatism).

It is no accident that *gesta episcoporum* and *gesta abbatum* flourished in the Carolingian and Ottonian worlds, where relations between secular rulers and local ecclesiastical institutions were so important. Carolingians depended upon support from ecclesiastical institutions and access to their resources. Likewise, monasteries and bishoprics benefited from Carolingian patronage and protection. Imperial and royal patronage created the nucleus for a collection of charters, which, in turn, provided the basis for an institution's history. The *gesta* were the final products of a process in which bishops and monks defined their place in the Carolingian world, based in large part upon their cartularies.

Histories of episcopal institutions—*gesta episcoporum*—were not unknown to Italy. After all, the Roman *Liber Pontificalis* was the prototype for the genre. Apart from ninth-century episcopal histories of Ravenna, Grado, and Naples, however, there were few *gesta episcoporum* in Italy.[9] Initiative for writing institutional histories belonged to central Italian monasteries during the eleventh and twelfth centuries. Gregorio di Catino's chronicle of Farfa is one of the most notable examples. During the late eleventh and early twelfth centuries he compiled two cartularies, the first containing copies of titles to property, the second containing copies of concessions of property by the abbey. Using these cartularies, Gregorio wrote his chronicle, following the familiar pattern of episcopal and monastic histories, that is, an integration of documents and narrative organized around a series of prelates. The chronicles of San Vincenzo of Volturno, San Clemente of Casauria, and San Benedetto of Montecassino were written around the same time.[10] The chronicles of Farfa and San Vincenzo are especially interesting because they demonstrate how monastic chroniclers sought to protect and assert monastic interests by anchoring historical memory to a powerful patron. Farfa was attempting to assert authority over San Vincenzo. Because the patrons of Farfa and San Vincenzo were the emperor and pope, respectively, Farfa based its claims on imperial privileges while San Vincenzo asserted its independence through papal privileges.[11] Not surprisingly, the historical memory of each monastery involved a justification of its own interests as well as a defense of its patron's power.

Episcopal Biographies

Episcopal contributions to the flourish of historical writing during the eleventh and twelfth centuries were quite different. Bishops and cathedral canons produced few institutional histories. Their principal contribution was hagiography, or biographies of saintly bishops, which bore little or no relation to collections of charters. These biographies belong to the transitional period following the disintegration of the Italian kingdom, when cities began to emerge as autonomous political entities. As discussed earlier, some form of episcopal lordship was the vehicle for this transition to the world of the communes.

Episcopal biographies proved to be more adaptable than *gesta abbatum* and *gesta episcoporum* to this reconfiguration of the political order. The examples of Farfa and San Vincenzo suggest that historical memory generated from such sources justified the political order of the royal or comital patrons who granted the most important charters in monastic cartularies. Episcopal biographies ignored charters and the political order upon which they depended, for this order was beginning to pass away. Stories of saints (usually bishops) written in episcopal circles exalted the bishop as the symbol of civic unity in a way that dislodged civic identity from what remained of the Italian kingdom. For example, eleventh-century bishops of Padua were responsible for discovering and translating the relics of Saint Massimo, the second bishop of Padua, the three Innocents martyred by Herod, and the body of Luke the evangelist to the cathedral. Eleventh-century accounts recording the discovery and translation of these and other relics emphasized the bishop's dominant role in these events. Moreover, these accounts portrayed the discovery of relics as the resurrection of the city's ancient glory, lost in the intervening period of spiritual and material decay, that is, the period of the Italian kingdom. The bishopric thus emerged as the principal promoter for reconstructing a civic identity. This spiritualization of the city's history reflected the new political reality of eleventh-century Padua, where the bishops exercised temporal and spiritual authority over the city.[12]

Emergence of the cathedral and episcopal complex to a central position in the urban landscape was yet another manifestation of episcopal lordship. During the early Middle Ages, the cathedral often was located at the edge of the city. With urban growth and the expansion of city walls, many cathedrals became the physical center of town. Many comital and royal palaces moved beyond the city wall, leaving the bishop's palace as the only palace in the city.[13] These changes in the urban landscape were physical expressions of the new centrality of bishops in the political and spiritual landscape of the cities.

The bishops' role as nuclei of communal formation is evident as well in the biographies of Gregorian bishops, that is, bishops who were faithful supporters of the papacy during the Investiture Controversy. These biographies of bishops from the recent past demonized the politics of lay signorial domination. In the world of the *gesta episcoporum*, bishoprics were institutional intermediaries, linking local networks of private power to a larger public institution, whether comital, royal, or imperial. The stories of Gregorian bishops erased this political framework.[14]

The bishopric's identity, once uprooted from its traditional political framework, was a hotly contested issue. Although opposition to lay investiture of bishops facilitated communal autonomy by hastening the fragmentation of imperial authority, there was nothing consciously pro-communal in Gregorian ideology. Indeed, some of the earlier Gregorian episcopal biographies, such as those of Mauro of Cesena and Rodolfo of Gubbio, both written by Peter Damian, have a strong monastic strain that makes them ill suited for the formation of a civic identity around the bishop.[15] Two late-eleventh-century biographies of the Luccan bishop Anselmo II, one in prose, probably written by one of Countess Matilda's chaplains or a member of Anselm's *familia*, the other in verse, written by Bishop Rangerio of Lucca (1087–1112), illustrate the same lack of concern for urban interests. Neither attempted to integrate the city into Anselmo's spirituality. If Anselmo was responsible for civic identity, it was because he alienated the people of Lucca, confirming them in their opposition to the papacy and Countess Matilda. In both biographies, Anselmo's sanctity is exclusively a function of his role in papal politics after his exile from Lucca.[16]

Later biographies began to recast images of Gregorian bishops as civic lords. Biographies of Bishop Bruno of Segni (1079–1123) and Bishop Ubaldo of Gubbio (1129–1160) softened universal claims of the papacy and emphasized elements of sanctity around which civic interests could coalesce. Bishop Ubaldo pacified factional violence in Gubbio and protected the city by negotiating a peace with Frederick Barbarossa. Bishop Bruno of Segni protected his city from Count Arnulfo, its powerful lord, who terrorized the city from his castle in the countryside. Shortly before his death, Bruno prophesied that the city would remain free from tyranny. The reforming bishop and city thus were partners in building a peaceful community free from signorial domination.[17]

From Episcopal Biography to Communal Chronicle

These episcopal biographies belong to the political rupture of the eleventh century and the early crystallization of civic identity around the bishopric. During the twelfth and early thirteenth centuries, the commune grew from an embryo developing within the bishopric to a mature institution exercising guardianship over the local church. In the midst of this transformation, episcopal biographies gave way to communal chronicles as expressions of communal consciousness. Among the most interesting transitional forms between episcopal biographies and communal narratives are groups of early-twelfth-century Pisan annals and historical poems, all written by clerics.[18] Two historical poems, the *Carmen in Victoriam Pisanorum* and the *De bello Ballearico sive rerum in Majorica Pisanorum* (also known as the *Liber Maiorichinus*), celebrate eleventh-century Pisan naval victories against Moslems in North Africa and the Balearic Islands. Both texts were written by cathedral canons. The canons' interest in celebrating the city's military victories is complicated. In 1092 Pope Urban II elevated the Pisan see to metropolitan status over the island of Corsica. He justified this privilege by referring to the city's many naval victories over the Saracens.[19] During the early decades of the twelfth century, as Pisa and Genoa competed for control over Corsica, the latter pressured the papacy to revoke this privilege. Interests of the bishopric and nascent commune thus were tightly connected. The city's military successes justified its bishop's metropolitan status, which in turn strengthened the city's claims to Corsica.

While cathedral canons celebrated the city's military prowess, they assumed a defensive posture against the emerging commune. One-tenth of the *Carmen* focuses on the actions of Ugo Visconte, a deputy of the Tuscan margrave who shared authority over the city with the bishop. The author thus had an interest in maintaining the older feudal order against the emerging commune. This same tension appears in the *Liber Maiorichinus*. The bishop assumed a role of leadership, but real control belonged to the *patres*, a group of twelve nobles appointed by the people of Pisa to lead the campaign.[20] The poem offered an ideal of cooperation between the bishop and an emerging consular aristocracy (the *patres*) when the relation between the two was changing from cooperation between equals to subordination of the religious to the secular. The canons who wrote these poems were trying to arrest this development.

It is a short step from these historical poems to early communal chronicles. The earliest, and among the most interesting, is the Genoese chronicle. In 1152 Caffaro, a member of the consular aristocracy, presented his chronicle to the communal council. The council commissioned a public notary to transcribe the chronicle into a public register, thus making his chronicle the official history of the commune. The continuation of this chronicle later became one of the official tasks of the communal chancery.[21] In the 1180s Bernardo Maragone, a Pisan city official, wrote a similar communal chronicle of Pisa.

In certain respects the renaissance of historical writing came full circle with communal chronicles. Like the *gesta abbatum* and *gesta episcoporum*, these chronicles were closely related to collections of official documents, in this case communal registers. The differences, however, are more striking than the similarities. These communal registers contained a wide variety of documents that recorded the city's property, rights, and jurisdiction in the countryside. By documenting the newly created and autonomous jurisdiction of the city, these registers functioned as tools for both forgetting and remembering. They reduced the old order of the Italian kingdom to a faint memory. Civic chronicles that were based on these registers focused almost exclusively on local and contemporary history, reflecting the reality of autonomous communal politics and the novelty of the commune as a political framework for historical consciousness. This focus on contemporary history represents the culmination of a process that began with the disintegration of regional and supra-regional authority, that is, the political configuration in which the *gesta episcoporum* and *gesta abbatum* flourished.[22] Equally important, many of the communal chronicles were written by public notaries who participated in the compilation of communal registers. Chronicles, like the registers upon which they were based, therefore reflected the interests of those who compiled them.

A HISTORY OF EARLY-THIRTEENTH-CENTURY ORVIETAN HISTORY

Orvietan historical texts reflect the general development of Italian historical writing in the twelfth and thirteenth centuries. They are, however, an oddity, falling between the boundaries of the genres that were most typical of this period. Their unusual character makes them all the more interesting, for they illustrate the experimental and contingent nature of a process in which the legal-notarial class became custodians of historical memory in the Italian communes. The historical reflections that Bishop Ranerio scribbled into the margins of Bishop Giovanni's *quaterni* are the key to understanding the development of Orvietan historical consciousness and its relation to the broader revival in Italian historical writing. It will therefore be helpful to begin with a close examination of Ranerio's margin comments.

The Historical Reflections of Bishop Ranerio

Bishop Ranerio, like most of his predecessors, was a career churchman. He had been a cathedral canon for over fifteen years before becoming bishop. He was, however, also from a family of prominent judges.[23] Prudenzio, Ranerio's father, was one of two judges who recorded testimonies in the dispute between the bishops of Orvieto and Sovana.[24] He appears in ten other episcopal documents between 1181 and 1225, six times as a judge redacting documents and four times as a witness.[25] It is worth noting that Prudenzio recorded documents of his own clients in registers well before

Bishop Giovanni incorporated this technology into episcopal administration. Therefore one may reasonably consider his work a model for Giovanni's innovations. Guido di Prudenzio, Ranerio's brother, was the second judge in the Orvieto-Sovana dispute.[26] Guido played a conspicuous role in communal politics as well, serving as a consul in 1212–1213.[27]

Coming from a family of judges, Ranerio looked at the world and thought of documents. In light of his family's history, it comes as no surprise that one of Ranerio's first actions as bishop was to survey the register compiled by Bishop Giovanni. As he looked through this register, he recorded his reflections on the episcopal past and on the present condition of the bishopric in marginal comments scattered throughout. He was engaged in the process of extracting history from a register in much the same way that notaries like Caffaro had done in other cities.

Altogether Ranerio's comments consist of ten passages ranging from forty to more than six hundred words. The ten passages fall into three categories. There are various comments on specific entries in the register. Second, there is a catalog of bishops, supplemented with historical information drawn from the first category of comments. The catalog begins with Bishop Guilielmo (1103–1136) and ends with Ranerio's election. Finally, there is a long reflection on the present condition of the bishopric, which is more or less a summation of the first two categories.

The revolutionary effect of Bishop Giovanni's administrative innovations begins to manifest itself in Ranerio's comments. Before Giovanni incorporated developments in notarial technology into episcopal administration, no Orvietan bishop could have reflected on the episcopal past in the manner that Ranerio did, that is, by paging through a notebook. The most striking characteristic of this new style of historical reflection is its negative portrayal of the episcopal past. Ranerio's history of the bishopric was a story of small accomplishments swallowed by larger failures. In order to build a new past that the bishopric and commune could share, the old past had to be forgotten, or at least marginalized. Just as recently developed notarial registers facilitated a new past among communal chroniclers—that is, one that erased the memory of the old Carolingian order— Giovanni's *quaterni* facilitated a forgetting of those aspects of the past that impeded an adjustment to the new world of the commune.

For all intents and purposes, Ranerio's memory of the episcopal past began with Bishop Guilielmo, about whom he had little to say.[28] Ranerio remembered the episcopate of Guilielmo's successor, Bishop Ildibrando, as the beginning of a decline in the bishop's authority and a loss of episcopal documents and property. "Ildibrando, who previously was the manager of the bishopric during the vacancy, succeeded Guilielmo. And he had a disagreement with the canons, by whom he was charged with a lapse in the flesh, and was unjustly compelled to give them episcopal possessions."[29] Ranerio provided more detail concerning Ildibrando's dispute with the canons in another comment. "In the time of Ildibrando, who was from Valloclis, of the family of Beccario, and manager of the vacant see, there was a great disagreement and battle between him and Archpriest Ranerio along with his canons, because Ildibrando had the parish clergy celebrate the divine office in the major church against the protests of the canons. With the church restored [to the cathedral canons], a certain priest Ranerio, who was part of the episcopal family and a parish priest, was stricken with grief and set fire to episcopal documents."[30]

Ranerio had very little to say about Ildibrando's successors, Guiscardo and Milo, apart from the length of their tenure as bishops. After Milo's death in 1161, the bishopric was vacant for seven years. Ranerio recalled, "After his [Milo's] death, Rocco, the prior of San Costanzo [the church of the cathedral canons], held the see, which was vacant for seven years and during which time it was invaded. The archdeacon held it with the canons, although at first he had no share in it. Then the possessions of the bishopric endured great ruin at the hands of Rocco, because the ones who were supposed to be custodians of the vacant see and pastors, rather were destroyers and wolves, usurping the family possessions, leaving practically nothing remaining."[31] Thus, after the death of Milo, the canons completed the usurpation of episcopal property that they had begun during the episcopate of Ildibrando.

When Rustico became bishop after the disastrous seven-year vacancy, the bishopric continued to suffer, due in part to the papal schism (1159–1177) and the conflict between Frederick Barbarossa and Pope Alexander III, which plunged central Italy into chaos. "During the time of Bishop Rustico there was a schism between Pope Alexander III and Emperor Frederick. And he [Rustico] was the

Catholic bishop and Pietro, of the family of Homodeo, was the schismatic. This Rustico gave to his supporters many episcopal possessions in Mealla, Bolsena, Sant' Abundo, Val Orvietano, and other places."[32]

The little that Ranerio had to say about Bishops Riccardo, Matteo, and Giovanni was positive. Bishop Capitano, Ranerio's immediate predecessor, did not fare so well. Although Capitano took care of the cathedral by restoring its bells, he neglected other important responsibilities. According to Ranerio, Capitano lost practically all of the episcopal documents in the archive. As a result, the bishopric lost control over important pieces of property.[33] Capitano thus presided over another period of decline for the bishopric.

What accounts for this overwhelmingly negative portrait of the episcopal past? The most immediate answer is the poor condition in which Ranerio found the bishopric in 1228. Ranerio concluded his historical reflections with a rather dismal summation of the bishopric's financial condition.[34] The poverty of the bishopric, however, is not the most important element in this lament, especially when one considers that Ranerio was prone to exaggerate his financial woes. At the beginning of a document of February 1230 in which Ranerio commissioned the collection of tithes throughout the diocese, he complained that episcopal wealth had grown so meager that there were scarcely enough resources to support the bishop and his *familia* for more than three months.[35] There is no doubt that episcopal finances were tight, but the bishopric did not exhaust its wealth in May 1230.

Ranerio's depressing portrait of the episcopal past considers documentation and wealth in equal measure. Immediately preceding his concluding remarks about the bishopric's poverty is his complaint about the loss of documents by Capitano and others. Ranerio's lament concerning the poverty of the bishopric is equally noteworthy. Although the bishopric was poor, it *seemed* wealthy. To whom? To Ranerio's predecessors and other members of the clergy who paid no attention to documents and who therefore could not account for ecclesiastical property and revenues. Herein lies the revolutionary effect of the new memory that Bishop Giovanni gave to the bishopric. Ranerio judged past bishops on their ability to preserve records, because he perceived notarial documents to be the most effective tool for preventing the appropriation of episcopal property for private uses.

The novelty of Ranerio's historical reflections is especially clear in his attitude toward Bishop Capitano. While Ranerio never explicitly says that his predecessor was inept, the image of Capitano that emerges from Ranerio's comments is less than flattering. Capitano paid little attention to episcopal documents, losing practically all of them. By the end of his tenure, the bishopric was desperately poor. It is, however, difficult to believe that Capitano was the inept bishop that Ranerio's comments suggest. He began his episcopate in 1213 as an experienced churchman, having served as a cathedral canon for more than thirty years. He first appears in Orvietan documents in 1182, witnessing the settlement of a dispute.[36] By 1201 he was archdeacon, a position he held until becoming bishop in 1213.[37] In 1205 Pope Innocent III sent him along with Bishop Matteo to root out heresy in Viterbo.[38] Capitano seems to have been an active bishop. He obtained recognition from Orvietan communal officials that the castle of San Vito, one the most important possessions of the bishopric, was exempt from taxation.[39] He defended rights of the bishopric in the church of Santa Maria in Acquapendente and in the baptismal church of Stennano.[40] He appears in approximately ten other entries, obtaining acknowledgment from tenants who held property from the bishopric that they owed an annual rent.[41] Nevertheless, Capitano was a failure from Ranerio's perspective because he did not pay proper attention to documents, which, for Ranerio, was synonymous with a lack of attention to the bishopric. Ranerio's claim that Capitano paid little attention to documents probably is accurate. Capitano does not seem to have shared Giovanni's enthusiasm for enregistering documents. Apart from a few entries, he added little to the register.

Was Capitano a competent bishop? The answer is yes and no. He was a product of the twelfth-century Orvietan church, and compared to his twelfth-century counterparts, he probably would measure favorably. From Ranerio's perspective, however, Capitano left the bishopric with a false sense of well-being. However rich the see may have appeared, much of its wealth was inaccessible and indefensible because it was poorly documented. Bishop Giovanni's administrative innovations created a new standard of vigilance for an Orvietan bishop. While Capitano would have made a good twelfth-century bishop, he had the misfortune of being elected in 1213. By then the rules had changed, and he no longer measured favorably.

What precisely had changed? The legal culture of notaries and judges transformed the self-understanding of the bishopric. In certain respects Ranerio thought about the episcopal past more like a lawyer than a bishop. There is, however, an important religious component to this lawyerly attention to documents. The new style of episcopal administration was part of an attempt to accommodate lay religious interests, especially those of the *popolo*, who objected to the diversion of ecclesiastical resources to noble families that offered their military services to the bishop. The *Passio* attempted to address these problems on the bishop's own terms. Ranerio's margin comments indicate that *popolani* interests ultimately succeeded in dictating the terms of the accommodation.

The Transition to a Civic Historical Consciousness

Ranerio's historical reflections, which in large part represented an exercise in forgetting, mark an important transition in the development of Orvietan historical consciousness. This becomes clear when they are placed in the context of other Orvietan historical texts. The *Passio*, which is the earliest extant Orvietan historical account, falls somewhere between episcopal biographies and the Pisan historical poems within the framework of Italian historical writing I have described. Like the Pisan historical poems, the *Passio* offered an ideal of cooperation between bishopric and commune when this relationship was in crisis. Giovanni's image of Pietro was a peculiar blend of conservatism and innovation, an attempt to drag the new world of the commune back into the twelfth century, when it was under the tutelage of the bishopric. It was a bold attempt to achieve something that was no longer possible. The twelfth-century view of the past, which the *Passio* sought to revive, had to be forgotten. This process of forgetting is clear in Ranerio's historical reflections.

While Ranerio's comments reflect the process of forgetting, the development of a positive vision of the past is found in other Orvietan texts. The earliest evidence of an Orvietan communal narrative comes from historical notes recorded in 1216 on a blank folio of a codex belonging to the cathedral chapter. Ranerio himself may have written these notes when he was a cathedral canon.[42] In addition to an extensive account of Pope Innocent III's visit to Orvieto in

1216 to preach the crusade, there is a short passage that reads like an entry to a chronicle.

> In the year of the Lord, 1216, fourth indiction. During that same time there was a great flood, in the month of May . . . before the feast of Sant'Urbano . . . so that the river Palea flooded . . . And it caused the death of many men, crops, and cattle. Certain ancients recount that in the time of Pope Hadrian . . . the same river flooded. From the coming of Hadrian to the coming of Innocent, according to the accounts of the elders, sixty years had passed.
>
> In that same year, on the feast of the birth of San Giovanni Battista, the army of Orvietans, having gathered at Balneo, [took] Count Ildebrando III into its protection to defend him against his brothers. . . .
>
> The number of those from the city and its district receiving the cross was more than 2,000 men and women.[43]

On the same folio there is a more extensive account of Innocent's preaching and the enthusiastic response he received in Orvieto.

These two texts represent the transition from biography to communal history in Orvieto. They contain some of the memorable collective experiences that constitute the story of a city, such as papal visits, participation in crusades, natural disasters, and important political treaties. Pope Hadrian IV's visit to Orvieto in 1156 and the treaty he concluded with the Orvietans the following year mark the first official recognition of the Orvietan commune. The reference to Count Ildibrando is important as well. During the early decades of the thirteenth century, Orvieto virtually tripled its territory, mostly at the expense of Count Ildibrando's family.[44]

The earliest extant communal chronicle, which is little more than a list of consuls and *podestà* from 1194 to 1224, was written within a decade of these fragments.[45] The addition of a list of communal magistrates to a commonly acknowledged group of important events marks the final step in the transition to a civic historical consciousness. The memory of civic events could now be put into the framework of civic chronology. The fragment in the cathedral chapter's register and the list of magistrates complement each other very nicely. That both churchmen and notaries played such an important role in the development of historical memory demonstrates that the formation of a new historical consciousness did not leave the church behind. Rather, the church was a vital part of the process. During the early decades of the thirteenth century, the bishopric and commune began to share a new type of past because *popolani* interests had infiltrated both in the form of notarial registers.

In August 1228, approximately one month before Ranerio was consecrated as bishop of Orvieto, he went to the castle of Parrano, fearing that some of its residents were attempting to usurp episcopal property there. The document that records his visit begins with a peculiar statement: "Rumors of the past often cause one to fear what is about to happen."[46] Apparently these words resonated in Ranerio's consciousness. Toward the end of one of his margin comments on the condition of the bishopric, he wrote, "rumors of the past ought to make prelates take caution in the future."[47] This is an apt summation of the significance of the legal-notarial class as custodians of civic historical consciousness. By shaping the past, they altered the way Orvietans approached the future.

CHAPTER EIGHT

THE CONVERGENCE
OF ECCLESIASTICAL REFORM
AND COMMUNAL CULTURE

NOTARIES SHAPED THE HISTORICAL CONSCIOUSNESS OF BOTH the Orvietan commune and the bishopric, and paved the way for the latter to adjust to the new political realities of the former. Was the bishopric deflected from the path of reform in the process? From the papacy's perspective, communes were a menace, for they refused to conform to the papal vision of political and religious authority. In a letter dated 1198, addressed to the officials of various central Italian communes, Pope Innocent III described the proper relation between spiritual and secular authority as follows: "Just as God, the creator of the world established two great lights in the sky, a greater light to rule the day and a lesser light to rule the night, thus for the firmament of the universal church, which is called by the name of heaven, he instituted two great offices, namely pontifical authority and kingly power, the greater which rules over souls like the day and the lesser which rules over the body like the night. Moreover, just as the moon draws its light from the sun . . . thus royal authority draws the splendor of its office from papal authority."[1] Much to Innocent's dismay, central Italian communes never internalized this elegant image of papal authority. All too often they defied the papacy and pursued their own political interests. Orvieto itself spent several years of Innocent's pontificate under papal interdict because its political goals clashed with those of the papacy.

Pope Innocent III viewed communes with considerable suspicion, fearing that their political interests were obstacles to ecclesiastical reform. Time would prove that his suspicions were misplaced, at least in the case of Orvieto, where communal development advanced the cause of reform. This convergence of communal development and ecclesiastical reform, which resulted from the renegotiation of Orvietan religious and political interests, reached its culmination with the episcopate of Bishop Ranerio. As notaries constructed a legal and administrative framework to regulate the competition between nobles and *popolani*, Bishop Ranerio used the same notaries and notarial technologies to regulate access to ecclesiastical property. As a result, episcopal and communal development shared a common logic during the early decades of the thirteenth century. There were other forces influencing the bishopric as well. Ranerio was deeply influenced by ecclesiastical reform traditions that culminated in the Fourth Lateran Council. He was a jealous defender of episcopal authority, determined to impose order upon the diocese. When Ranerio died in 1248, the Orvietan church was a better organized and more efficiently administered institution.

The convergence of these two traditions gave birth to a new Orvietan saint—Ambrogio of Massa. Like Ranerio, Ambrogio possessed the unique ability to synthesize potentially incompatible interests. This mendicant priest, who was known for his austerity and humility, addressed lay expectations for purity and engagement far better than either the common life or Pietro Parenzo. He could compete effectively with Cathar perfect for the laity's admiration without disengaging them from the church or the world of matter. In different ways, both he and Ranerio reaffirmed the idea that matter, including ecclesiastical property, could have spiritual value if directed toward spiritual uses.

THE ORVIETAN CHURCH AND ECCLESIASTICAL
REFORM TRADITIONS

The Fourth Lateran Council

On April 10, 1213, Innocent issued the bull *Vineam Domini Sabaoth*, calling for an ecumenical reform council.

> Many beasts are trying to destroy the vineyard of the Lord of Hosts. Their assault against it has grown so strong that thorns have largely overtaken the vines. And now, bemoaning, we report that the vines themselves are spoiled and corrupt, bearing wild fruit instead of grapes. . . . After mature and frequent deliberation with our brothers and with other prudent persons, as is appropriate for such a matter, on their council we have decided the following. Because it is a matter of the common condition of all believers, following the custom of the Holy Fathers, in view of the well-being of souls, we will convoke a General Council at an opportune time to root out vices and implant virtues, correct abuses and reform morals, suppress heresy and fortify the faith, to calm discords and affirm peace, to subdue oppression and encourage liberty.[2]

On November 11, 1215, more than four hundred bishops, along with many abbots, canons, and representatives of secular rulers, gathered in the Lateran basilica. Twenty days later the council produced a blueprint for ecclesiastical reform consisting of seventy-one canons.[3] This blueprint was the culmination of a reform tradition extending back to the second half of the eleventh century.[4] The council was principally concerned with institutional and moral reforms that would make the church an effective framework for the care of souls. Such reforms would allow the church to integrate the laity into a lifelong regimen of pastoral care and sacramental grace. This ambitious reform program included an aggressive campaign against heresy that threatened to separate the laity from the church.

Ecclesiastical Reform and the Orvietan Church on the Eve of Ranerio's Episcopate

In 1228, when Bishop Ranerio first entered the episcopal palace, he noted that there was a copy of the *concilium Innocentii* (presumably the Fourth Lateran Council) in the bishop's chamber.[5] This copy of the decrees of the Fourth Lateran Council in the episcopal palace is a token of the profound influence of ecclesiastical reform traditions on episcopal consciousness. During the late twelfth and early thirteenth centuries, effects of this reform tradition became increasingly evident in the Orvietan church. Prosecution of Orvietan heretics, as described in the *Passio*, conformed to the canon law on heresy. In particular, the confiscation of heretics' property recalls the bull of Pope Lucius III, *Ad abolendam*, and canon 27 of the Third Lateran Council.[6] Maestro Giovanni's argument for Pietro's sanctity was based in part on canon 27, which promised that those who died in combat against heretics would receive remission of all their sins.[7] After Pietro's death, punishment of heretics according to *lese magistatis crimine*, or treason, recalls Innocent's bull *Vergentis in senium*.[8]

The canon law of marriage was another important aspect of the church's attempt to integrate all aspects of lay activity into the framework of pastoral care. Bishop Giovanni adjudicated a number of marriage disputes. In most cases, extant documents merely record decisions without describing arguments of the parties involved. There is, however, one dispute described in detail, in which Riciadonna, an Orvietan noblewoman, sought release from a marriage to Oderisio, claiming that she had never agreed to marry. Giovanni decided the dispute based on the canon law of marriage. In particular, the central question of the dispute was whether Riciadonna had given present consent when Oderisio asked for her hand in marriage. Giovanni decided that she had not consented and released her.[9]

The bishop's court was a clear and direct link between writings of canonists and everyday lives of Orvietans. In another case brought before Bishop Giovanni, a priest Ildibrando claimed that a certain Pietro stole his cloak and several other possessions. Because Ildibrando did not want to plead his case before a secular judge, he had his brother Brunaccio plead the case for him. The secular judge ordered the dispute to be resolved through judicial combat. When Bishop Giovanni learned of the matter, he nullified the decision on grounds that judicial combat tempted the Lord and that it was not a true judgment.[10] Giovanni's decision reflected growing disenchantment among twelfth- and early-thirteenth-century canonists concerning trial by combat. It was three years after Giovanni's decision that canon eighteen of the Fourth Lateran Council prohibited the clergy from participating in judicial ordeals.[11]

The aspects of pastoral care that most intrigue historians are the very ones that are most hidden from view. How well did clergy instruct the laity concerning faith and sacraments? How often did laypersons hear sermons, and from whom? How often did they attend mass and go to confession? Did bishops visit churches in the diocese regularly? What type of training did clergy receive?[12] There are only hints in the Orvietan documents. Ranerio held a synod in the first year of his episcopate. Whether his predecessors convened annual synods as prescribed in canon six of the Fourth Lateran Council is impossible to tell.[13] How closely did Orvietan bishops monitor the clergy's moral life? In 1234 Ranerio disciplined two priests of Santa Maria in Allerona for living with concubines.[14] The Orvieto-Sovana dispute offers plenty of evidence that Orvietan bishops disciplined clergy concerning issues of property, tithes, and jurisdiction, but provides little evidence of moral discipline. Witnesses in the same dispute recalled bishops from both dioceses traveling through the region, confirming children, consecrating churches, and collecting tithes. When Bishop Capitano exchanged the tithes and burial offerings of San Donato for those of Santa Maria in Stiolo, he demanded that his right of hospitality be respected in both churches when he went to confirm children.[15] This would suggest that he traveled around the diocese performing pastoral duties. Unfortunately, it is impossible to tell how frequently Orvietan bishops made these visits. The earliest record of an episcopal visitation describes that of Bishop Costantino (1250–1256) to the church of San Gregorio of Soalto in 1256. Upon arriving, Costantino preached a sermon and then reprimanded the priests, *conversi*, and oblates for not recognizing episcopal jurisdiction.[16] There probably was little that was new in Costantino's visit, apart from its being recorded in the episcopal register.

There are, however, many examples in which the Orvietan church fell short of the ideal. Bishop Ranerio's punishment of the two priests living with their concubines is a good example of the diligence a bishop was supposed to exercise over the moral life of the clergy, but the two priests themselves were hardly representative of reform ideals. Bishop Capitano granted tithes of a church in Stiolo to a layman.[17] Bishop Giovanni did not succeed in eliminating the judicial ordeal in Orvieto. In 1226 a judge, advised by the communal council, commanded that a case of theft be decided by a duel.[18] In that same year, Pope Honorius reformed the monastery of Santi Severo and Martiro, one of the wealthiest and most powerful monasteries in Orvieto, replacing the black monks, or Benedictines, with Praemonstratensians. Bishop Ranerio commented that reform was necessary because Capitano had failed to correct the monks, who abused the rule and held their abbot in slight esteem.[19]

The Lament of Honorius: The Disappointing Progress of Reform (Part I)

Examples in which the Orvietan church, or any other local church for that matter, fell short of the ideals and canons of the ecumenical reform councils are too numerous to count. Five years after the Fourth Lateran Council, Pope Honorius III measured the church's condition against the canons of the Fourth Lateran Council and was appalled. On November 22, 1219, Pope Honorius sent a letter to bishops and abbots in the Tuscan patrimony, lamenting their lack of attention to the canons of the Fourth Lateran Council and the deplorable condition of the church. The letter, which is filled with images of excrement, disease, and infection, demonstrates the enduring appeal of those currents of reform that tended to value purity above all else. It was this same fear of pollution that fueled the reform of the common life in the eleventh century. It must have struck a chord in Ranerio, for he had it copied into the episcopal register.[20]

Honorius began the letter with a passionate declaration of his frustration with the progress of ecclesiastical reform. If God could cause Aaron's staff to bud, then the Lord's own vineyard would be flourishing had its keepers obeyed the admonitions and statutes of the General Council. The bridegroom desired grapes from the vineyard, but grapes were withering on the vine because the vineyard's keeper had neglected to gather them.

First among the culprits were bishops, who neglected to use the spiritual sword to correct and punish those who endangered souls of the faithful. "Indeed, certain ministers of the altar, like beasts of burden, not only decay in manure, but like the people of Sodom, preach their own sin and do not conceal it, causing people to rush headlong into snares. Certain prelates of churches, who received the double-edged swords in their hands for executing punishment, do not correct the accusers wandering among the people, do not cut off the rotten members, and do not exclude the diseased and infectious sheep from the fold. They do not bind or cure the bruised and swelling wound or protect it with oil or plaster."[21] Instead of caring for their flocks, many prelates used ecclesiastical property at their disposal to enrich their own families: "And like the hands of pitiful women that cook their little children, these [bishops] dissipate and consume the property committed to them. They disperse the stones of the sanctuary at the head of all the plazas. They promote unworthy people and they give ecclesiastical stipends to the pernicious, gathering in their churches an assembly of blood relations."[22]

Monks were equally culpable. Canon twelve of the Fourth Lateran Council prescribed triennial provincial chapters or councils of monks and regular canons to regulate those living the cloistered life.[23] Much to the disappointment of Honorius, monks failed to use these tools to maintain monastic discipline. "There are many monks who flee the yoke. They break the bonds and like the dung of the earth are made contemptible. They do not correct and punish their subjects; they [their subjects] do not celebrate the chapters according to the statute of the General Council, with the result that deeds performed in the shadows are not made known in the light. For this reason, in fact, heresies grow stronger."[24]

In light of this neglect, Honorius called bishops and abbots to renew their commitment to the canons of the Fourth Lateran Council and to exercise greater vigilance against heretics. "We command and sternly admonish that . . . [your] minds be returned with new earnestness, through doubled anxiety, that from now on you especially observe the statutes of the aforementioned council that regard the health of souls and that you cause them to be inviolably observed by your subjects. . . . Moreover, watch out most readily for the depraved heretic, taking care if perhaps he enters into [your] boundaries, to thoroughly uproot that which is like a cancer. It multiplies like a serpent and as the dragon draws down the stars from the sky, he plots against the woman, desiring to devour the son that she conceived."[25]

While protecting the church from pollution, prelates were to ensure that clergy and ecclesiastical property under their watch remained devoted to the care of souls. "And let him not forbear a close brother or friend who, holding the statutes of the council in slight esteem, rejects honesty of habits or life, or does not observe clerical modesty in tonsure, vestments, and other things, guarding anxiously lest you confer benefices on the unworthy. And do not permit anyone, after the General Council, to have a baptismal church or parish held in benefice to which care of souls is attached unless perhaps he has a special indulgence from the apostolic see concerning this."[26] For the monks, the call to renewed vigilance meant fulfillment of their obligation to convene the prescribed provincial chapters. "Let not the abbots of the black order fail to celebrate provincial councils this year, just as it was established in the Council. And we want and command to be informed concerning these [provincial councils] so that we can commend careful attention to good things and punish the negligence of the perverse."[27] According to Honorius, the key to reforming the church was effective oversight by using tools such as provincial councils. The one thing lacking was the will of prelates to use them.

Honorius concluded his lamentation with an indictment of priests who irreverently handled the Eucharist and exposed it to the danger of pollution. "Certainly seeing that the manna in the silver-covered arc of the covenant, prefiguring the silver vessel containing the full deity of the body of Christ, was placed in the Holy of Holies so that it would be neatly conserved, we are much grieved and saddened that in most provinces priests, holding in contempt the canonical sanctions, rather divine judgment, preserve the holy Eucharist incautiously and uncleanly, and handle it without reverence, as if they did not fear the Creator . . . or dread the Judge of all. And yet the apostle fearfully threatens the one who tramples under foot the Son of God or who brings the blood of the testament into pollution, that he will deserve a worse punishment than the transgressors of the Mosaic Law who were struck with the sentence of death."[28] Finally, he commanded priests to store the Eucharist reverently and in a clean and safe place and described the proper comportment for priests celebrating mass or carrying the host to the sick.

The Lament of Ranerio:
The Disappointing Progress of Reform (Part II)

Ranerio shared Honorius's frustration with the progress of reform. After reflecting on the past of the Orvietan church, he somberly meditated on its present and future in the longest of his margin comments. Honorius's letter and Ranerio's meditation form an interesting polyphonous lament. While both lines in the polyphony evoke a sense of frustration, Ranerio's lament is more personal and parochial. It anchors the moral and theological tone of Honorius's lament to the earth, or more specifically, the commune. Completely absent are concerns about purity and pollution. This is not because Ranerio ignored them. Rather, he transformed them into sentiments more congruent with the expectations of those under his care. Instead of fearing contact with the world, Ranerio affirmed a fundamentally spiritual quality in the mundane.

Ranerio began by recalling the first days of his episcopate.[29] "In 1228 A.D., first indiction, on February 24, on the feast of Santa Romana, the Orvietan bishop Capitano died. He was elected in the year of the Lord 1213, in the month of January, succeeding Maestro Giovanni, who had been bishop for a year and three months. After the death of Domino Capitano, in the same year, on April 8, Ranerio was elected as bishop, and on April 15 [the election] was confirmed by Pope Gregory IX, during the second year of his pontificate. In that same year, on September 24, [Ranerio] was marked with the gift of consecration by the same pope in the city of Perugia." The precise chronology, including a reference to indiction and papal year, lends a notarial flavor to the passage, as does Ranerio's reference to himself in the third person.

Continuing the chronology from his election and confirmation, Ranerio remembered the first time he celebrated solemn mass in the cathedral. His thoughts then turned to the first time he entered the episcopal palace and the things that he found there.

Celebrating the first solemn mass in the cathedral church on the feast of San Severo, he entered the episcopal palace on April 20. And diligently inquiring into the movable property, these are the principal things that he found. In the chapel: old vestments of the bishop, certain vestments of the archdeacon, two book cases

and other chests, a book of gospels and a book of epistles, both
beautifully decorated with silver, a missal, a book of ordinations,
and other similar books, a book of antiphons for night and day,
broccarda [a book of legal maxims], a book of various explana-
tions, three *raseria* of wheat, one and a half *raseria* of spelt, one
lame mule, nine wine casks, seven empty and two full of wine.
Concerning other furniture and equipment, the bishopric had
been miserably despoiled, the very bishopric for which God,
with the help of the blessed virgin and all the saints, had thought
worthy to provide.[30]

When Honorius thought about the church, his mind roamed across a
landscape of Old Testament images. Ranerio's mind fixed upon the
things in front of him. Within the cathedral complex, spirit and matter were tightly compressed. The distance between celebrating mass
and counting possessions was not great. The same God who provided
the bread and wine for the Eucharist gave the bishopric vestments,
books, wheat, furniture, and even a lame mule.[31] The tone of
Ranerio's concerns was more immediate and practical. He was more
concerned about what was missing than what might be polluted.

From the list of movable property and the disturbing realization
that certain things were missing, his thoughts turned to the *quaterni*
in front of him. "No instrument was found in these *quaterni* or elsewhere, recording contracts executed in the time of Bishop Capitano.
And the inventory made by Domino Maestro Giovanni was forgotten for the most part, and the possessions and revenues were diminished, as well as the prescribed rights of the bishopric in the
churches. The archdeacon usurped many things from the bishopric
contrary to old customs." Ranerio grasped the significance of
Giovanni's *quaterni*. He thought of the world in terms of a legal
grammar. Documents, like nouns, made it possible to keep track of
things. Bishop Capitano did not understand this. His casual disregard
of documents left episcopal rights and possessions without an
anchor, ready to drift into oblivion.

From disappearing documents and things, Ranerio's thoughts
took a sudden leap. "The laudable order of Praemonstratensians was
placed in the church of Saints Severo and Martiro by Pope Honorius
in March 1226, as it pleased the Lord, while Domino Lombardo was
prior [of the cathedral chapter] and Maestro Mariano was archdea-

con. The black monks [Benedictines] had been expelled because they had not been corrected by the bishop. With the abbot held in slight esteem, the monks abused the rule." Here the concerns of Honorius and Ranerio converged. Monastic discipline was fundamental to diocesan order. As will become apparent, Ranerio exerted considerable effort throughout his episcopate to establish his authority over several important monasteries in the region. His vigilance over churches and monasteries under his authority was an extension of his diligence in counting objects in the episcopal palace.

The memory of Honorius led Ranerio's thoughts back to books, for one especially valuable book disappeared during Honorius's visit to Orvieto in 1220. Ranerio's thoughts then returned to the episcopal palace and his predecessors who were responsible for these physical tokens of the bishopric.

> Beyond the books mentioned above, the bishopric had a very good book of the *Moralia*, which was lost when Pope Honorius III entered our city in 1220 and stayed for three months. Bishop Riccardo, who was from Gaeta and was bishop for twenty-four years, had the aforementioned books of gospels and epistles copied, and renovated the episcopal palace. Bishop Matteo, from Orvieto, succeeded him, and dedicated a very beautiful chapel [in the episcopal palace] to the honor of San Silvestro, while renovating the stairs of the palace. And after nine and a half years as bishop, he yielded his soul to the Creator. Maestro Giovanni, a man of letters, succeeded him, renewing the contract with Parrano and regathering property in Mealla, while making the present inventory. And after one year and three months in the bishopric, he went to be with the Lord. Domino Capitano, who renewed the bells with the cathedral canons, was bishop for almost sixteen years when he passed from this earthly prison to the celestial homeland.

Unfortunately, there came a time when a bishop's soul abandoned his body and returned to the Lord, leaving such things as books, chapels, property, and bells as physical tokens of his activity.

Capitano's soul, like so many other things, reminded Ranerio of documents, for when the soul of a bishop departed, there remained no anchor for episcopal possessions apart from legal instruments.

"All the instruments recording contracts made during the time of the aforementioned Bishop Capitano were lost. Whence the bishopric from old times suffered terrible loss from certain priests of the episcopal *familia* and servants, who burned many old and useful instruments." Documents compensated for the transient souls of bishops. Bishop Capitano, however, did not appreciate this. Apparently he saw no need to carefully preserve his documents. As a result, when Ranerio became bishop, there was no easily accessible record of his predecessor's activity.

As Ranerio surveyed the task before him, therefore, he sounded more like a notary than a bishop. "Lest the charters made during the time of the aforementioned bishop be lost, I, Ranerio [bishop] elect, will devote myself, with the help of divine grace and the blessed eternal virgin Mary, to recovering the lost instruments from notaries and to diligently guard them in the episcopal archive, as rumors of the past ought to make prelates take caution in the future, and what is possessed in common is easily neglected, and this is almost a natural vice, just as the legitimate sanction proclaims." Not only would Ranerio be a diligent custodian of documents, he would admonish his clergy to do the same: "Moreover, certain possessions bound in pledge in the past and the present were held by creditors almost as if they possessed them, because none of the instruments documenting the pledges were available. Concerning these matters, let the clergy act with caution. If they commissioned documents for pledging property, let them also guard them with a sense of shrewdness and care, lest opportunity for corruption of property be afforded to creditors, so that neither by pretext nor good faith can they allege anything against the church." These admonitions for clergy to act more cautiously in the future arose from the sad condition of the bishopric in the present. "The Orvietan bishopric, however, is bound in many types of servitude both to clergy and laity. It is stripped of almost all its possessions except Vinea and Caio. Seemingly wealthy and located in the city, in fact it is pressed on all sides with the contemptible burden of poverty." It was not that the bishopric had no claim to wealth. Rather, this wealth was too entangled in a morass of ill-documented counterclaims. As a result, the bishopric had lost control over its economic resources.

The reflections of Ranerio and Honorius share a common sense of frustration. For both, the deplorable condition of the church reflected a lack of diligence on the part of bishops and abbots to use institutional and administrative mechanisms that were available to them. It is, however, the difference between the two lamentations that makes the polyphony so interesting. Honorius reflected on the church from above and appears to have been unaware of political and social realities at the local level. He knew only one obstacle: the lack of will to follow the instructions of the Fourth Lateran Council and to use the institutional mechanisms it prescribed, such as episcopal synods and triennial monastic councils. Ranerio's reflections were anchored in local realities. He was therefore more aware of local resources that could be applied to the reform effort. For example, while Honorius was disappointed at the failure of bishops and abbots to use synods and provincial councils, Ranerio was appalled at the failure of bishops to carefully document ecclesiastical possessions. He appreciated the potential for extra-ecclesiastical resources, like the class of legal professionals, to advance the cause of reform. He was also more in tune with lay spiritual aspirations to which the local church had to respond. In Ranerio's comments, a fear of disorder—of the diversion of things from their intended use—replaced Honorius's fear of pollution. These two fears were not necessarily incompatible, but Ranerio's concern to rightly direct the use of ecclesiastical resources was more amenable to local concerns. To begin with, it was the mirror image of one of the principal political goals of the *popolo*, that is, to prevent noble families from misappropriating communal property. Equally important, Honorius's fear of pollution, which tended to convey an image of a cloistered church in a defensive posture, seemed out of step with lay aspirations for more active engagement in the local parish. Ranerio seemed more at home in the world. His comments reveal an ability to see spiritual potential in the mundane. After all, the lame mule was among the things that God left to the bishopric, and he called on the Virgin's help to recover lost documents.

THE COMMUNE AND REFORM

These differences are significant. Whether consciously or subconsciously, Ranerio was open to the potential for communal development to advance the process of ecclesiastical reform in ways that

Popes Innocent III and Honorius III were not. The unwillingness of communes like Orvieto to march in step with papal politics cloaked the positive effect that communal development could have on ecclesiastical reform. The commune's emergence as a political and economic center of gravity and the corresponding readjustment of its relation with the bishopric bolstered episcopal authority in two ways. The general gravitation of people and resources toward the city facilitated efforts to strengthen episcopal authority over rural churches and monasteries. Moreover, legal professionals provided bishops with more effective tools for administering the people and property under their care.

The Bishopric, the Commune, and the Countryside

The emergence of the commune exerted an unsettling effect on the rural population by drawing people and resources into the city. In some respects, urbanization and the reconfiguration of rural settlements hurt the bishopric economically. More often, it facilitated the expansion of episcopal authority by drawing rural monasteries and churches toward the bishopric. In 1230 Ranerio commissioned the investigation and collection of episcopal revenues throughout the diocese. After listing various regions in which he wanted to document and collect revenues, he concluded with a rather pessimistic assessment of what he expected to collect. "Although the produce, revenues, and tithes are expected to decrease rather than increase, because little by little these places are deserted by [their] inhabitants, nonetheless, we command that the produce, revenues, and tithes of the aforementioned *mensa* be recorded and counted."[32] As populations moved, the layout of the ecclesiastical landscape and the configuration of episcopal revenues changed. For example, Ranerio commented in the margin of Bishop Giovanni's inventory that the church of San Pietro in Vetere had once been a baptismal church (and therefore the center of an ecclesiastical district). It apparently lost this status by 1226, when Bishop Capitano gave it to the Franciscans and relinquished episcopal claims to certain of its revenues.[33]

Part of the decline in population about which Ranerio complained resulted from migration to newer and more dynamic settlements in the countryside. Much of it was due to urbanization. The first half of the thirteenth century was a period of tremendous population growth in the city.[34] This explains Ranerio's persistent complaints about the cathedral canons' urban property. Once they had established their control over the bulk of urban revenues, an influx of people from the countryside would mean a transfer of wealth from bishop to chapter.

Urbanization had a positive effect on the bishopric as well, creating an unmistakable momentum in the diocese toward the episcopal center. The reconfiguration of the countryside created a difficult environment for many rural churches and monasteries, many of which looked to the bishop for support amidst their troubles. This centripetal force is especially evident in Ranerio's relations with several monasteries in the region.

In Orvieto, as elsewhere, relations between bishops and monks were fraught with ambiguity.[35] During the late eleventh century, monasteries began to possess an increasing number of private churches, a fact that often resulted in conflicts between bishops and monks concerning their respective rights and jurisdictions. During the twelfth century, Italian bishops sought to recover their losses. This potential for conflict was fully realized in Ranerio's relation with the monastery of San Sepolcro near Acquapendente. When Ranerio became bishop in 1228, the dispute between Orvietan bishops and San Sepolcro was almost a century old. San Sepolcro was one of the sources of conflict between the bishops of Orvieto and Sovana, even though the monastery claimed to be immediately subject to the papacy and therefore beyond the jurisdiction of either bishop.

Ranerio refused to allow San Sepolcro to escape episcopal jurisdiction. In his diocesan synod of November 1228, he threatened to excommunicate anyone offering assistance to the monks.[36] The principal source of contention was episcopal jurisdiction over seven churches in the western portion of the Orvietan diocese belonging to the monastery.[37] Ranerio submitted the dispute to the papacy in 1231.[38] There is no record of the outcome in the episcopal register.

Other monasteries were less reluctant to accept episcopal authority. In 1245 the monks of San Nicolo of Monte Orvetano donated their monastery to the bishopric.[39] The donation followed a series of conflicts between Ranerio and the monks concerning mismanagement of their property.[40] This same gravitation toward the bishopric is evident in Santa Maria of Mazapalo, a hermitage near Acquapendente. In 1237 the economic and spiritual condition of the hermitage was decaying. Its prior therefore donated the hermitage to the bishopric. The donation included seven churches and one hermitage subject to Santa Maria.[41] Apparently the hermitage's fortunes continued to decline, for in 1239, Pope Gregory IX appointed the monks of San Guilielmo to reform Santa Maria.[42] The circumstances surrounding these events are unclear. The documents of 1237 and 1239 may belong to a struggle between San Guilielmo and Santa Maria, whose prior donated the hermitage to the bishopric, to escape subjection to San Guilielmo. In any case, it is clear that the hermits considered Bishop Ranerio the safest refuge from their troubles.

The case of another monastery, Santa Maria in Silva, offers an interesting explanation for this gravitation toward the bishopric. In 1230 Abbot Graziano relinquished his rights in the church of Santa Croce in Rasa to the bishopric, "because the same church is located in the Orvietan diocese and is oppressed by tyranny of laymen, with its possessions and other things having been seized, and because the Orvietan bishop has episcopal jurisdiction [over it] and is obligated by the law of the commune to defend it."[43] The convergence of three forces compelled Abbot Graziano to surrender Santa Croce of Rasa to Bishop Ranerio: the tyranny of laymen, episcopal jurisdiction, and communal statutes.

Typically it was one or more of these three forces that caused rural monasteries to gravitate toward the bishopric. Eleven years after the submission of Santa Maria in Silva, a similar convergence of forces occurred in the same region of Rasa. Fordivoglia, the count of Rotacastello, along with several family members, attacked the monastery and castle of San Vito, set fire to portions of it, and took several monks hostage and beat them. San Vito belonged to the bishopric; therefore Ranerio vigorously defended it. He called upon the commune for help, and in January 1241 the Orvietan bailiff outlawed the counts of Rotacastello.[44] Later that month Bishop Ranerio excommunicated them.[45] The "tyranny of laymen" forced the monastery to look to the combined protection of bishopric and commune.

The canonry of Sant' Hyppolyto offers yet another example of the bishop's protecting rural churches and monasteries from the "tyranny" of rural aristocrats. Ranerio expended considerable resources and efforts during the early years of his episcopate to defend Sant' Hyppolyto against Filippo di Manfreduccio, a rural noble. In 1229 Ranerio compiled a list of over fifty separate expenses, mostly related to legal proceedings, that the bishopric incurred in defense of the canonry.

Communal development was an important factor in each of these cases, either directly or indirectly. The migration of people and wealth from the countryside to the city would explain the economic decay of monasteries such as San Nicolo of Monte Orvetano and Santa Maria in Mazapalo, as well as the tyranny of laymen such as the counts of Rotacastello and Filippo di Manfreduccio, who found that they were competing for diminishing economic resources in the countryside.[46] This is not to say that the entire countryside was in crisis. Rather, it is likely that these monasteries and powerful families were located in regions that were left behind in the economic and demographic transformations that accompanied rapid urbanization.

Communal development offered a cure for instability as well. The city's growing economic and political power compelled people to look to it for solutions. For rural churches and monasteries, this meant looking to the bishop. As Abbot Graziano recognized, the bishop operated within the framework of the commune's increasingly sophisticated legal apparatus. If communal statutes obligated the bishop to defend the churches under his jurisdiction, it also bound the commune to support the bishop in this task. Indeed, when communal officials took the oath of office, they swore to protect the local church.[47] The commune's actions against Fordivoglia and the counts of Rotacastello demonstrate that they took this oath seriously. Such cooperation between commune and bishop was not uncommon, as examples from Lucca and Florence suggest.[48]

Bishops, Notaries, and the Countryside

While communal development created a gravitational force drawing the diocese inward toward episcopal jurisdiction, there were equally strong forces drawing episcopal property away from the bishop. For example, in 1215 Bishop Capitano borrowed forty-two lire from Martino di Giovanni and several others to redeem property and tithes held in pledge by Ranerio di Stefano in San Gervasio. Capitano pledged the same property and tithes to his new creditors.[49] Thirty years later Bishop Ranerio redeemed this property from Aldovino Coglapecora, who held it in pledge against a loan he had made to Martino di Giovanni. Apparently Aldovino held the document that recorded the earlier transaction between Capitano and Martino di Giovanni, for he returned this document to Bishop Ranerio along with the property in 1246.[50] Memory of this transaction thus fled the episcopal archive and followed the property and tithes in San Gervasio through a series of exchanges. Ranerio was determined to eliminate the drift of ecclesiastical property away from the church. In a diocesan synod of 1228, he threatened to excommunicate anyone who alienated ecclesiastical property without consent of the bishop.[51] He regularly exacted oaths from rectors, priors, and abbots to obey this injunction.[52] When they disobeyed, he carried out his threat and excommunicated them.[53]

On the whole, Ranerio effectively managed these centrifugal forces. When he first entered the episcopal palace in 1228, he began counting and making lists of everything that he saw. When he finished counting things inside, he turned his attention outside and spent most of his twenty-year episcopate enumerating episcopal possessions and the many pieces of the diocese. More than one hundred churches, monasteries, and hospitals appear in the *quaterni* compiled by Bishops Giovanni and Ranerio. Approximately sixty appear in Ranerio's documents alone. Thus, during the first half of the thirteenth century, the Orvietan church emerges from the shadows for the first time.[54]

The document in which he commissioned an investigation of episcopal revenues is one of the most interesting examples of this emergence. In addition to listing the most important possessions of the bishopric (the castle communities of San Vito and Parrano and various communities in the Val di Lago), the document lists eleven of the seventeen baptismal churches and ecclesiastical districts that appear in episcopal registers.[55] It thus provides a broad summary, albeit incomplete, of the episcopal *mensa* and the diocese. Beyond this broad overview of episcopal revenues, there are several detailed surveys of ecclesiastical property. Bishop Giovanni compiled an inventory of episcopal property and commissioned inventories of the monastery/castle community of San Vito, the fraternity of Santi Apostoli, and the baptismal churches of Stennano and Ficulle.[56] Ranerio supplemented Giovanni's inventory with another extensive survey of episcopal property.[57] He had an inventory of San Nicolo in Pizallo copied into the register[58] and probably commissioned other inventories that were not copied. For example, he commanded the abbot of San Nicolo of Monte Orvetano to compile an account of the monastery's revenues and expenses, although the result of this effort is not recorded.[59]

The commune thus exerted a centralizing force on the countryside that greatly facilitated Ranerio's efforts to bring the diocese more firmly under episcopal jurisdiction. At the same time, the commune's legal-notarial culture provided a more powerful technology for administering ecclesiastical property. It is here that communal development converged with the ecclesiastical reform traditions that formed the basis of Honorius's lamentation.

Legal-Notarial Culture and the Common Life

The influence of notarial technologies on the bishopric went beyond mundane matters of administration. In a few cases, communal legal culture contributed to important changes in the trajectory of ecclesiastical reform itself. Disenchantment with the common life and the underlying assumptions about purity provide one of the most interesting examples. At the end of Ranerio's comment concerning his determination to gather lost documents is the following curious passage: "Rumors of the past ought to make prelates take caution in the future, and what is possessed in common is easily neglected, and this is almost a natural vice, just as the legitimate sanction proclaims."[60] The connection between rumors of the past and property held in common is not immediately apparent. As is often the case with Ranerio, a trail of documents leads from one to the other. The phrase concerning property held in common echoes a maxim found at the beginning of five separate inventories of property compiled by the cathedral chapter in 1218. "How easily are the things held in common consigned to oblivion. Because it is a natural fault that what is held in common is neglected, and with the memory of men enveloped in shadows of forgetfulness, and because it is not possible to effectually preserve the past, it is proper and in harmony with reason that ecclesiastical possessions, which are easily neglected, be redacted in public documents for the perpetual memory of those in the future."[61] Ranerio certainly knew of these inventories, as he was a cathedral canon in 1218 when they were compiled.

The formula concerning property held in common echoes a comment of Azo, a late-twelfth- and early-thirteenth-century glossator on

Roman law: "Note that it is a natural defect for what is possessed in common to be neglected."[62] Azo's words reflected a growing prejudice among medieval jurists against property held in common. According to Azo and other jurists, both secular and ecclesiastical, co-ownership often prohibited the effective supervision of property, because a co-owner could not act contrary to the wishes of his or her partner. In the words of Azo, "One is thought to have nothing, who does not have all."[63]

Whether Ranerio and the Orvietan canons were familiar with Azo's work is impossible to demonstrate. They were, however, familiar with the tradition of legal studies to which Azo belonged. Among the items that Ranerio listed in his inventory of the episcopal palace was a book of *broccarda*, or legal maxims derived from Roman law that generally circulated in lesser centers of legal study outside of Bologna. Apparently this book did not simply gather dust in the episcopal archive. The quotation regarding common property suggests that the bishop and cathedral canons were familiar with its contents and even used it as a guide for ecclesiastical reform.

The aversion to common property just mentioned is a curious sentiment for the Orvietan cathedral canons, for they themselves still lived according to the common life. As noted earlier, eleventh-century reformers believed that the common life was necessary to separate the clerical lifestyle more clearly from that of the laity, thus freeing clergy from pollution that came from worldly entanglements. Despite these good intentions, this ideal of separation seemed increasingly out of step with lay aspirations by the mid-twelfth century. During the first half of the thirteenth century, the common life gradually fell into disuse among the cathedral canons. A document of 1221 speaks of a compromise between the head of the cathedral chapter and certain canons to correct abuses of the chapter's common property.[64] Apparently the compromise had little effect in the long run, for in 1246 the canons divided their common property into prebends.[65] Ranerio clearly had no love for the common life. As he reflected on the history of the twelfth-century bishopric, he claimed that cathedral canons used the common life as a pretense for usurping episcopal property.[66] According to Ranerio, it fostered an intolerable lack of definition that provided an opportunity for usurpation.

By the thirteenth century, the danger of losing touch with the laity was felt more urgently than the danger of being polluted by contact with the world in which they lived. As laypersons became more actively engaged in the life of the church, they were sometimes dismayed to find that resources that should have been available to foster the church's spiritual life had been misappropriated. Ranerio's concern to use documents to anchor ecclesiastical possessions and his appropriation of legal-notarial culture were more responsive to lay spiritual aspirations than was the common life.

Ecclesiastical Reform and the Transformation of Communal Culture

By the 1240s the bishopric had largely adjusted to the world of the communes and had gone a long way toward adapting the church's evangelical traditions to the political and social ideals of urban society. This is not to say that tensions plaguing the bishopric at the beginning of the thirteenth century had disappeared. Cathars maintained a strong presence in Orvieto. Nevertheless, the convergence of ecclesiastical and communal culture placed the bishopric in a better position to meet these challenges.

This transformation is evident in two very different saints who emerged in the midst of two similar periods of political and religious turmoil. In 1200 the Orvietan bishopric looked to Pietro Parenzo to rescue Orvieto from its political and religious crisis. Giovanni cast Pietro Parenzo as the model Christian knight, wielding the secular sword on behalf of the church. In short, he was a sanctification of the very mixture of politics and religion that heretics, radical reformers, and at least some Orvietans found so objectionable. Orvietans looked to an entirely different type of saint in 1240—the Franciscan Ambrogio of Massa.

During the middle decades of the thirteenth century, Orvietans confronted a political and religious crisis similar to that at the turn of the century.[67] Relations between Orvieto and the papacy were generally positive between 1216 and 1230. The Tuscan patrimony was not the center of Pope Honorius III's attention. As pressure of papal state building eased, relations between Orvieto and the papacy were amicable. Members of the de Iudice, a Roman family loyal to the papacy, served as *podestà* of Orvieto from 1216 to 1218, and again in 1226 and 1230. Tensions resumed when Pope Gregory IX began to tighten the reigns of papal government.[68] In November 1230, Gregory wrote to the council and people of Orvieto complaining that they had violated the papacy's rights in the Val di Lago and Acquapendente, the same region over which Pope Innocent III and the Orvietans had clashed thirty years earlier. "We do not deny but that we grieve greatly because of the land of the Roman church that you hold for so long by forceful occupation . . . but we are burdened with much greater grief when we consider the danger of souls, which we do not doubt will result from the detention of the aforementioned land . . . because, in fact, you are bound out of a debt of fidelity, by a sworn oath, to be helpers in conserving and protecting the patrimony of St. Peter. It is evident that you dangerously provoke the Lord against you, having become invaders, violators of trust, rebels against us, and oppressors of our *fideles*."[69] In 1232 Orvieto was at odds with the papacy once again. This time, Gregory excommunicated the Orvietans and Florentines for refusing papal arbitration in their war against Siena.[70] In 1234 he sent another letter to the Orvietans demanding that they respect papal claims in the Val di Lago.[71] As in 1198, Orvietans were recalcitrant. An Orvietan chronicler writing in the second half of the thirteenth century recalled, "1236. Rogello Salvi of Florence [was *podestà*]. During this time Tebaldo of Rieti, a papal chaplain, came to Bolsena. The tails of his horses were cut in derision and he was expelled, because he wanted to invade the Val di Lago for the Roman church."[72]

Just as territorial disputes with the papacy fostered heresy around 1200, these disputes coincided with a bout of heresy that took place during the 1230s. An overly aggressive campaign against heretics by papal inquisitors during the late 1230s only heightened tensions. Orvietans called on a Roman aristocrat and staunch opponent of Gregory IX, Gregorio Pagure, to be their *podestà* in 1238. The pope had excommunicated him several years before for supporting Frederick II.[73] The following year, several Orvietans broke into the Dominican convent and beat Fra Ruggiero, who was the head of the inquisition in Orvieto.[74]

To further complicate matters, tensions between Pope Gregory IX and Emperor Frederick II were mounting. In 1239 Gregory excommunicated the emperor. One year later, Frederick descended upon central Italy, intent on subduing it.[75] Orvieto apparently survived this conflict without committing firmly to either side.[76] Nevertheless, as in the papal-imperial conflicts of the late twelfth century, the dispute between Frederick II and Gregory fueled fires of factional violence in Orvieto. An Orvietan chronicler recalled that in 1241, "there was a great battle among all the Orvietans."[77]

Faced with internal political tensions, heresy, and the tricky business of steering between papal and imperial politics, Orvietans again needed a saint. In 1240 the *podestà*, council, and *popolo* wrote to Pope Gregory to tell him of miracles performed by Ambrogio of Massa, a local Franciscan who died that same year. Pope Gregory commissioned Bishop Ranerio and Bishop Gualcherino of Sovana to investigate these miracles.[78]

Despite similarities between the crises of the late twelfth and mid-thirteenth centuries, the saints who emerged to address these crises could not have been more different. Fra Pandolfo, himself a former bishop of Sessa and longtime companion of Ambrogio, testified to the following signs of Ambrogio's sanctity: "His flesh never saw corruption neither through his own [actions] or through others, after he acquired the religious habit. He was obedient to his superior in all things, merciful with regard to penitents. . . . he was anxious in collecting alms for the needs of the friars . . . and he willingly sang mass and delighted in the divine office."[79] Fra Bartolomeo testified that he knew Ambrogio "to be obedient without murmuring and patient in tribulation, acting compassionately toward the poor and sick . . . and [that] during his entire life as a friar, he persevered in the purity and chastity of his body until he died."[80] Other friars recalled that he was diligent in fasting and devoted to the Virgin Mary. If a cause for dispute arose, he humbly submitted. The laity testified only to his miracles. Nevertheless, it is clear that his manner of life left an impression on them as well, for as he lay dying, Orvietans began to gather around his bed hoping for miraculous cures.

Ambrogio's story is an eloquent testimony to the convergence of the commune's political culture with ecclesiastical reform traditions. The initiative for his canonization came from the commune, not the bishop or cathedral chapter. The *podestà*, communal council, and *popolo* had no need for a saint to instruct them how and when to use the sword. They chose someone whose devotion to God exemplified compassion, humility, self-discipline, and obedience. As a preacher and confessor, he actively engaged the laity. He ministered to the physical and spiritual needs of people within the body politic, leaving political matters to communal officials. There is not the slightest hint of political ambition in his actions.

While compatible with the political ideals of the commune, his spirituality complemented developments in the bishopric quite well. His austerity matched that of Cathar perfect, but he did not denigrate the mundane. His engagement with the world complemented Ranerio's sentiments that the physical world possessed a spiritual quality, if rightly used. He engaged the laity as a preacher and as a confessor. He dealt compassionately with the poor and sick. All the while, he affirmed the ecclesiastical hierarchy. He expressed obedience to superiors, offering a counterexample to the wandering and undisciplined monks mentioned by Honorius and Bishop Ranerio.

Why was Ambrogio, who was the child of ecclesiastical reform, such an appealing figure to Orvietan political officials? An Orvietan *podestà* of 1232 offers the most insightful response. In 1232 Pope Gregory IX was about to excommunicate Orvieto and Florence for not accepting papal arbitration in their war against Siena. In the midst of negotiations, the *podestà* consulted with the communal council, then responded to the papacy, "It was acknowledged to be true that the Roman Church was their [the Orvietans'] queen and mother, both in spiritualities and temporalities, and that in no way had they proposed to withdraw from the mandates of the Church, as from their lord, if it were not that they swore with the Florentines for the preservation of their rights, fearing the power of the Sienese, who were wanting to take away [their] land."[81] No doubt there is an element of flattery in these words. The Orvietan *podestà* wanted to appease Pope Gregory without capitulating. There is still much truth in the response of the *podestà*. The Roman Church indeed was the commune's mother and queen. In 1157 the Orvietan commune was born when it swore fidelity to the papacy and received official recognition as a political body. At the risk of belaboring the analogy, if the church was the commune's mother, the bishopric was the womb in which it developed. By 1240, when communal officials wrote to Pope Gregory concerning Ambrogio, they had long since outgrown their dependence on the bishopric. Nevertheless, ecclesiastical reform traditions were buried deep within the memory of the Orvietan community because the commune developed from within the bishopric.

This same convergence of communal and ecclesiastical cultures is evident in Ranerio's successor, Bishop Costantino, who was a very different person from Ranerio. Costantino was a Dominican friar with scholastic training.[82] Before he became bishop, he wrote a commentary on the gospel of Luke. This commentary is interesting because in various comments he expressed his commitment to the ideal of spiritual poverty that Orvietans found so attractive in Ambrogio. "The religious life, this is what one ought to buy, with all having been left behind, denouncing the world with a strong hand, that one might build an altar there to the Lord."[83] Throughout his commentary he criticized the worldliness of the clergy. "Prelates and preachers ought to be prepared whenever and wherever they are asked concerning the faith . . . but oh! today many prelates know better how to respond concerning hunting and games of chess, and priests know more about where to buy good wine than about the articles of the faith."[84] The tone of many of Costantino's criticisms recalls that of Pope Honorius's letter, which Bishop Ranerio found so compelling.

Bishop Costantino's mendicant spirituality fit equally well within the administrative framework and centralizing momentum that Ranerio established. Costantino completed the sixteenth *quaternus*, which Ranerio had left unfinished, and compiled two more of his own.[85] Like Ranerio, he was a jealous defender of episcopal authority. In 1252 he complained before the General Council of the commune about attacks against the monastery and castle community of San Vito.[86] In 1256 he visited the church of San Gregorio of Soalto, demanding that they respect episcopal authority.[87] This is the first record of an episcopal visitation in the episcopal registers and represents an interesting application of notarial administrative techniques to the care of souls. Finally, it is worth noting that the first appearance of episcopal vicars in Orvieto is recorded in Costantino's documents.[88] This use of officially appointed episcopal representatives marks the early stages in the development of the professional diocesan bureaucracy that would become so common throughout the Italian church.[89]

Intuitively bureaucratization and mendicant spirituality belong to opposite ends of the spectrum, and yet they converged in Bishop Costantino.[90] Like Ranerio, he demonstrates the convergence of two worlds that seem to have little to do with each other. What do a *quaternus* recording episcopal revenues, a proto-communal chronicle, the lamentation of a pope about ecclesiastical reform, and the story of a sick person weeping and praying for deliverance at the tomb of a saint have in common? The most immediate answer is Bishop Ranerio, for all four of them appear in records he compiled. More fundamentally, they all belong to a common process of political and ecclesiastical development set in motion when the nascent commune first began to expand its power through the bishopric. Even as the bishopric and commune became increasingly distinct institutions, their common origin left an enduring mark on both institutions; hence the convergence of ecclesiastical reform and communal development.

CONCLUSION

TWO SAINTS, PIETRO PARENZO AND AMBROGIO OF MASSA, trace the developments in the bishopric described in this study. Among Fra Pandolfo's memories of Ambrogio were the saint's feet, which were worn and had large cracks because he wore no shoes, regardless of the season or the weather. At night he poured candle wax into the cracks of his feet, presumably to close the wounds.[1] For Fra Pandolfo and his fellow friars, Ambrogio's feet were tokens of perfect obedience to the rule of St. Francis.[2] For us, they mark a transformation in the way Orvietans addressed political and religious tensions at the core of their society. Pietro Parenzo rode into Orvieto in 1200 on a horse, a symbol of military might. He came bearing the sword and he died by the sword. Ambrogio arrived in Orvieto with bare feet. Instead of using the sword to force laypersons into their officially designated place, he engaged them with his humility, compassion, and discipline. He marks a resolution to the Orvietans' struggle to define the relation between their political and religious interests in the context of communal formation.

The process that culminated in the convergence of the bishopric and commune began long before the crisis in their relationship around 1200. It began as the bishopric emerged as one of the most important substitutes for public authority following the collapse of the Carolingian state. As a substitute for local public authority, the bishopric became a field for a tug-of-war between a variety of political and religious interests.

What did this tug-of-war look like in motion? During the twelfth century, the role of noble families in this coalition of interests was especially important. As landowners themselves, they had a vested interest in a stable political order. At the same time, they were the warrior class whose military skills were essential for pacifying the *contado*. As they fought on behalf of the bishopric, commune, and papacy, they received payment for their services from the revenues of each of these institutions. In periods of intense conflict, such as the Alexandrian schism during the 1160s and 1170s, payments to noble families for their military services could create a considerable drain on ecclesiastical revenues. Moreover, these families often were reluctant to relinquish their claim to property they held in pledge, for access to ecclesiastical wealth was an important component of their own power.

This almost inevitable diversion of episcopal resources away from spiritual uses created tremendous conflict between the bishopric's political and religious interests. In this respect, the Orvietan bishopric was typical of ecclesiastical institutions throughout Europe. The three Lateran Councils of the twelfth century consistently affirmed the ideal that the laity should not exercise control over ecclesiastical property.[3] Nevertheless, bishoprics, monasteries, and local churches could not protect their property without the military services of the nobility, and these services were expensive.

Several religious responses emerged from this tension. Despite the prominent strain of pacifism in earlier Christian traditions, there emerged an image of the Christian knight, sanctifying violent activity in defense of the church. According to this ideal, the military activity of the nobility, if rightly directed, could be a spiritual exercise that offered eternal reward.[4] Knightly spirituality became part of the ideology of Italian communes as members of the warrior class settled in cities during the tenth and eleventh centuries. In Orvieto, as in other communes, many of these nobles were episcopal clients and members of the early consular aristocracy. This was the ideal of Pietro Parenzo, although by the time he arrived on the stage, this ideology was becoming outdated.

The accommodation between the bishopric and the ruling elite modified both parties. On the one hand, the image of the Christian knight constrained the egoistic tendencies of the church's protectors that were most threatening to the church (admittedly with only limited success). On the other hand, this accommodation modified the church's understanding of violence and war through the conscious adoption of a militaristic ethos into the body of medieval Christian traditions. It was in part this "militarization" of the bishopric (both in its use of human resources and in the adaptation of its traditions) that made it such an effective tool for drawing the countryside into the orbit of the city.

This accommodation between the bishopric and aristocratic families provoked a response from other elements in Orvietan society that resulted in further constraints on noble violence and brought further modifications to the religious traditions of the church. Certain reformers criticized the accommodation between the church and the knightly class as a distortion of the apostolic life. Not only were ecclesiastical resources diverted from spiritual uses, the relationship between the bishop and knightly aristocracy entangled the bishop in politics. Some of the disaffected laity found an alternative spirituality in Catharism. Others appealed to the voluntary poverty and renunciation of political power by Jesus, the apostles, and a long list of Christian ascetic heroes as the purest tradition of medieval Christianity. Both alternatives struck a chord, especially among the *popolo*, who were disconcerted by the movement of ecclesiastical wealth away from spiritual uses and into the coffers of noble families. Political motives complemented religious ones, for the spiritual ideology of the knight leveraged the political power of the nobility against the *popolo*. The result was a massive disaffection with episcopal authority among the *popolo* and a pressure for reform to which the bishop had to respond.

Thus, during the early decades of the thirteenth century, we begin to see what we might call a "popolization" of the bishopric. The growing influence of the *popolo* can be attributed to several factors. First, by 1200 the commune had expanded and matured sufficiently to become its own field of power. While nobles and *popolani* could still leverage their political power through the bishopric, the commune became the principal field where political actors pursued their political interests. As a result, the force of religious interests tugging at the bishopric increased relative to that of political interests. The bishop now had no choice but to respond to *popolani* religious disaffection. Second, the ability of the *popolo* to appeal to evangelical traditions allowed them to exert more pressure on the bishopric than would otherwise have been possible. The result was a tremendous change in episcopal administration that reflected the religious interests of the *popolo*. Legal professionals helped bishops to establish a more efficient legal and administrative framework to protect episcopal property from being exploited for private use. As a result, there was a noticeable increase in the efficiency of episcopal administration during the opening decades of the thirteenth century. By diminishing the flow of ecclesiastical resources to the nobility, they leveraged their own political power as well. Ambrogio of Massa, the Franciscan saint who embraced apostolic poverty and the ideal of active engagement with the laity, was the saint who leveraged the *popolo*'s ability to assert influence on the bishopric. He represented an alternative to Pietro Parenzo, who embodied the accommodation between the bishopric and the knightly aristocracy.

The prominent role of notaries and ecclesiastical officials in shaping the city's spiritual and secular ideals raises important questions for historians of medieval Italian cities. The standard model for communal development posits a fundamental opposition between nobles and the *popolo* and between the commune and the bishop. By the fourteenth century, *popolo* and bishops were the clear losers. There is a great deal of truth to this model, but it often overlooks the community of interests that emerged from the competition and the extent to which *popolo* and bishopric defined this new community of interests. Protecting communal and ecclesiastical property and restraining violence were among the common interests that maintained a sense of community even in the midst of fierce competition. There was no debate about whether these were worthy goals. The competition arose over defining the terms and establishing the mechanisms for achieving the goals. Nowhere in Italy did the *popolo* succeed in establishing an enduring regime, but in their competition with the nobility, they influenced the way nobles thought about and exercised power in relation to both the commune and the bishopric.[5] The central role of Orvietan bishops as a conduit for the notarialization of the city's historical memory suggests that they too were important participants in negotiating the community of interests that held the commune together.

In sum, the bishopric shaped the political and religious cultures of the commune, and it affected their convergence because it was a field where these interests cooperated and competed to establish order. By "convergence of cultures," I certainly do not intend to evoke images of the peaceable kingdom. This culture was not a carefully crafted script deposited in the collective memory of the community. Rather, it operated as a tension or tug of conscience triggered by an individual or group's pursuit of political and religious interests. Canons of ecumenical councils and laypersons listening to Cathar preachers reminded the bishopric and papacy of the dangers inherent in ecclesiastical wealth and its political entanglements. The ideal of the Christian knight reminded aristocrats that their military skill required a larger justification than their own private interests. The economic benefits of a stable countryside to Orvietans, noble and non-noble alike, reminded those laypersons attracted to Catharism that they could not afford to be as pessimistic as the itinerant preachers about the material world and its political realities. The convergence of ecclesiastical and political cultures did not remove the tensions. It did, however, create norms that constrained Orvietans as they pursued their political and religious interests. These norms, which emerged from an awareness of those pulling from the opposite direction, made Orvieto a community, or a civil society, as opposed to a mere geographical space where groups with irreconcilable interests engaged in interminable conflict.

In the introduction, I suggested that a careful study of a local Italian bishopric had much to tell us about fundamental developments in high medieval society. I would also suggest that what we have witnessed in this study of the Orvietan bishopric is a model of the twofold process of European state building in its early stages—the processes of establishing territorial domination and constructing norms that transform the people inhabiting a territory into a community. Orvietan bishops and urban elites began establishing the city's domination over the countryside through a patchwork of agreements with rural lords and communities. The papacy built upon this achievement by drawing Orvieto and its recently won territory into its own patchwork of territorial authority. Bureaucratization was the process of converting this patchwork of agreements into a more uniform system of authority; this was the work of centuries. Individuals and groups, both conquerors and conquered, who found themselves in the same patchwork had to create institutional mechanisms for regulating the inevitable competition of interests. Once created, these mechanisms needed constant adjustment. As the example of Orvieto demonstrates, this process was fraught with difficulty and contingency—in the High Middle Ages, there were more failures than successes. Civil society was not the peaceable kingdom. It was a community that succeeded in creating, maintaining, and adjusting bureaucratic mechanisms that both regulated the inevitable competition of interests and established norms that bound competitors into community.

APPENDIX

The Authorship of the Passio

FROM THE TEXT OF THE *PASSIO* ITSELF, IT IS CLEAR THAT A Maestro Giovanni wrote the legend and that he was a cathedral canon. With the exception of a short addendum written in 1216, the *Passio* was probably written within a year of Pietro's death (i.e., 1199/1200).[1] The Maestro Giovanni who wrote the *Passio* almost certainly is the same Maestro Giovanni who became bishop of Orvieto in 1211.

Natalini raised two objections to the identification of Bishop Giovanni as the author of the *Passio*. First, the person who in 1216 added the list of miracles to the original legend identified the original author as *magistro Ioanne, fonte scientie litterarum* without commenting that the author of the *Passio* later became bishop. According to Natalini, it is hard to imagine that the author of the addendum would have failed to mention this if indeed Maestro Giovanni was the same person as Bishop Giovanni. More important, Natalini argued that the Maestro Giovanni who wrote the *Passio* was a cathedral canon and the son of Giovanni Fortis. Bishop Giovanni, on the other hand, was from the Bolognese family of Castelli. This argument assumes that Bishop Giovanni was never an Orvietan cathedral canon, for if Maestro Giovanni di Castelli (assuming there was such a person) and Maestro Giovanni di Giovanni Fortis were both canons, then Maestro Giovanni of the *Passio* could have been either.

Natalini is correct in identifying Maestro Giovanni, the cathedral canon, as the son of Giovanni Fortis.[2] That Bishop Giovanni was from the Bolognese family of Castelli is doubtful. The source of this information is apparently the list of Orvietan bishops found in Ughelli's *Italia Sacra*.[3] Where Ughelli obtained the information is unclear. He only writes, "Joannes Castellius Bononiensis, *ut quidam scribunt.*" Because Ughelli's list of Orvietan bishops contains many inaccuracies, it is reasonable to suspect that his undocumented identification of Bishop Giovanni's family is also inaccurate. It must also be noted that an earlier list of bishops compiled by Marabottini considered Bishop Giovanni as a native Orvietan.[4]

The fatal weakness in Natalini's argument is that he assumes Bishop Giovanni was not a cathedral canon before becoming bishop. It is, however, clear that Bishop Giovanni was a canon. A list of bishops compiled by Seraphyno, the notary who executed many of Bishop Giovanni's documents, reads, "Eodem die illo [Bishop Matteo, Bishop Giovanni's predecessor] sepulto, electus est Magister Johannes canonicus et intravit palatium in die Sancti Luce."[5]

Bishop Ranerio referred to Bishop Giovanni as a *vir litteratus*,[6] echoing the reference to Giovanni, the author of the *Passio* (*magistro Ioanne, fonte scientie litterarum*), found in the addendum to the *Passio*. In light of these arguments, there is no good reason to doubt that the Maestro Giovanni who wrote the *Passio* is the same Maestro Giovanni who became bishop of Orvieto in 1211.

ABBREVIATIONS

ACO	Archivio Capitolare di Orvieto
ASO	Archivio de Stato di Orvieto
AVO	Archivio Vescovile di Orvieto
COD / Lat I, II, III	*Conciliorum Oecumenicorum decreta / Concilium Laternaense I, II, III.* Ed. Giuseppe Alberigo.
MGH LL	*Leges Langobardorum, Monumenta Germaniae Historica.*
MGH SS	*Monumenta Germaniae Historica. Scriptores.*
PL	*Patrologia cursus completus, Series Latina.* Ed. Jacques-Paul Migne.

INTRODUCTION

1. Edwin Muir, "The Sources of Civil Society in Italy," *Journal of Interdisciplinary History* 29:3 (Winter 1999): 381. This article is, in part, a commentary on Robert D. Putnam's book *Making Democracy Work: Civic Traditions in Modern Italy* (Princeton, 1993), which traces the success of modern regional governments in Italy to the development of civic traditions during the Middle Ages.

2. Robert Brentano, *A New World in a Small Place: Church and Religion in the Diocese of Rieti, 1188–1378* (Berkeley, 1994), p. 4.

3. Ibid., p. 17.

4. Muir, "The Sources of Civil Society in Italy," pp. 383–84.

5. Representative of these studies is Carlo Guido Mor and Heinrich Schmidinger, eds., *I poteri temporali dei vescovi in Italia e in Germania*

(Bologna, 1979). Especially important is the article by Giovanni Tabacco, "Vescovi e comuni in Italia," ibid., pp. 253–81. See also Eugenio Dupré Theseider, "Vescovi e città nell'Italia precomunale," in *Vescovi e diocesi in Italia nel Medioevo (sec IX–XIII)*, Atti del II convegno di storia della chiesa in Italia (Rome, 1964), pp. 55–110; Pierre Racine, "Evêque et cité dans la royaume d'Italie: Aux origines des communes italiennes," *Cahiers de Civilisation Médiévale* 27:1–2 (1984): 129–39.

6. Representative of these studies are Pierre Racine, "Città e contado in Emilia e Lombardia nel secolo XI," in *L'evoluzione delle città italiane nell'XI secolo*, ed. Renato Bordone and Jörg Jarnut, Atti della settimana di studio 8–12 settembre 1986 (Bologna, 1988), pp. 99–136; George Dameron, *Episcopal Power and Florentine Society, 1000–1320* (Cambridge, Mass., 1991); Duane Osheim, *An Italian Lordship: The Bishopric of Lucca in the Late Middle Ages* (Berkeley, 1977).

7. Hagen Keller, *Signori e vassali nell'Italia delle città (secoli IX–XII)*, trans. Andrea Piazza (Turin, 1995), p. xv; Jean-Claude Maire Vigueur, *Comuni e Signorie in Umbria, Marche e Lazio* (Turin, 1987), p. 64.

8. John M. Najemy, "The Dialogue of Power in Florentine Politics," in *City States in Classical Antiquity and Medieval Italy*, ed. Anthony Molho, Kurt Raaflaub, and Julia Emlen (Ann Arbor, 1991), pp. 269–87. See also Philip Jones, *The Italian City-State: From Commune to Signoria* (Oxford, 1977), pp. 583–630.

9. Bernard of Clairvaux, "De Consideratione," IV.3.6, *PL*, 182: 776.

10. While I find Weber's model of prophetic religions useful for describing the broad framework of this study, I have no intention of attempting a Weberian analysis.

11. Max Weber, *Economy and Society*, ed. and trans. Guenther Roth and Claus Wittich (Berkeley, 1978), 1:439–67.

12. Chris Wickham, "Debate: The Feudal Revolution," *Past and Present* 155 (1997): 196–208. For other participants in the debate, see Thomas Bisson, "The Feudal Revolution," *Past and Present* 142 (1994): 6–42; and the responses by Dominique Barthélemy, Stephen White, and Timothy Reuter, "Debate: The Feudal Revolution," *Past and Present* 152 (1996): 196–223; 155 (1997): 179–208. Other important contributions to discussions concerning the feudal revolution include J. P. Poly and E. Bournazel, *The Feudal Transformation, 900–1200*, trans. Caroline Higgit (London, 1991); Susan Reynolds, *Fiefs and Vassals: The Medieval Evidence Reinterpreted* (Oxford, 1994).

13. For an introduction to the writings of Pierre Bourdieu, see Pierre Bourdieu and Loïc J. D. Wacquat, *An Invitation to Reflexive Sociology* (Chicago, 1992). For a discussion of the concept of *habitus*, see Pierre

Bourdieu, *Outline of a Theory of Practice*, trans. Richard Nice (Cambridge, 1977), pp. 72–95.

14. Three works particularly important for this study are Carol Lansing, *Power and Purity: Cathar Heresy in Medieval Italy* (Oxford, 1997); Daniel Waley, *Mediaeval Orvieto: The Political History of an Italian City-State, 1157–1334* (Cambridge, 1957); Elisabeth Carpentier, *Orvieto à la fin du XIIIe siècle: Ville et campagne dans le cadastre de 1292* (Paris, 1986). Lansing's book is a social history of the Cathar communities in Orvieto and provides valuable information on the religious and political climate of the city during the twelfth and thirteenth centuries. Waley's study is a political history. Because of the paucity of sources for the twelfth and early thirteenth centuries, it is heavily weighted toward the late thirteenth and early fourteenth centuries. Carpentier's book is a social history focusing on the relation between the city and the surrounding countryside. Based on an analysis of the 1292 *catasto*, a survey of rural property owners, it is principally concerned with the late thirteenth century. Although both books focus on a later period, they offer useful information for the early development of the commune. Carpentier also wrote a social and political history of Orvieto for the two decades leading up to the Black Death. See Carpentier, *Une ville devant la peste: Orvieto et la peste noire de 1348* (Paris, 1962). Other important studies include Lucio Riccetti, *La città costruita: Lavori pubblici e immagine in Orvieto medievale* (Florence, 1992); and Marilena Rossi Caponeri and Lucio Riccetti, *Chiese e conventi degli ordini mendicanti in Umbria nei secoli XIII–XIV: Inventario delle fonti archivistiche e catologo delle informazioni documentarie* (Perugia, 1987). This last study offers a helpful introduction to the archival collections in Orvieto. Many useful articles concerning medieval Orvieto can be found in the *Bollettino dell'Istituto Storico Artistico Orvietano*. Finally, Fumi's *Codice Diplomatico*, which contains over eight hundred pages of edited documents dating between the eleventh and fifteenth centuries, is fundamental to the study of medieval Orvieto.

15. Carpentier, *Orvieto*, p. 237.

16. Osheim, *An Italian Lordship*, pp. 2, 71.

17. Luigi Fumi, ed., *Codice Diplomatico della città d'Orvieto: Documenti e regesti dal secolo XI al XV e la carta del popolo*, Documenti di Storia Italiana, 8 (Florence, 1884).

18. Marlene Polock, "Der Prozess von 1194 zwischen Orvieto und Sovana um das Val di Lago," *Quellen und Forschungen aus Italienischen Archiven und Bibliotheken* 70 (1990): 46–150.

19. Pericle Perali, ed., *La cronaca del vescovado Orvietano (1029–1239) scritta dal vescovo Ranerio (cronachette, notizie, e inventari)* (Orvieto, 1907).

· 20. M. T. Clanchy, *From Memory to Written Record: England 1066–1307*, 2d ed. (Oxford, 1993), p. 67.

21. John W. Baldwin, *The Government of Philip Augustus: Foundations of French Royal Power in the Middle Ages* (Berkeley, 1986), pp. 412–18.

22. C. Stephen Jaeger, *The Envy of Angels: Cathedral Schools and Social Ideals in Medieval Europe, 950–1200* (Philadelphia, 1994), pp. 5, 7.

23. Ibid., p. 323.

CHAPTER 1. CAROLINGIAN BEGINNINGS

1. Jones, *The Italian City-State*, pp. 69–70.

2. Chris Wickham, "The Other Transition: From the Ancient World to Feudalism," *Past and Present* 103 (1984): 3–36; Chris Wickham, *Early Medieval Italy: Central Power and Local Society, 400–1000* (Ann Arbor, 1989), pp. 40, 74–77; Giovanni Tabacco, *The Struggle for Power in Medieval Italy: Structures of Political Rule*, trans. Rosalind Brown Jensen (Cambridge, 1989), pp. 77–78.

3. Wickham, *Early Medieval Italy*, pp. 38, 42.

4. Ibid., p. 136.

5. Ibid., p. 36.

6. Ennio Cortese, *Il diritto nella storia medievale* (Rome, 1995), 1:166–70. Wickam, *Early Medieval Italy*, pp. 38, 39, 43; Pierre Riché, *Education and Culture in the Barbarian West from the Sixth through the Eighth Century*, trans. John J. Contreni (Columbia, S.C., 1976), pp. 409–11.

7. Ottorino Bertolini, "I vescovi del 'regnum Langobardorum' al tempo dei Carolingi," in *Vescovi e diocesi in Italia nel medioevo (sec. IX–XIII)*, Atti del II Convegno di storia della Chiesa in Italia (Padua, 1964), pp. 1–26.

8. Tabacco, *The Struggle for Power in Medieval Italy*, p. 115.

9. Wickham, *Early Medieval Italy*, pp. 47–50; Rosamond McKitterick, *The Frankish Kingdoms under the Carolingians, 751–987* (New York, 1983), pp. 135, 170–71.

10. François Bougard, *La justice dans le royaume d'Italie de la fin du VIIIe siècle au début du XIe siècle* (Rome, 1995), pp. 49–50; McKitterick, *The Frankish Kingdoms under the Carolingians*, p. 69; Wickham, *Early Medieval Italy*, p. 53.

11. Tabacco, *The Struggle for Power in Medieval Italy*, pp. 82–84; Wickham, *Early Medieval Italy*, pp. 77–78; Thomas F. X. Noble, *The Republic of St. Peter: The Birth of the Papal State, 680–825* (Philadelphia, 1984), pp. 6–12, 244–45.

12. Tabacco, *The Struggle for Power in Medieval Italy*, pp. 91–92, 95, 100.

13. Osheim, *An Italian Lordship*, p. 2.

14. Giovanni Tabacco, "L'ambiguità delle istituzioni nell'Europa costruita dai Franchi," *Rivista storica italiana* (1975): 401–38; Tabacco, *The Struggle for Power in Medieval Italy*, p. 125; Giuseppe Sergi, "Vescovi, monastery, aristocrazia militare," *La Chiesa e il potere politico dal medioevo all'età contemporanea*, in *Storia d'Italia, annali 9*, ed. Giorgio Chittolini and Giovanni Miccoli (Turin, 1986), pp. 73–98.

15. Wickham, *Early Medieval Italy*, p. 56; Tabacco, *The Struggle for Power in Medieval Italy*, p. 126.

16. Charlemagne, Louis the Pious, Lothar, and Louis II issued immunities to the monasteries of Farfa, San Salvatore in Brescia, San Vincenzo al Volturno, Montecassino, Bobbio, Sesto, Santa Maria Theodota in Pavia, San Michele in Orte, San Ambrogio in Milan, San Zeno in Verona, San Salvatore in Monte Amiata, and Nonantola; and to the bishoprics of Reggio, Modena, Benevento, Aquileia, Grado, Cremona, Novara, Padua, Fiesole, and Bergamo. Engelbert Mühlbacher, ed., *Die Urkunden Pippins, Karlmanns und Karls des Grossen*, nos. 99, 133, 135, 147, 156, 158, 175, 200, 234, 255, *MGH, Diplomata Karolinorum*, vol. 1 (1906; reprint, Munich, 1991); Konrad Wanner, ed., *Die Urkunden Ludwigs II*, nos. 1, 9, 13, 14, 31, 44, 53, 60, 72, 103, 119, 129, *MGH, Diplomata Karolinorum*, vol. 4 (Munich, 1994).

17. Tabacco, *The Struggle for Power in Medieval Italy*, p. 127.

18. McKitterick, *The Frankish Kingdoms under the Carolingians*, pp. 91–92.

19. Bougard, *La justice dans le royaume d'Italie*, pp. 140–52. For example, in Rothar's edict, the *sculdahis* or the *gastald* was responsible for exacting monetary fines for the king's court from those who violated a grave. In the laws of Liutprand, legal cases begin with a complaint made to the *sculdahis*. Within the context of the tribunal, the *sculdahis* participate in the decision, but are subordinate to a presiding judge (*iudex*), who renders the judgment. Friedrich Bluhme, ed., *Leges Langobardorum*, Rot. 15, Liut. 26, *MGH, Leges*, vol. 4 (1868; reprint, Stuttfart, 1984); Katherine Fischer Drew, trans., *The Lombard Laws* (Philadelphia, 1973), pp. 55, 156.

20. Bougard, *La justice dans le royaume d'Italie*, p. 160.

21. Alfred Boretius, *Capitularia Regum Francorum*, no. 20, c. 5; no. 89, c. 6, 10, *MGH, Legum Sectio II*, vol. 1 (1888; reprint, Hannover, 1984); Bougard, *La justice dans le royaume d'Italie*, pp. 236–38.

22. Boretius, *Capitularia Regum Francorum*, no. 89, c. 8, 10; no. 163, c. 1; no. 178, c. 6.

23. Ibid., no. 96, c. 1; no. 91, c. 8.

24. Ibid., no. 77, c. 1; Boretius, *Capitularia Regum Francorum*, vol. 2, no. 203, c. 5.

25. The principal edition of Italian *placita* is Cesare Manaresi's *I placiti del 'regnum Italiae,'* vols. 92, 96, 97, *Fonti per la storia d'Italia* (Rome, 1955–1960). For discussions of the *placita*, see Hagen Keller, "I placiti nella storiografia degli ultimi cento anni," *Fonti medioevale e problematica storiografia*, Atti del congresso internazionale tenuto in occasione del 90 anniversario della fondazione dell' istituto storico italiano (Rome, 1976), 1:41–68; Keller, "Der Gerichtsort in oberitalienischen und toskanischen Städten. Untersuchungen zur Stellung der Stadt im Herrschaftssystem des Regnum Italicum vom 9. bis 11. Jahrhundert," *Quellen und Forschungen aus italienischen Archiven und Bibliotheken* 49 (1969): 1–72; Chris Wickham, "Land disputes and Their Social Framework in Lombard-Carolingian Italy, 700–900," in *The Settlement of Disputes in Early Medieval Europe*, ed. Wendy Davies and Paul Fouracre (New York, 1986), pp. 105–24. Also helpful are discussions in Charles Radding, *The Origins of Medieval Jurisprudence: Pavia and Bologna, 850–1150* (New Haven, 1988).

26. Keller, "Der Gerichtsort in oberitalienischen und toskanischen Städten," pp. 2–11.

27. Maureen Miller, *The Bishop's Palace: Architecture and Authority in Medieval Italy* (Ithaca, 2000), pp. 13–14, 55.

28. Keller, "Der Gerichtsort in oberitalienischen und toskanischen Städten," pp. 12–19.

29. Ibid., p. 19.

30. Ibid., pp. 18–19.

31. Harry Bresslau, *Manuale di diplomatica per la Germania e l'Italia*, trans. Anna Maria Voci-Roth (Rome, 1998), pp. 534–40; Mario Amelotti and Giorgio Costamagna, *Alle origini del notariato italiano*, Studi storici sul notariato italiano (Roma, 1975), pp. 23–29, 159–71; Armando Petrucci, "Il notariato italiano dalle origini al secolo XIV," in *Notarii. Documenti per la storia del notariato italiano* (Milan, 1958), pp. 3–11.

32. For example, Liutprand demanded that charters conform to either Lombard or Roman law. Ratchis demanded that documents of sale designate whether the purchase price had been paid, in order to prevent the seller from regaining title to the property based on a claim of nonpayment. Bluhme, ed., *Leges Langobardorum*, Liut. 91, Rat. 8.

33. Ratchis refers to the writer in the above-mentioned law as a *scriba publica*. Ibid., Rat. 8.

34. Boretius, *Capitularia Regum Francorum*, vol. 2, no. 202, c. 5.

35. Boretius, *Capitularia Regum Francorum*, vol. 1, no. 40, c. 3; Bresslau, *Manuale di diplomatica per la Germania e l'Italia*, pp. 541–42.

36. Janet Nelson, "Literacy in Carolingian Government," in *The Uses of Literacy in Early Medieval Europe*, ed. Rosamond McKitterick (Cambridge, 1990), p. 286.

37. Boretius, *Capitularia Regum Francorum*, vol. 2, no. 201, c.13; vol. 1, no. 158, c. 13, 15; Bresslau, *Manuale di diplomatica per la Germania e l'Italia*, pp. 565–66.

38. For Lothar's capitulary, see Boretius, *Capitularia Regum Francorum*, vol. 1, no. 163, c. 6; Radding, *The Origins of Medieval Jurisprudence*, p. 41; Riché, *Education and Culture in the Barbarian West*, pp. 404–11.

39. Paul Kehr, ed., *Karoli III. Diplomata*, no. 50, *MGH, Diplomata Regum Germaniae Ex Stirpe Karolinorum*, vol. 2 (Berlin, 1937), pp. 83–85; Jean Pierre Delumeau, *Arezzo: Espace et sociétés, 715–1230. Recherches sur Arezzo et son contado du VIIIe au début du XIIIe siècle* (Rome, 1996), 1:162, 230.

40. Wickham, *Early Medieval Italy*, pp. 60–63.

41. Ibid., pp. 168–71, 177–81. For a discussion of the importance of Italian politics to the German kings, see Timothy Reuter, *Germany in the Early Middle Ages, 800–1056* (New York, 1991), pp. 122–23, 168–74. For Berengar II, see Pierre Riché, *The Carolingians: A Family Who Forged Europe*, trans. Michael Idomir Allen (Philadelphia, 1993), pp. 241–42, 269–71.

42. Tabacco, *The Struggle for Power in Medieval Italy*, pp. 152–58. Wickham, *Early Medieval Italy*, p. 172.

43. Luigi Schiaparelli, ed., *I Diplomi di Berengario I, Fonti per la storia d'Italia*, vol. 35 (Rome, 1903). Berengar granted rights to build castles to the *vicedominus* and other citizens of Novara (no. 76, 102), the bishop of Padua (no. 82), the abbess of Santa Teodota of Pavia (no. 84), a royal *fidelis* in Reggio-Emilia (no. 94), and the abbess of Santa Giulia in Brescia (no. 110).

44. Schiaparelli, no. 112. While this grant to Cremona is the most extensive, Berengar granted immunities, the right to build castles, and fiscal property and rights to numerous bishops in northern Italy: Mantua (no. 12), Modena (no. 24), Luni (no. 31), Monza (no. 47), Asti (no. 51), Treviso (no. 52), Como (no. 77), Padua (no. 82, 101, 103), and Novara (no. 123).

45. Wickham, *Early Medieval Italy*, pp. 174–76.

46. Bougard, *La justice dans le royaume d'Italie*, p. 275.

47. Bresslau, *Manuale di diplomatica*, pp. 568–69; Radding, *The Origins of Medieval Jurisprudence*, pp. 47–48.

48. Bougard, *La justice dans le royaume d'Italie*, pp. 281–84; Radding, *The Origins of Medieval Jurisprudence*, pp. 48–49.

49. Keller, "Der Gerichtsort in oberitalienischen und toskanischen Städten," pp. 47, 61; Bougard, *La justice dans le royaume d'Italie*, pp. 277–78; Miller, *The Bishop's Palace*, pp. 140–41.

50. Petrucci, "Il notariato italiano," p. 25.

51. Ibid., pp. 12–13; Amelotti and Costamagna, *Alle origini del notariato italiano*, pp. 200–203.

52. Petrucci, "Il notariato italiano," p. 25.

53. Wickham, *Early Medieval Italy*, pp. 180–81; Reuter, *Germany in the Early Middle Ages*, pp. 269–73.

54. Noble, *The Republic of St. Peter*, pp. 3–12, 15–60.

55. Ibid., pp. 153–83.

56. Giovanni Tabacco, "La Toscana meridionale nel medioevo," in *L'Amiata nel medioevo*, ed. Mario Ascheri and Wilhelm Kurze (Rome, 1989), p. 2.

57. Noble, *The Republic of St. Peter*, p. 166.

58. Pierre Toubert, *Les structures du Latium medieval: Le Latium méridional et la Sabine du IXe à la fin du XIIe siècle* (Rome, 1973), 2:980–98; Daniel Waley, *The Papal State in the Thirteenth Century* (New York, 1961), pp. 6–9.

59. Paul Fabre and Louis Duchesne, eds., *Le Liber Censuum de l'Eglise romaine* (Paris, 1889–1952), 1:363–64, 368, 371.

60. Tabacco, "La Toscana meridionale," p. 9.

61. Wickham, *Early Medieval Italy*, pp. 172–73, 181–85.

62. The classic study of *incastellamento* is Toubert, *Les structures du Latium medieval*, 1:303–550. For the importance of *incastellamento* in Roman and Lombard Tuscany, see Maire Vigueur, *Comuni e signorie*, pp. 1–8; Delumeau, *Arezzo: Espace et sociétés*, 1:178–91; Chris Wickham, *The Mountains and the City: The Tuscan Appenines in the Early Middle Ages* (Oxford, 1988), pp. 292–306.

63. Wickham, *Early Medieval Italy*, pp. 188–89; Tabacco, *The Struggle for Power in Medieval Italy*, pp. 132–33.

64. Tabacco, *The Struggle for Power in Medieval Italy*, pp. 324–31. For a more general discussion of bishops' assuming comital authority, see Enzo Petrucci, "Attraverso I poteri civili dei vescovi nel medioevo. A proposito degli atti di un recente convengo," *Rivista di storia della chiesa in Italia* 32:2 (1980): 518–45; Pierre Racine, "Evêque et cité dans le royaume d'Italie," pp. 129–39; Tabacco, "Vescovi e comuni in Italia," pp. 253–82; Eugenio Dupré Theseider, "Vescovi e città nell'Italia precomunale," pp. 55–110.

65. For a discussion of the nature of episcopal authority in central Italy, see S. Mochi Onory, *Ricerche sui poteri civili dei vescovi nelle città umbre durante l'alto medioevo* (Bologna, 1930), pp. 130–93; Maire Vigueur, *Comuni e Signorie in Umbria, Marche e Lazio*, pp. 72–73.

66. Delumeau, *Arezzo: Espace et sociétés*, 1:264–72; Tabacco, *The Struggle for Power in Medieval Italy*, p. 174.

67. Jones, *The Italian City State*, pp. 80–81.

68. Keller, *Signori e vassali*, pp. 13, 79, 251–52.

69. Ibid., pp. 148, 326–27.

70. Ibid., pp. 14–18, 326–27; Delumeau, *Arezzo: Espace et sociétés*, 1:428–51.

71. Maire Vigueur, *Comuni e signorie in Umbria, Marche e Lazio*, p. 73.

72. Osheim, *An Italian Lordship*, p. 16; Giovanna Nicolaj, "Storie di vescovi e di notai ad Arezzo fra XI e XII secolo," in Patrizia Cancian, ed., *La memoria delle chiese: Cancellerie vescovili e culture notarili nell'Italia centro-settentrionale (secoli X–XIII)* (Turin, 1995), pp. 97–99.

CHAPTER 2. BUILDING AN EARTHLY CITY:
THE BISHOPRIC AND ORVIETAN TERRITORIAL EXPANSION

1. See Catherine Boyd, *Tithes and Parishes in Medieval Italy: The Historical Roots of a Modern Problem* (Ithaca, 1952), pp. 49–55; Cinzio Violante, "Pievi e parrocchie nell'Italia centrosettentrionale durante i secoli XI e XII," in *Le istituzioni ecclesiastiche della 'societas christiana' dei secoli XI–XII. Diocesi, pievi, e parrocchie* (Milan, 1977), pp. 643–799; Toubert, *Les structures du Latium medieval*, 2:859–61; Dameron, *Episcopal Power and Florentine Society*, p. 23; Andrea Castagnetti, "Il peso delle istituzioni: Strutture ecclesiastiche e mondo rurale. L'esempio Veronese," in *Le campagne italiane prima e dopo il mille: Una società in trasformazione*, ed. Bruno Andreolli et al. (Bologna, 1985), pp. 257–73.

2. The following discussion is based on Boyd, *Tithes and Parishes in Medieval Italy*; Violante, "Pievi e parrocchie nell'Italia centrosettentrionale durante i secoli XI e XII," pp. 643–799; Chris Wickham, *The Mountains and the City*, pp. 93–110.

3. Osheim, *An Italian Lordship*, pp. 11–12.

4. Delumeau, *Arezzo: Espace et sociétés*, 1:538.

5. Violante, "Pievi e parrocchie nell'Italia centrosettentrionale durante i secoli XI e XII," pp. 778–85; Delumeau, *Arezzo: Espace et sociétés*, 1:535–36; 547–48.

6. Giovanni Tabacco, "Vescovi e monasteri," pp. 105–23.

7. See chapters 6 and 8 for a discussion of this dispute.

8. Mauro Ronzani, "Aspetti e problemi delle pieve e delle parrocchie cittadine nell'Italia centro-settentrionale," in *Pievi e parrocchie in Italia nel basso medioevo (sec. XIII–XV)* (Rome, 1984), p. 307.

9. Miller, *The Bishop's Palace*, pp. 19–20; Dameron, *Episcopal Power and Florentine Society*, p. 23.

10. Carpentier, *Orvieto*, pp. 31–39.

11. For a helpful discussion of the development of cathedral clergy, see Maureen Miller, *The Formation of a Medieval Church: Ecclesiastical Change in Verona, 950–1150* (Ithaca, 1993), pp. 42–59; Yoram Milo, "From Imperial Hegemony to the Commune: Reform in Pistoia's Cathedral Chapter and its Political Impact," in *Istituzioni ecclesiastiche della toscana medioevale* (Lecce, 1980), pp. 87–107; Toubert, *Les structures du Latium médiéval*, 2:803–06; Osheim, *An Italian Lordship*, p. 15.

12. J. M. Wallace-Hadrill, *The Frankish Church* (Oxford, 1983), pp. 174–76; Delumeau, *Arezzo: Espace et sociétés*, 1:490.

13. Miller, *The Bishop's Palace*, pp. 80–84; Miller, *The Formation of a Medieval Church*, pp. 58–59; Mauro Ronzani, "La plebs della città. La problematica della pieve urbana in Italia centro-settentrionale fra il IX e il XIV secolo," in *Chiesa e città*, ed. Cosimo Damiano Fonseca and Cinzio Violante (Potenza, 1990), pp. 28–31; Toubert, *Les structures du Latium médiéval*, 2:846–54; Osheim, *An Italian Lordship*, pp. 15–17; Dameron, *Episcopal Power and Florentine Society*, pp. 49–50.

14. For a good discussion of the dynamic between bishops and cathedral chapters in Lazio, see Toubert, *Les structures du Latium médiéval*, 2:804–54. The relationship between the bishop and cathedral clergy in Lazio parallels that in Orvieto in many ways. For an example of these developments outside of Italy, see Everett Crosby, *Bishop and Chapter in Twelfth-Century England: A Study of the Mensa Episcopalis* (Cambridge, 1994). For the early development of the cathedral church and its clergy, see Ronzani, "La plebs della città. La problematica della pieve urbana in Italia centro-settentrionale fra il IX e il XIV secolo," pp. 23–43. Also see Cosimo Damiano Fonseca, "'Ecclesia Matrix' e 'conventus civium': L'ideologia della cattedrale nell'età comunale," in *La pace di Costanza, 1183* (Bologna, 1984), pp. 135–49.

15. AVO Cod B 85v.

16. Vincenzo Natalini, "Il Capitolo del duomo di Orvieto ed i suoi statuti inediti (1260–1458)," *Rivista di storia della chiesa in Italia* 9 (1955): 181–82.

17. See John Gilchrist, "Was There a Gregorian Reform Movement in the Eleventh Century?" *Canadian Catholic Historical Association: Study Sessions* 37 (1970): 1–10; Ovidio Capitani, "Esiste un 'età gregoriana'?" *Rivista di storia e letteratura e religiosa* I (1965): 454–81; Cinzio Violante, "La réforme ecclésiastique du XIe siècle: Une synthèse progressive d'idées et de structures opposées," *Le Moyen Age* 97:3–4 (1991): 355–65; Giles Constable, *The Reformation of the Twelfth Century* (Cambridge, 1996), p. 4.

18. See Bernard Schimmelpfennig, *The Papacy*, trans. James Sievert (New York, 1992), pp. 131–32.

19. I. S. Robinson, *The Papacy, 1073–1198: Continuity and Innovation* (Cambridge, 1990), pp. ix–x.

20. Gerd Tellenbach, *The Church in Western Europe from the Tenth to the Early Twelfth Century*, trans. Timothy Reuter (Cambridge, 1993), pp. 119–20, 140.

21. Tellenbach, *The Church in Western Europe*, p. 140.

22. Malcolm Lambert, *Medieval Heresy: Popular Movements from the Gregorian Reform to the Reformation*, 2d ed. (Oxford, 1992), pp. 35–38.

23. Jean Leclercq, "La spiritualité des chanoines réguliers," in *La vita comune del clero nei secoli XI e XII*, Atti della Settimana di studio: Mendola, settembre 1959 (Milan, 1962), p. 119.

24. Giovanni Miccoli, "Pier Damiani e la vita comune del clero," in *La vita comune del clero nei secoli XI e XII*. Atti della Settimana di studio: Mendola, settembre 1959 (Milan, 1962), pp. 204–10.

25. Ibid., pp. 190–91.

26. For a helpful discussion of the rule of St. Augustine, see Miller, *The Formation of a Medieval Church*, pp. 82–83; Carlo Egger, "Le regole seguite dai canonici regolari nei secoli XI e XII," in *La vita comune del clero nei secoli XI e XII*, Atti della Settimana di studio: Mendola, settembre 1959 (Milan, 1962), 2:9–12.

27. For a discussion of these changes in Orvieto, see chapter 3. See also Delumeau, *Arezzo: Espace et sociétés*, 1:751.

28. For Ranerio's comment, see AVO Cod B 83r, Perali, *La cronaca*, VI, p. 10.

29. Cosimo Damiano Fonseca, "Canoniche regolari, capitoli cattedrali e 'cura animarum,'" in *Pieve e parrocchie in Italia nel basso medioevo (sec XIII–XV)* (Rome, 1984), pp. 267–68; Michele Maccarrone, "I papi del secolo XII e la vita comune e regolare del clero," in *La vita comune del clero nei secoli XI e XII*, Atti della Settimana di studio: Mendola, settembre 1959 (Milan, 1962), pp. 381–82.

30. Miller, *The Formation of a Medieval Church*, pp. 85, 105; Osheim, *An Italian Lordship*, p. 21.

31. Heinrich Fichtenau, *Heretics and Scholars in the High Middle Ages, 1000–1200*, trans. Denise A. Kaiser (University Park, Pa., 1998), pp. 123–25.

32. Constable, *The Reformation of the Twelfth Century*, pp. 77–84; Tellenbach, *The Church in Western Europe*, p. 130.

33. Dameron, *Episcopal Power and Florentine Society*, p. 66; Osheim, *An Italian Lordship*, pp. 70–73.

34. Chris Wickham, "Paesaggi sepolti: Insediamento e incastellamento sull'Amiata, 750–1250," in *L'Amiata nel medioevo*, ed. Mario Ascheri and Wilhelm Kurze (Rome, 1989), pp. 116–20.

35. For the early history of the Aldobrandeschi, see Gabriella Rossetti, "Gli Aldobrandeschi," in *I ceti dirigenti in Toscana nell'età precomunale* (Pisa, 1981), pp. 151–64; Wickham, *Early Medieval Italy*, pp. 73–74; Osheim, *An Italian Lordship*, p. 14.

36. Wilhelm Kurze, "I momenti principali della storia di S. Salvatore e Monte Amiata," in *L'Amiata nel medioevo*, ed. Mario Ascheri and Wilhelm Kurze (Rome, 1989), p. 36; Wickham, "Paesaggi sepolti," p. 130.

37. Delumeau, *Arezzo: Espace et sociétés*, 1:360.

38. *PL*, 144:401. See also Amleto Spicciani, "I Farolfingi: Conti di Chiusi e Conti di Orvieto," *Bullettino senese di storia patria* 92 (1985): 30.

39. AVO Cod B 100v; Fumi, *Codice Diplomatico*, XIV, pp. 9–10.

40. AVO Cod B 85v; Polock, "Der Prozess," pp. 133–34. Please note that my citation of pages in AVO Codice B differs from that of Polock. In 1987, Marilena Rossi-Caponeri and Lucio Riccetti renumbered the folii in Codice B in preparation for *Chiese e conventii degli ordini mendicanti in Umbria nei secoli XIII–XIV.* I have followed this most recent numeration. Polock uses the older numeration. As a result, the numeration of the dispute in her edition is 83r–89r instead of 80r–86r.

41. AVO Cod B 85v; Pericle Perali, ed., *La cronaca* (Orvieto, 1907), VII, p. 11. Because Perali published his edition of Ranerio's marginal comments before the most recent numeration of Codice B, his citations, like Polock's, will differ from mine by three pages.

42. Spicciani, "I Farolfingi," p. 21.

43. Ibid.

44. Ibid., p. 33.

45. Ibid., p. 58.

46. AVO Cod B 101v; Fumi, *Codice Diplomatico*, XXVII, pp. 17–18. Fageto is located near Santa Maria de Rasa, approximately 20 km northeast of Orvieto. Civitella is a little over 25 km northeast of Orvieto. Pornillo is about 20 km northeast of Orvieto. Mucarone is located near Morrano, approximately 7 km north of Orvieto. The location of the remaining locations is uncertain. Waley, *Mediaeval Orvieto*, p. 1, suggests that Vagno is the Vaiano located 8 km south of Orvieto. For Fracta, there is a villa Fratte near Mimiano, about 10 km east of Orvieto.

47. The six transactions are recorded in AVO Cod B 107v (Fumi, *Codice Diplomatico*, XI, pp. 7–8); 126v (Fumi, XII, pp. 8–9); 100v (Fumi, XIV, pp. 9–10); 100v (Fumi, XV, pp. 11–12); 128v (Fumi, XVI, pp. 12–13); 101v (Fumi, XXVII, pp. 17–18); 103r (Fumi, XXVIII, p. 18).

48. AVO Cod B 100v; Fumi, *Codice Diplomatico*, XV, pp. 11–12.

49. AVO Cod B 128v; Fumi, *Codice Diplomatico*, XVI, pp. 12–13.

50. Spicciani, "I Farolfingi," pp. 53, 58.

51. Osheim, *An Italian Lordship*, pp. 24–25.

52. See Wickham, *Early Medieval Italy*, p. 186.

53. See Cinzio Violante, "Quelques caractéristiques des structures familiales en Lombardie, Emile et Toscane aux XIe et XIIe siècles," in *Famille et parenté dans l'occident medieval*, ed. Georges Duby and Jacques Le Goff (Rome, 1977), pp. 94–96. See also Spicciani, "I Farolfingi," p. 11.

54. Pierre Toubert argues that in medieval Italy, where the Latin style of naming was abandoned, personal names were no longer recognizable as part of a large family group. Only in the twelfth century did Italian families begin to attach a stable family name to individual names. See Toubert, *Les structures du Latium médiéval*, 1:695–701. In the case of the Farolfingi, around the end of the twelfth century, certain branches of the family appear to have assumed a stable family name based on a toponym, e.g., the counts of Sarteano, descendents of Manente I. The Counts of Montemarte derived their family name from the castle of Montemarte, located in the region between Orvieto and Todi.

55. For example, see Paolo Cammarosano, *La Familia dei Berardenghi: Contributo alla storia della società senese nei secoli XI–XIII* (Spoleto, 1974), p. 123ff.

56. AVO Cod B 100v; Fumi, *Codice Diplomatico*, XIV, pp. 9–10. Bolsena is approximately 15 km southwest of Orvieto.

57. Toubert, *Les structures du Latium médiéval*, 2:1091–98.

58. Tabacco, *The Struggle for Power in Medieval Italy*, pp. 208–12. See also Dameron, *Episcopal Power and Florentine Society*, pp. 132–33.

59. For the dispute between Siena and Arezzo, see Delumeau, *Arezzo: Espace et sociétés*, 1:475–87; Cammarosano, *La famiglia dei Berardenghi*, pp. 66, 134–39; Guy P. Marchal, "De la mémoire communicative à la mémoire culturelle. La passé dans les témoignages d'Arezzo et de Sienne (1177–1180)," *Annales* 56:3 (May–June 2001): 563–89. For the fluidity of diocesan boundaries in general, see Brentano, *A New World in a Small Place*, pp. 81–106.

60. Delumeau, *Arezzo: Espace et société*, 1:504.

61. AVO Cod B 82r; Polock, "Der Prozess," p. 110.

62. For a detailed introduction to the dispute, see Marlene Polock's introductory essay to her edition of the dispute in "Der Prozess."

63. That the dispute lasted for almost a century and was repeatedly brought to judgment was not uncommon for the Middle Ages. The fluidity of political structures made it possible for parties in a dispute to seek justice from a variety of political and religious authorities. In the absence of an effective enforcement mechanism, the success of a judgment depended solely on the willingness of the parties in the dispute to abide by it.

64. See the testimony of Arlotto di Berizo, AVO Cod B 85r; Polock, "Der Prozess," p. 130.

65. AVO Cod B 81v; Polock, "Der Prozess," p. 96.

66. AVO Cod B 82v; Polock, "Der Prozess," p. 98.

67. Dameron, *Episcopal Power and Florentine Society*, p. 70; Osheim, *An Italian Lordship*, p. 71.

68. AVO Cod B 84v; Polock, "Der Prozess," p. 126.

69. See the testimony of Priest Girardo of Grotte, AVO Cod B 84r; Polock, "Der Prozess," pp. 122, 124.

70. AVO Cod B 81r; Polock, "Der Prozess," pp. 103–4. The monastery of San Sepolcro was a persistent problem for the Orvietan bishops. During the opening decades of the thirteenth century, the bishops of Orvieto were involved in a long and bitter dispute with the monastery of San Sepolcro, which refused to submit to the diocesan authority of the bishop of Orvieto. AVO Cod B 93r–94v.

71. Even Dono, the archdeacon of Orvieto, recognized that the Bishop of Sovana owned the church of Santa Romana. AVO Cod B 83r; Polock, "Der Prozess," p. 116.

72. The bishop of Orvieto granted certain revenues of San Stefano to the abbot of San Sepolcro. The ability of the Orvietan bishop to concede revenues from San Stefano would suggest that the church was under his authority. AVO Cod B 107r; Fumi, *Codice Diplomatico*, XXXI, pp. 19–20.

73. Several witnesses referred the uprooting of populations and to a "time of war" during Ildibrando's episcopate. See the testimony of Priest Pagano, AVO Cod B 83v; Polock, "Der Prozess," p. 119.

74. From the little evidence that is available, the effect of castle building on diocesan structure in Orvieto was different from that in Lazio described by Pierre Toubert. See Toubert, *Les structures du Latium médié-val*, 2:793 ff. In Lazio incastellation led to a dissolution of the system of baptismal churches and dependent chapels. As the example of Grotte suggests, incastellation may have caused a relocation of the baptismal church, but did not necessarily alter its role as a center of diocesan administration.

75. AVO Cod B 84r; Polock, "Der Prozess," pp. 124–25. Priest Amideo testified that the settlers from these two places came during the episcopate of Ildibrando. AVO Cod B 85r; Polock, "Der Prozess," pp. 131–32. The statement "later, if you want to give to another, then you can do so" is difficult to interpret. Presumably the bishop of Orvieto was saying that first the settlers must pay him tithes. Beyond this, they could make other payments to the bishop of Sovana if they so wished.

76. AVO Cod B 84v; Polock, "Der Prozess," p. 127.

77. AVO Cod B 84v; Polock, "Der Prozess," pp. 127–28. There is some confusion among the witnesses concerning the chronology of events and whether Santa Romana or San Stefano was destroyed. The two most detailed accounts of the attack are those of Martinozzo (quoted above), an Orvietan

knight, and Priest Amideo. The account that I have presented follows Martinozzo's testimony, which makes more sense within the context of the other witnesses. Amideo testified that it was the baptismal church of San Stefano that was destroyed. This is certainly an error, for San Stefano belonged to the Orvietan bishopric. Amideo is confused in his chronology as well. He places the destruction of the church before the episcopate of Ildibrando. Yet he says that the settlers from Terzano and Argazano came to Grotte during the episcopate of Ildibrando. AVO Cod B 85r; Polock, "Der Prozess," p. 131.

78. See the testimony of Lambertucio di Trocta. AVO Cod B 84v; Polock, "Der Prozess," p. 128. According to this witness, Priest Rustico (the future Bishop Rustico?) destroyed the altar.

79. See the testimony of Priest Rollando. AVO Cod B 84v; Polock, "Der Prozess," p. 129.

80. AVO Cod B 84v–85r; Polock, "Der Prozess," p. 129.

81. AVO Cod B 82r; Henry V stopped in Acquapendente on his way to Rome. See Polock, "Der Prozess," p. 111, n. 52.

82. Ibid. Count Ugolino, a Farolfing, was the son of Count Bernardo I, who in 1115 donated the church of Santa Cristina in Bolsena to Bishop Guilielmo. Ugolino participated in this donation.

83. AVO Cod B 83v; Polock, "Der Prozess," pp. 120–21.

84. Ibid. See also the testimonies of Dono, the archdeacon, and Priest Ranerio of Rosano. AVO Cod B 83r; Polock, pp. 115, 117–18.

85. The date of the case at Pitigliano is difficult to establish. Polock dates the hearing around 1140/1144. See Polock, "Der Prozess," p. 50. I am inclined to place the hearing around 1150 for the following reasons. Because almost all of the Orvietan conquests in the southwest occurred during the episcopate of Ildibrando (1140–1155), it seems that the expansion of Orvieto into the region was only beginning in the early 1140s. Moreover, Priest Stefano, who was present at Pitigliano, mentioned that Bishop Ildizo did not continue to pursue the case after Pitigliano because of his sickness. AVO Cod B 80v; Polock, "Der Prozess," p. 103. This suggests that the hearing took place not long before Ildizo died in 1151.

86. AVO Cod B 83v; Polock, "Der Prozess," p. 119. This passage is the only mention of an episcopal advocate in Orvieto. The advocate was an official who represented the bishop in judicial matters. In some cities, the office was an important means of exercising power and came to be dominated by a single family. See Osheim, *An Italian Lordship*, pp. 31ff. In Orvieto, the office apparently was filled on an ad hoc basis.

87. See Polock, "Der Prozess," pp. 51–52. Also see James A. Brundage, *Medieval Canon Law* (London, 1995), p. 131.

88. AVO Cod B 107r; Fumi, *Codice Diplomatico*, XXXI, pp. 19–20.

89. Sandro Carocci, "Le *comunalie* di Orvieto fra la fine del XII e la metà del XIV secolo," *Mélanges de l'École française de Rome, moyen âge–temps modernes* 99 (1987): 703.

90. Ibid., p. 715.

91. Tabacco, *The Struggle for Power in Medieval Italy*, pp. 219–20.

92. AVO Cod B 85v; Polock, "Der Prozess," p. 136.

93. Delumeau, *Arezzo: Espace et sociétés*, 1:483.

CHAPTER 3. THE CONNECTEDNESS OF THINGS: EPISCOPAL REFORM AND STATE BUILDING

1. AVO Cod B 69v; Perali, *La cronaca*, I, p. 5.

2. AVO Cod B 73r; Perali, *La cronaca*, IV, p. 7.

3. AVO Cod B 81r; Polock, "Der Prozess," p. 104.

4. See the testimony of Priest Amideo, AVO Cod B 85r; Polock, "Der Prozess," p. 131.

5. No reasons are given for his exile. AVO Cod B 81r; Polock, "Der Prozess," p. 104.

6. AVO Cod B 69v; Fumi, *Codice Diplomatico*, XXXII, p. 20.

7. AVO Cod B 83r; Perali, *La cronaca*, VI, p. 10.

8. AVO Cod B 85v; Perali, *La cronaca*, VII, pp. 10–11.

9. Georges Duby, "Les chanoines reguliers et la vie économique des XIe et XIIe siècles," in *La vita comune del clero nei secoli XI e XII*, Atti della Settimana di studio: Mendola, settembre 1959 (Milan, 1962), pp. 73–80.

10. See Carpentier, *Orvieto*, pp. 31–39.

11. Étiene Hubert, *Espace urbain et habitat à Rome du Xe siècle à la fin du XIIIe siècle* (Rome, 1990), pp. 134–35, 279.

12. These are very rough approximations based on the breakdown of entries recording recognitions of property in the episcopal and capitular registers (Codici A, B, and C for the bishop and the Codice di San Costanzo for the chapter). The number of documents broken down by region does not necessarily translate into a breakdown of the size or value of property according to region. Nevertheless, the breakdown of documents does provide a general indication of the relative concentration of episcopal and capitular property in the city. A "recognition" is a type of document in which a holder of a particular piece of property acknowledges before a notary that he/she owes an annual *pensio*, or rental payment, to the bishop or chapter.

13. Miller, *The Formation of a Medieval Church*, pp. 46–47.

14. Mauro Ronzani, "Aspetti e problemi delle pievi e delle parrocchie cittadine nell'Italia centro-settentrionale," pp. 307–49.

15. Miller, *The Formation of a Medieval Church*, pp. 58–61. For a detailed discussion of parish rights and the parish as a framework for the care of souls, see William M. Bowsky, *"Populus Sancti Laurentii*: Care of Souls, a Parish, and a Priest," in *Miscellanea Domenico Maffei*, ed. Antonio Garcia y Garcia and Peter Weimar (Goldbach, 1995), 4:147–91.

16. Vincenzo Natalini, *San Pietro Parenzo. La leggenda scritta dal Maestro Giovanni canonico d'Orvieto* (Rome, 1936), p. 158.

17. Mauro Ronzani, "L'organizzazione della cura d'anima nella città di Pisa (secoli XII–XIII)," in *Istituzioni ecclesiastiche della Toscana medioevale* (Lecce, 1980), pp. 72–75; Violante, "Pievi e parrocchie nell'Italia centrosettentrionale durante i secoli XI e XII," pp. 763–64. See also Susan Reynolds, *Kingdoms and Communities in Western Europe, 900–1300*, 2d ed. (Oxford, 1997), pp. 79–100.

18. Horst Fuhrman, *Germany in the High Middle Ages, c. 1050–1200*, trans. Timothy Reuter (Cambridge, 1986), pp. 100–101.

19. Delumeau, *Arezzo: Espace et sociétés*, 2:986.

20. Fuhrman, *Germany in the High Middle Ages*, pp. 117–27.

21. Peter Partner, *The Lands of St. Peter: The Papal State in the Middle Ages and the Early Renaissance* (London, 1972), p. 127; Waley, *The Papal State in the Thirteenth Century*, p. 8.

22. Robinson, *The Papacy, 1073–1198*, pp. 369–87.

23. See Robinson, *The Papacy*, pp. 13–15; Partner, *The Lands of St. Peter*, pp. 178–82; Paolo Brezzi, *Roma e l'impero medioevale (774–1252)* (Bologna, 1947), pp. 318–26.

24. AVO Cod B 85r; Polock, "Der Prozess," p. 131.

25. The only other occurrence of "error" in the testimonies clearly refers to a papal schism. Priest Giovanni of Plano Castagnano (apparently a pro-imperial partisan) described the schism during the pontificate of Alexander III as "the error of Alexander." AVO Cod B 81v; Polock, "Der Prozess," p. 109.

26. See Robinson, *The Papacy (1073–1198)*, pp. 10, 49. See also Partner, *The Lands of St. Peter*, pp. 168–76. For the events in Viterbo, see G. Signorelli, *Viterbo nella storia della chiesa* (Viterbo, 1907), 1:122.

27. AVO Cod B 100r; Fumi, *Codice Diplomatico*, XXIII, p. 15.

28. AVO Cod B 105r; Fumi, *Codice Diplomatico*, XXIX, pp. 18–19.

29. AVO Cod B 101v; Fumi, *Codice Diplomatico*, XXVII, pp. 17–18.

30. AVO Cod B 85r; Polock, "Der Prozess," p. 130.

31. *Liber Censuum*, 1:380–82. For the importance of castles in papal efforts to reestablish authority over the patrimony, see Toubert, *Les structures du Latium médiéval*, 2:1075ff.

32. See Renato Stopani, *La Via Francigena: Una strada europea nell'Italia del medioevo* (Florence, 1988), p. 61.

33. AVO Cod B 81r; Polock, "Der Prozess," p. 104. The exile can be dated to sometime between 1153 and 1154. Stefano recalled that he was ordained a deacon by Bishop Pietro of Sovana (1153–1175) during Ildibrando's exile. In 1154 Ildibrando is back in Orvieto restoring the canons to the cathedral. AVO Cod B 69v; Fumi, *Codice Diplomatico*, XXXII, pp. 20–21.

34. AVO Cod B 83r; Polock, "Der Prozess," pp. 115–16.

35. AVO Cod B 69v; Fumi, *Codice Diplomatico*, XXXII, p. 20.

36. Boso, "Vita Hadriani IV," *Le Liber Pontificalis*, ed. Louis Duchesne and Cyrille Vogel, Bibliothèque des Ecoles française d'Athènes et de Rome, ser. 2 (Paris, 1955), 2:390.

37. Robinson, *The Papacy*, pp. 460–65.

38. Boso, "Vita Hadriani IV," pp. 393–95; 389–90.

39. Ibid., 2:395. Hadrian stayed in Orvieto for at least two weeks and possibly as many as twelve weeks. See Waley, *Mediaeval Orvieto*, p. 2.

40. Fumi, *Codice Diplomatico*, XXXVI, pp. 23–24.

41. Maccarrone, "I papi del secolo XII e la vita comune e regolare del clero," pp. 378–80.

42. Ranerio appears in two documents prior to 1156: one in 1137 that recorded the donation of Count Otto (AVO Cod B 101v; Fumi, *Codice Diplomatico*, XXVII, pp. 17–18), and one in 1154, when Bishop Ildibrando restored the cathedral to the canons (AVO Cod B 69v; Fumi, XXXII, pp. 20–21). In both documents he is called "archpriest." He is twice called "prior," but only after 1156; that is, in retrospect, after he was no longer head of the cathedral canons. In a document dated 1157, he is listed among the witnesses as "Ranerio, the former prior of San Costanzo." AVO Cod B 102r; Fumi, XXXVII, p. 25. In 1194 Priest Amideo, a witness in the Sovana dispute, referred to Ranerio as the prior of San Costanzo. AVO Cod B 85r; Polock, "Der Prozess," p. 131.

43. See discussion of common life in chapter 1.

44. See AVO Cod B 102r; Fumi, *Codice Diplomatico*, XXXVII, XXXVIII, p. 25.

45. Fumi, *Codice Diplomatico*, p. 26. For the terms of the agreement, see Waley, *Mediaeval Orvieto*, pp. 2–3. See also Reynolds, *Fiefs and Vassals*, p. 234. Reynolds comments that in this agreement there is no reason to suppose a connection to the academic law of fiefs. Whether or not this was the case in 1157 is a matter of speculation. In 1200 the Orvietan cathedral canon, Maestro Giovanni, who seems to have had some form of legal training, thought of Orvieto as a fief and the Orvietans as vassals of the papacy. It is, however, impossible to tell whether his interpretation reflects the understanding of the Orvietans in 1157, or whether it is his own invention. See discussion of Maestro Giovanni in chapter 5.

46. Toubert, *Les structures du Latium médiéval*, 2:1127–35.

47. Corciano is about 7.5 km north of Città Castellano and about 12.5 km south/southeast of Orte. Boccaleone sold the castle to Boso, the representative of Hadrian IV, in August 1158. *Liber Censuum*, 1:385.

48. Santa Cristina is located about 12 km southwest of Orvieto.

49. Rocca di San Stefano is located near Proceno, less than 5 km northwest of Acquapendente.

50. Rocca Ripeseno is located less than 5 km west/northwest of Orvieto.

51. Boso, "Vita Hadriani IV," *Liber Pontificalis*, 2:396.

52. *Liber Censuum*, 1:383–84.

53. See discussion of Farolfingi in chapter 1.

54. *Liber Censuum*, 1:389–90.

55. Ibid., 1:389.

56. Ibid., 1:389–90.

57. Ibid., 1:394–95.

58. See Robinson, *The Papacy*, pp. 246–47.

CHAPTER 4. THE UNTENABILITY OF EPISCOPAL LORDSHIP: BISHOPRIC AND COMMUNE IN THE LATE TWELFTH CENTURY

1. Toubert, *Les structures du Latium medieval*, pp. 1130–31.

2. Waley, *Mediaeval Orvieto*, pp. 4ff.

3. Maire Vigueur, *Comuni e signorie*, pp. 63, 95–96; Tabacco, *The Struggle for Power in Medieval Italy*, pp. 185–88; Daniel Waley, *The Italian City-Republics*, 3d ed. (New York, 1988), pp. 32–36.

4. AVO Cod B 101v; Fumi, *Codice Diplomatico*, XXVII, pp. 17–18.

5. Fumi, *Codice Diplomatico*, p. 26.

6. For a discussion of the *launegild*, see Cortese, *Il diritto nella storia medievale*, 1:161–62.

7. See Tabacco's analysis of the Cremonese *capitanei* for a penetrating discussion of this point in *The Struggle for Power in Medieval Italy*, pp. 324–31.

8. Waley, *Mediaeval Orvieto*, p. 4, n. 3.

9. AVO Cod B 102r; Fumi, *Codice Diplomatico*, XXXVII, p. 25.

10. AVO Cod B 103v; Fumi, *Codice Diplomatico*, XVII, pp. 13–14.

11. AVO Cod B 84v; Polock, "Der Prozess," p. 129.

12. AVO Cod B 84v; Polock, "Der Prozess," pp. 127–28.

13. For example, see AVO Cod B 102v; Fumi, *Codice Diplomatico*, XVIII, p. 14;. AVO Cod B 101v; Fumi, *Codice Diplomatico*, XXV, XXVI,

pp. 16–17; AVO Cod B 103r; Fumi, *Codice Diplomatico*, L, p. 35; AVO Cod B 100v; Fumi, *Codice Diplomatico*, XLVI, p. 32.

14. AVO Cod B 70r; Fumi, *Codice Diplomatico*, XLVII, pp. 32–33.

15. AVO Cod B 69v; Perali, *La cronaca*, I, p. 5.

16. Rocco appears rather than the bishop because the see was vacant in 1157.

17. AVO Cod B 80r; Fumi, *Codice Diplomatico*, XL, pp. 27–28.

18. Sant' Andrea was located in the central plaza where the communal palace would later be built. Several important submissions to Orvieto were executed in the church of Sant' Andrea. See Fumi, *Codice Diplomatico*, XXXIX, XLI, XLII, pp. 26–29.

19. Maire Vigueur, *Comuni e signorie*, p. 97.

20. Ibid., pp. 77–78. For a discussion of the relation between the *popolo* and nobility, see also John Koenig, *Il popolo dell'Italia del Nord nel XIII secolo* (Bologna, 1986); Waley, *The Italian City-Republics*, pp. 131–43.

21. Maire Vigueur, *Comuni e signori*, pp. 139–44.

22. See Lansing, *Power and Purity*, pp. 25–30.

23. Carpentier, *Orvieto à la fin du XIIIe siècle*, p. 195.

24. For information on the economic life of the guilds, see Carpentier, *Une ville devant la peste*, pp. 44–63.

25. It is safe to assume that the archpriest of the cathedral chapter belonged to the ruling class. Ildibrando was from the Becarrio, a noble family.

26. See Delumeau, *Arezzo: Espace et sociétés*, 2:1011–1108 for a detailed and informative discussion of imperial policy in central Italy under Frederick Barbarossa and his son Henry VI.

27. Boso, "Vita Alexandri III," *Liber Pontificalis*, 2:403–404.

28. Fuhrman, *Germany in the High Middle Ages*, pp. 135–67, 174.

29. For a more detailed account of the papal-imperial conflicts during the second half of the twelfth century, see Partner, *The Lands of St. Peter*, pp. 203–23; Robinson, *The Papacy*, pp. 473–524.

30. AVO Cod B 69v; Perali, *La cronaca*, II, p. 6.

31. Michele Maccarrone suggests that Pietro was an antibishop in Orvieto, chosen by Frederick Barbarossa. Michele Maccarrone, "Orvieto e la predicazione della crociata," *Studi su Innocenzo III* (Padua, 1972), p. 23. There is, however, no mention of Frederick's involvement in this affair. Furthermore, none of the witnesses in the Sovana dispute mention an antibishop in Orvieto. Given the ambiguity of Ranerio's comment and the absence of any other reference to an antibishop in Orvieto, it is probably better to identify Pietro, the "schismatic" bishop, as Bishop Pietro of Sovana, who was in fact an imperial partisan and supporter of the antipope Victor IV. Paganutio testified that Pietro was compelled by Count Ildibrando Novello

to become a schismatic. Later, Pietro returned to the church and received penance from the bishop of Castro. AVO Cod B 80v; Polock, "Der Prozess," pp. 101–102.

32. AVO Cod B 81r; Polock, "Der Prozess," pp. 104–105.

33. AVO Cod B 84r; Polock, "Der Prozess," p. 125. Polock notes that the occasion for Pietro's trip was the antipope Calixtus III's stay in Viterbo between 1170 and 1172. In 1170 Count Ildibrando Novello, who exercised comital authority over much of the diocese of Sovana, was *podestà* of Viterbo. Polock, p. 148, n. 37.

34. AVO Cod B 82v; Polock, "Der Prozess," p. 97.

35. AVO Cod B 82v, 84r; Polock, "Der Prozess," pp. 115, 123.

36. AVO Cod B 84r; Polock, "Der Prozess," p. 124.

37. Delumeau, *Arezzo: Espace et sociétés*, 2:1131–39.

38. Fumi, *Codice Diplomatico*, XXXIX, pp. 26–27.

39. AVO Cod B 82v; Polock, "Der Prozess," p. 113. Ranerio and Jacobo inherited Mezzano, Latera, Juliano, Pitigliano, Sorano, Sala, Farnese, Castilione, Petralla, and Merona from their father, Count Bartolomeo. Count Ranerio then donated the castles of Latera, Mezzano, and Juliano to his brother Jacobo. See Gasparo Ciacci, *Gli Aldobrandeschi nella storia e nella divina commedia* (Rome, 1935), 2:75, 94–95, CCXVIII. Also see Polock, "Der Prozess," pp. 76–77. Ranerio and Jacobo's father was the Count Bartolomeo in whose jurisdiction the first hearing at Pitigliano was held. AVO Cod B 83v; Polock, "Der Prozess," p. 119.

40. In his opening argument, the syndic representing the Orvietan bishopric claimed that the property of Ranerio di Bartolomeo belonged to the bishopric. AVO Cod B 82v; Polock, "Der Prozess," p. 98.

41. AVO Cod B 85r; Polock, "Der Prozess," p. 129. He is, in fact, one of the witnesses in the 1168 act of submission. He appears along with his brother as "Rubertus et Marinus filii Mendici." Fumi, *Codice Diplomatico*, XXXIX, p. 27.

42. AVO Cod B 85r; Polock, "Der Prozess," pp. 129–30. For Arlotto as a consul representing the commune in the 1168 act of submission, see Fumi, *Codice Diplomatico*, XXXIX, p. 27.

43. See Waley, *Mediaeval Orvieto*, pp. xxi, 4, 6, 17–19, 22–23, 60–63.

44. AVO Cod B 82v; Polock, "Der Prozess," p. 113. The *lambardi* were a rural aristocracy who, although subject to a superior such as a count or a commune, enjoyed privileges exempting them from the fiscal burdens to which the rural population was subject. In many cases they exercised legal jurisdiction over their land. Some of the *lambardi* settled in the city and formed the ruling class of the nascent communes. Those who remained in the countryside usually constituted the knightly class of the rural communes. See Andrea Castagnetti, "Il potere sui contadini. Dalla signoria

fondiaria alla signoria territoriale. Comunità rurali e comuni citadini," in *Le campagne italiane prima e dopo il mille. Una società in trasformazione*, ed. Bruno Andreolli, Vito Fumagalli, and Massimo Montanari (Bologna, 1985), pp. 229–30.

45. AVO Cod B 70r; Fumi, *Codice Diplomatico*, XLVII, pp. 32–33. Although it is not certain that Stefano was the son of the Tebalduccio who fought against Count Ildibrando and the bishop of Sovana, there is good reason to affirm the connection. Tebalduccio had a sister named Stefania, indicating that Stefano was among the stock of family names.

46. On October 3, 1212, Pope Innocent III wrote a letter to the consuls and *podestà* of the commune asking them to assist Bishop Giovanni in recovering land from the sons of Stefano di Tebalduccio. In this letter Innocent mentioned that Stefano first laid claim to the land during the schism. AVO Cod B 111v. Stefano's receipt of this property from Rustico is confirmed by Bishop Ranerio's comment concerning the pledge of episcopal property by Rustico in Mealla, which is where San Gervasio is located. Bishop Ranerio almost certainly had Stefano in mind when he commented that Rustico pledged a considerable amount of episcopal property in order to secure loyal support during the schism.

47. The document that recorded the pledge of property is no longer extant. We know about the pledge because in 1181, Bishop Riccardo received the baptismal church in Stiolo and the episcopal tenants in Caio back from Rocco. AVO Cod B 107r; Fumi, *Codice Diplomatico*, LII, p. 35.

48. Vincenzo Natalini, ed., *San Pietro Parenzo*. Hereafter cited in text as *Passio*.

49. Natalini, *Pietro Parenzo*, p. 154.

50. For the origins and early spread of Catharism, see Malcolm Lambert, *The Cathars* (Oxford, 1998), pp. 19–59. Much of the general discussion that follows is based on Lambert's study, to which I refer the reader for its vast bibliography on the subject. For Catharism in Italy and, more particularly, in Orvieto, I rely on Carol Lansing, *Power and Purity*, which provides a detailed and insightful study of the Cathars in a local social context.

51. Lambert, *The Cathars*, p. 55.

52. Ibid., pp. 21, 141.

53. Malcolm Lambert, *Medieval Heresy*, p. 118.

54. See Lansing, *Power and Purity*, pp. 84ff; Lambert, *The Cathars*, p. 76; Lorenzo Paolini, "Italian Catharism and Written Culture," in *Heresy and Literacy, 1000–1350*, ed. Peter Biller and Ann Hudson (Cambridge, 1994), pp. 95–98.

55. Apparently they belonged to a group of laypersons who participated in the prayers of the confraternity. Natalini, *Pietro Parenzo*, p. 154.

56. See Constable, *The Reformation of the Twelfth Century*, p. 74; Fichtenau, *Heretics and Scholars*, p. 50.

57. For the common mixing of beliefs, see Lansing, *Power and Purity*, pp. 92–95.

58. See discussion of Bishop Ildibrando's agreement with the cathedral canons in chapter 2.

59. Natalini, *Pietro Parenzo*, p. 166.

60. For an interesting discussion of this aspect of reform, see Amy G. Remensnyder, "Pollution, Purity, and Peace: An Aspect of Social Reform between the Late Tenth Century and 1076," in *The Peace of God: Social Violence and Religious Response in France around the Year 1000*, ed. Thomas Head and Richard Landes (Ithaca, 1992), pp. 280–307.

61. For the role of confraternities in combating heresy, see Lambert, *The Cathars*, pp. 176–80.

62. AVO Cod B 78r. Regarding the other twelfth-century bishops, Bishop Guilielmo (1103–1136) was from the Martinotii, a prominent Orvietan family. AVO Cod B 73r. The family of Bishop Ildibrando (1140–1154), the Beccarii, were from Vallocli, about 10 km west of Orvieto. There is no mention of Bishop Gualfredo's (1156–1157) family or place of birth. Even the dates of the episcopate of Gualfredo are not certain. No documents survive from his episcopate, and the testimonies regarding the years of his episcopate vary considerably. Bishop Guiscardo (1157–1159) was from Orvieto. AVO Cod B 73r. Bishop Milo (1159–1161) was from Valmontone, approximately 6 km north of Orvieto. AVO Cod B 73r. Bishop Rustico (1168–1175) may have been from Orvieto. A Priest Rustico appears in several early-twelfth-century documents (AVO Cod B 101v and 102v, dated 1133 and 1127, respectively), donating a considerable amount of property to his relatives.

63. See Maccarrone, "Orvieto e la predicazione della crociata," p. 24.

64. S. Loewenfeld, ed., *Epistolae Pontificium Romanorum ineditae* (Leipzig, 1885), p.158, #275.

65. Ibid., p. 158, #276.

66. AVO Cod B 70r; Fumi, *Codice Diplomatico*, XLVII, pp. 32–33.

67. AVO Cod B 101r, 102v; Fumi, *Codice Diplomatico*, LI, LIII, pp. 34–36.

68. AVO Cod B 102v, 108r; Fumi, *Codice Diplomatico*, LVI, LVII, pp. 37–38.

69. Natalini, *Pietro Parenzo*, p. 155.

70. See Lansing, *Power and Purity*, p. 31.

71. For the various matters disputed by Pope Urban III and Frederick, see Robinson, *The Papacy*, p. 504. Also see Partner, *The Patrimony of St. Peter*, p. 218; Waley, *The Papal State*, pp. 23–24.

72. Delumeau, *Arezzo: Espace et sociétés*, 2:1095–1103.

73. *MGH, Constitutiones et Acta Publica Imperatorum et Regum*, ed. Ludwig Weiland, vol. 1, no. 322 (1893; reprint, Hannover, 1999).

74. For the question of whether Henry VI actually conquered Orvieto, see Luigi Fumi, "L'assedio di Enrico VI di Svevia Re de' Romani contro la Città di Orvieto (1186)," *Bollettino di Storia Patria* 12:203–16. Also see Waley, *Mediaeval Orvieto*, p. 9.

CHAPTER 5. LOOKING AT NEW THINGS IN AN OLD WAY:
PIETRO PARENZO AND THE CRISIS
OF EPISCOPAL AUTHORITY

1. See appendix for a discussion of the authorship of the *Passio*.

2. For a more detailed account of central Italian politics during the 1190s, see Waley, *The Papal State*, pp. 30ff; Partner, *The Lands of St. Peter*, pp. 229ff; Michele Maccarrone, "Orvieto e la predicazione della crociata," pp. 10–22.

3. *Die Register Innocenz III, Pontifikatsjahr, 1199/1200*, ed. Othmar Hageneder, Anton Haidacher, et al. (Vienna, 1964), 2:369, #194.

4. Traditionally the Roman prefect was the chief executive and judicial officer of the city, in theory appointed by the pope. The office declined in importance with the formation of the Roman commune as the senators assumed most of the prefect's duties. The fortunes of the office fluctuated in accordance with the pope's ability to enforce his will against the Roman senate. The office eventually became the privilege of Pietro di Vico's family. During the late twelfth century, the prefects were usually imperial supporters. In 1198 Innocent reestablished his authority over the prefect, from whom he received an oath of fealty. See Robinson, *The Papacy*, pp. 9, 11–14; Jürgen Petersohn, "Kaiser, Papst und Praefectura Urbis zwischen Alexander III. und Innocenz III. Probleme der Besetzung und Chronologie der römischen Präfektur im letzten Viertel des 12 Jahrhunderts," *Quellen und Forschungen aus italienischen Archiven und Bibliotheken* 60 (1980): 157–88.

5. "Gesta Innocentii Papae III," *PL*, 214: xxix–xxx. See also Maccarrone, "Orvieto e la predicazione della crociata," pp. 10–12.

6. See the testimony of Homodeo Pagani. AVO Cod B 85r; Polock, "Der Prozess," p. 130. Paganucio, another witness, recalled that Bishop Pietro of Sovana (1153–1175) confirmed children in Acquapendente approximately twenty years earlier (i.e., 1174). When asked if this was during the war between Orvieto and Acquapendente, he responded that he did not know. Nevertheless, the question suggests that there was a war close to the time of the events that he described. AVO Cod B 80v; Polock, "Der Prozess," p. 101.

7. Fumi, *Codice Diplomatico*, LXVIII, pp. 47–48.

8. "Gesta Innocentii Papae III," *PL*, 214:xxvii.

9. The following summary of Innocent's interaction with the Romans, Viterbo, and the Tuscan League is from the "Gesta Innocentii Papae III," *PL*, 214:clxxviii–clxxx. Also see Brezzi, *Roma e l'impero medioevale*, pp. 393–95; Signorelli, *Viterbo nella storia della chiesa*, 1:156–58.

10. See Waley, *The Papal State*, pp. 31–32, 38ff.

11. These rectors presumably are not papal rectors. Their preparations to fight a war against Innocent proves as much. They were probably the *podestà* of the individual communes.

12. AVO Cod B 79r; Fumi, *Codice Diplomatico*, LXXXIV, pp. 60–61. The document is dated 1211 and is a petition for reimbursement of various expenses from Viterbo, including expenses that certain Orvietans incurred while fighting on behalf of Viterbo against Rome.

13. The terms "rector" and "*podestà*" were used interchangeably in late-twelfth-century Italy. For Orvieto, see Waley, *Mediaeval Orvieto*, p. 10. These rectors, including Pietro Parenzo, should not to be confused with papal rectors, who were administrative officials in charge of provinces within the patrimony, such as Tuscany, Sabina, or the march of Ancona. See Waley, *The Papal State*, pp. 95ff.

14. See Waley, *The Italian City-Republics*, pp. 40–45.

15. Jean-Claude Maire Vigueur, "Nello stato della chiesa: Da una pluralità di circuiti al trionfo del guelfismo," in *I podestà dell'Italia comunale*, Parte I: *Reclutamento e circolazione degli ufficiali forestieri (fine XII sec.–metà XIV sec.)*, ed. Jean-Claude Maire Vigueur (Rome, 2000), 2:741–65; Sandro Carocci, "Barone e podestà. L'aristocrazia Romana e gli uffici comunali nel due-trecento," ibid., 2:847–75.

16. Natalini, *Pietro Parenzo*, pp. 153–56.

17. Lansing, *Power and Purity*, pp. 57, 151.

18. Natalini, *Pietro Parenzo*, pp. 157–58.

19. Ibid., p. 158.

20. Ibid., pp. 158–59.

21. Ibid., p. 166.

22. Ibid., pp. 178–79.

23. Ibid., pp. 179–80.

24. For Pope Hadrian's treaty with Orvieto, see chapter 3.

25. For the argument of the Orvietan jurist, see the discussion of the bishopric and the city in chapter 2.

26. Natalini, *Pietro Parenzo*, p. 170.

27. Ibid., p. 155.

28. Ibid., p. 156.

29. Ibid.

30. Ibid., p. 167.

31. Ibid., p. 155.

32. Fumi, *Codice Diplomatico*, LXX, p. 49.

33. AVO Cod B 88r; Fumi, *Codice Diplomatico*, LXXI, pp. 49–50.

34. The compromise may have involved an agreement in which Orvieto had the right to appoint a *podestà* in Acquapendente, so long as the *podestà* and officials of Acquapendente swore fidelity to the papacy. See Maccarrone, "Orvieto e la predicazione della crociata," p. 63. Also see Waley, *Mediaeval Orvieto*, p. 15.

35. *PL*, 215:673, 1086–87.

36. In 1205 Innocent sent a letter to Bishop Matteo concerning a marriage dispute. *PL*, 215:573–74. In 1207 Innocent referred a dispute between some citizens of Viterbo and the monastery of San Martino di Monte Viterbo to Capitano and Bishop Matteo. *PL*, 215:1255–56.

37. Fumi, *Codice Diplomatico*, LXXX, p. 56.

38. *PL*, 216:84.

39. The outcome of this dispute is uncertain. Waley suggests that Orvieto backed down and escaped the interdict. Waley, *Mediaeval Orvieto*, p. 16. Maccarrone suggests that Orvieto was indeed placed under interdict and remained so until Innocent visited Orvieto in 1216. During this visit Innocent released Orvieto from an interdict. Maccarrone, "Orvieto e la predicazione della crociata," pp. 62–66. It is hard to believe that Orvieto remained under interdict from 1209 until 1216. The interdict from which Orvieto was released in 1216 was more likely related to its alliance with Narni in 1214, as Narni was itself under interdict and causing considerable problems for Innocent. See Maccarrone, pp. 79ff.

40. To safeguard Bulgarello's oath, a *fideiussor* was appointed until the time that the excommunication was lifted. AVO Cod B 66v–67r.

41. See Maccarrone, "Orvieto e la predicazione della crociata," pp. 70–73, 79–85.

42. Lansing, *Power and Purity*, p. 151.

43. The account of Innocent's visit to Orvieto was recorded on a blank folio at the end of a codex belonging to the cathedral chapter. The text is edited by Maccarrone in "Orvieto e la predicazione della crociata," pp. 8–9.

44. Natalini, *Pietro Parenzo*, pp. 200–201. Also see Maccarrone, "Orvieto e la predicazione della crociata," pp. 140–42.

45. André Vauchez, "Il culto dei 'nuovi' santi in Umbria nei secoli XIII e XIV," in *Ordini mendicanti e società italiana, XIII–XV secolo* (Milan, 1990), pp. 186–93.

46. For a discussion of Pietro's family, see Natalini, *Pietro Parenzo*, pp. 134–50; Lansing, *Power and Purity*, pp. 32–33; Toubert, *Les structures du Latium medieval*, 2:1049.

CHAPTER 6. LOOKING AT OLD THINGS IN A NEW WAY: THE MAKING OF AN EPISCOPAL REGISTER

1. Delumeau, *Arezzo: Espace et sociétés*, 2:1253.

2. Brentano, *A New World in a Small Place*, p. 17.

3. See, for example, Clanchy, *From Memory to Written Record*; *Civiltà comunale: Libro, Scrittura, Documento*, Atti della società Ligure di storia patria, n.s., no. 29 (Genoa, 1989); *Il notariato nella civiltà Toscana*, Studi storici sul notariato italiano, no. 8 (Rome, 1985). For the role of notaries and lawyers in the Italian communes in a later period, see Lauro Martines, *Lawyers and Statecraft in Renaissance Florence* (Princeton, 1968).

4. Among the exceptions to this neglect are the articles in Patrizia Cancian, ed., *La memoria delle chiese: Cancellerie vescovili e culture notarili nell'Italia centro-settentrionale (secoli X–XIII)* (Turin, 1995).

5. Maureen Miller, *The Formation of a Medieval Church*, p. 104.

6. Gian Giacomo Fissore, "Problemi della documentazione vescovile astigiana per i secoli X–XII," in *La memoria delle chiese: Cancellerie vescovili e culture notarili nell'Italia centro-settentrionale (secoli X–XIII)*, ed. Patrizia Cancian (Turin, 1995), p. 43; Nicolaj, "Storie di vescovi e di notai ad Arezzo fra XI e XII secolo," pp. 95–111; Osheim, *An Italian Lordship*, p. 37.

7. The Orvietan notary Prudenzio redacted his documents into a register. In 1221 Guido di Prudenzio copied an agreement between Pope Clement III and Henry VI into a communal register (ASO Titolario Cod A 25v). He stated that he copied the treaty from the *protocollo seu abreviatura domini Prudentii iudicis* (i.e., from his father's notes, presumably in a register).

8. Bresslau, *Manuale di diplomatica per la Germania e l'Italia*, pp. 777–88; Armando Petrucci, "Modello Notarile e testualità," in *Notariato nella civiltà Toscana*, Studi storici sul notariato italiano, no. 8 (Rome, 1985), p. 131.

9. Clanchy, *From Memory to Written Record*, p. 70.

10. Baldwin, *The Government of Philip Augustus*, pp. 412–23.

11. Clanchy, *From Memory to Written Record*, p. 78.

12. See also Pierre Toubert, *Les structures du Latium médiéval*, 1:122–26; Paolo Cammarosano, *Italia medievale. Struttura e geografia delle fonti scritte*, 3d ed. (Rome, 1995), pp. 267–70.

13. Petrucci, "Il notariato italiano," p. 13.

14. Toubert, *Les structures du Latium médiéval*, 1:95–100, 128ff.

15. Clanchy, *From Memory to Written Record*, pp. 156–57.

16. Codice B contains a total of 19 *quaterni*. The entries in *quaterni* 1–6 and 17–19 date to the fourteenth century. *Quaterni* are the individual

gatherings that are bound together to make a register. A *quaternus* contains several parchments folded to make twice the number of folios. The size of *quaterni* 7–16 ranges between 4 parchments (8 folios) and 6 parchments (12 folios).

17. Eighty-two percent of these entries date between 1211 and 1248. Another 15 percent, which date before 1211, were nevertheless copied into the register between 1210 and 1248.

18. For a general description of the composition of Codice B, see Lucio Riccetti, "La cronaca di Ranerio vescovo di Orvieto (1228–1248). Una prima ricognizione," *Rivista di storia della chiesa in Italia* 43:2 (July–December 1989): 480–509.

19. AVO Cod B 100r; Fumi, *Codice Diplomatico*, XLV, pp. 31–32.

20. AVO Cod B 100v; Fumi, *Codice Diplomatico*, XVI, pp. 12–13.

21. AVO Cod B 66v–67r; Fumi, *Codice Diplomatico*, LXXXVII, pp. 62–63.

22. The inventory in the ninth *quaternus* contains a fairly extended description of revenues due from the castle of Parrano. AVO Cod B 77v. Apparently Bishop Giovanni did not possess a copy of prior agreements between the counts of Parrano and the Orvietan bishops from which to make an inventory of revenues due to the bishopric from Parrano.

23. AVO Cod B 70r–v.

24. Revenues due from Mealla and San Gervasio are also recorded in the inventory. AVO Cod B 77r.

25. AVO Cod B 111v; Fumi, *Codice Diplomatico*, XCV, p. 67. Fumi mistakenly dated this entry 1213 instead of 1212.

26. AVO Cod B 102v and 108r; Fumi, *Codice Diplomatico*, LVI, LVII, pp. 37, 38. AVO Cod B 102v records an agreement between Bishop Riccardo and Rainuccio di Dono concerning property in Mealla for which Rainuccio owed an annual payment. This piece of property is mentioned in Giovanni's inventory. AVO Cod B 77v. An agreement between Bishop Riccardo and Farolfo concerning three properties in Mealla that they held in common and for which Farolfo owed annual rents is found in AVO Cod B 108r.

27. AVO Cod B 67v. The *castaldus* was an official in rural communities subject to the bishop's temporal authority. His duties included managing and protecting episcopal property, collecting revenues, and in some cases policing.

28. AVO Cod B 101r, 103r, 107v, 108v; Fumi, *Codice Diplomatico*, XLVIII, LI, LIII, LIX, pp. 33, 34–35, 35–36, 39. Among the revenues granted to the *castaldus* were rents from land held by Tezalo di Rizuto, Donulo di Cognolo, and the sons of Blanco Arcidosso. All of these individuals appear in the above-mentioned documents concerning Corsula.

29. AVO Cod B 104r–v.

30. The earliest document concerning the dispute between San Sepolcro and the bishopric is dated 1210. AVO Cod B 107r. In reality this dispute is the residue of the Orvieto-Sovana dispute, as the monastery claimed to be in the diocese of Sovana, not Orvieto. San Sepolcro continued to offer resistance during the episcopate of Capitano. AVO Cod B 71r. The dispute became especially heated during the episcopate of Ranerio. AVO Cod B 93r, 94v, 98v, 121v. While I am inclined to attribute this *quaternus* to Giovanni, it is possible that Bishop Ranerio compiled it, given his interest in the dispute. His father and brother, Prudenzio and Guido, respectively, were the judges who recorded the testimonies of the 1194 proceeding that was copied into the tenth *quaternus*.

31. Jaeger, *The Envy of Angels*, p. 5.

32. Clanchy, *From Memory to Written Record*, pp. 66–67.

33. AVO Cod B 73r.

34. The context for this comment is the document recording Bishop Ildibrando's agreement with the cathedral canons in 1154. In the margin of the document in which Bishop Ildibrando restored the right of the canons to celebrate the divine office in the cathedral, Ranerio wrote that one of the parish priests was so distraught with the decision that he set fire to the episcopal archive. AVO Cod B 69v; Perali, *La cronaca*, I, p. 5.

35. AVO Cod B 73r.

36. AVO Cod B 78r; Perali, *La cronaca*, V, p. 8.

37. Brentano, *A New World in a Small Place*, p. 42; Osheim, *An Italian Lordship*, p. 31; Dameron, *Episcopal Power and Florentine Society*, p. 64.

38. AVO Cod B 84v; Polock, "Der Prozess," pp. 126–27.

39. AVO Cod B 83r; Polock, "Der Prozess," pp. 114–15.

40. AVO Cod B 83r; Polock, "Der Prozess," pp. 116–17.

41. Osheim, *An Italian Lordship*, pp. 33, 39–40; Dameron, *Episcopal Power and Florentine Society*, p. 65.

42. In 1243 Bishop Ranerio commanded the abbot of Monte Orvieto to gather the *castaldi* and *fideles* of the monastery and make them swear to act in good faith and to report any misdeeds that came to their attention. AVO Cod B 123v. Although this example is from the mid-thirteenth century, it provides a glimpse into the way in which large portions of the episcopal *mensa* must have been administered. It also indicates that the functions of *castaldi* extended beyond the mere administration of property and included policing. Also see AVO Cod B 87v, where Ranerio recorded a list of workers from the castle of Parrano who were denounced to the *castaldus*.

43. In a few places, the compiler wrote that a given person or persons *dicit* or *dicunt* that they held their property in *livello* from the bishop. See entries on AVO Cod B 75v.

44. AVO Cod B 84r; Polock, "Der Prozess," p. 123.

45. AVO Cod B 78r; Perali, *La cronaca*, V, p. 9.

46. See Mario Sensi, "Sinodi e visite pastorali in Umbria nel '200, '300, '400," in *Vescovi e diocesi in Italia dal XIV alla metà del XVI secolo,* ed. Giuseppina de Sandre Gasparini, Antonio Rigon, et al. (Rome, 1990), pp. 339ff.

47. Brentano, *A New World in a Small Place,* p. 119.

48. Maire Vigueur, *Comuni e signori,* pp. 112–13; Robert Brentano, "The Bishops' Books of Città di Castello," *Traditio* 16 (1960): 241–54.

49. For the expansion of Orvieto during these years, see Waley, *Mediaeval Orvieto,* pp. 17ff.

50. On aristocratic violence, see Maire Vigueur, *Comuni e signori,* pp. 88–89.

51. For a good discussion of the development of *popolani* institutions in Orvieto, see Lansing, *Power and Purity,* pp. 54–56. For the development of the council, see Waley, *Mediaeval Orvieto,* pp. 10, 39–40; Carpentier, *Orvieto à la fin du XIIIe siècle,* pp. 40–41.

52. Fumi, *Codice Diplomatico,* CCXIII, p. 144; CCXVI, p. 146.

53. A document of 1207 records the pledge of communal property to the *anterioni,* or chiefs of the regions. Fumi, *Codice Diplomatico,* LXXXIX, p. 55.

54. Consuls of the guilds of merchants, innkeepers, and hosiers represented the commune in a treaty with Narni. Fumi, *Codice Diplomatico,* XCVII, p. 68.

55. In Orvieto they were known as *libri memoriales.* Such registers were common throughout Italy. See Antonella Rovere, "I 'libri iurium' dell'Italia comunale," in *Civiltà Comunale: Libro, Scrittura, Documento,* Atti della società ligure di storia patria, n.s., no. 29 (Genoa, 1989), pp. 157–99. See also Cammarosano, *Italia medievale,* pp. 137–39.

56. Delumeau, *Arezzo: Espace et sociétés,* 2:1135.

57. Luigi Fumi, ed., "Cronaca Potestatum (1194–1322)," *Ephemerides Urbevetanae dal Cod. Vaticano Urbinate 1745,* Rerum Italicarum Scriptores 15:5 (Città di Castello, 1903), p. 142.

58. ASO Titolario Cod A 34r; Fumi, *Codice Diplomatico,* CLIII, p. 100.

59. Carocci, "Le comunalie di Orvieto," pp. 701–28.

CHAPTER 7. HOW THE PAST BECOMES A RUMOR:
THE NOTARIALIZATION OF HISTORICAL CONSCIOUSNESS

1. "Processus Canonizationis B. Ambrosii Massanii," *Acta Sanctorum,* vol. 66 (10 November) (Paris, 1863–1919), pp. 594–95. This example of the influence of written documentation on the spiritual imagination was, perhaps, not uncommon. See Clanchy, *From Memory to Written Record,* p. 188.

2. Although questions concerning the relative power of nobles and the *popolo* are beyond the scope of this study, the implications of this chapter are relevant to the question. Did the *popolo* succeed in establishing political institutions and administrative techniques that effectively represented their interests, or were these institutions simply a facade for personal power exercised by aristocrats through family ties and patronage? For an interesting discussion of how *popolani* institutions shaped the manner in which aristocratic power operated, see Najemy, "The Dialogue of Power in Florentine Politics," pp. 269–87. See also Philip Jones, *The Italian City-State*, pp. 583–630. While Jones acknowledges the importance of the *popolo* in shaping communal government, he argues that power remained essentially private and personal.

3. Several recent studies have demonstrated the importance of historical memory for the legitimization of power. See Patrick J. Geary, *Phantoms of Remembrance: Memory and Oblivion at the End of the First Millennium* (Princeton, 1994); Amy G. Remensnyder, *Remembering Kings Past: Monastic Foundation Legends in Medieval Southern France* (Ithaca, 1995).

4. Bishop Ranerio identified himself as the author by writing "Ran" at the end of each comment. At several points within the margin notes, he identified himself, leaving no doubt concerning the authorship of the comments.

5. Michel Sot, *Gesta Episcoporum, Gesta Abbatum*, Typologie des sources du moyen âge occidental, 37 (Turnhout, 1981), pp. 32ff. The *Liber Pontificalis* is a collection of papal biographies written by clergy close to papal administration. The first *Liber Pontificalis* was written under Pope Boniface (530–532). Subsequent authors added to the original, resulting in a collection of biographies up to 1431 (with a few gaps).

6. Sot, *Gesta Episcoporum*, p. 15.

7. Ibid., pp. 21, 27.

8. Ibid., pp. 16–18. Paul the Deacon, *Gesta episcoporum Mettensium*, ed. Georg Heinrich Pertz, *MGH SS* (Hannover, 1829), 2:261.

9. Sot, *Gesta Episcoporum*, p. 38.

10. Cammarosano, *Italia medievale*, pp. 91–92; Alessandro Pratesi, "Cronache e documenti," in *Fonti medioevali e problematica storiografica*, Istituto Storico Italiano per il Medio Evo (Rome, 1976), 1:337–50; Girolamo Arnaldi, "Cronache con documenti, cronache 'autentiche' e pubblica storiografia," in ibid., 1:351–74.

11. See Toubert, *Latium médiéval*, 1:77–87. For editions of the chronicles of Farfa and San Vincenzo, see Ugo Balzani, ed., *Chronicon Farfense di Gregorio di Catino, Fonti per la storia d'Italia* (Rome, 1903), vols. 33–34; Vincenzo Frederici, ed., *Chronicon Vulturnense del monaco Giovanni, Fonti per la storia d'Italia* (Rome 1925–1938), vols. 58–60.

12. Andrea Tilatii, "Dall'agiografia alla cronaca. Le *inventiones* degli antichi patroni padovanni. Fra interpretazione storiografia e sviluppo di una coscienza civica (secc. XI–XII)," in *La religion civique à l'epoque médiévale e moderne (Chrétienté et Islam)*, ed. André Vauchez (Rome, 1995), pp. 47–64. See also Jean-Charles Picard, *Le souvenir des évêques: Sepultures, listes épiscopales et culte des évêques en Italie du Nord des origins au Xe siècle* (Rome, 1988). For an edition of the translation story, see I. Daniele, "L'Historia inventionis sanctorum Maximi, Iuliani, Felicitatis et Innocentum," in *Atti e memorie dell'Accademia patavina di scienze, lettere ed arti*, n.s. 95 (1982–1983), 183–207.

13. Maureen Miller, *The Bishop's Palace*, pp. 126–56.

14. See Mario Nobili, "Il *Liber de Anulo et Baculo* del vescovo di Lucca Rangerio, Matilda e la lotta per le investiture negli anni 1110–1111," in *Sant'Anselmo vescovo di Lucca (1073–1086) nel quadro delle trasformazioni sociali e della riforma ecclesiastica*, ed. Cinzio Violante, Nuovi Studi Storici, 13 (Rome, 1992), pp. 157–206.

15. Miller, *The Bishop's Palace*, pp. 260–61; *Vita sancti Mauri episcopi Caesenatis et confessoris*, PL, 144:946–52; *Vita sancti Rodulphi episcopi Eugubini*, PL, 144:1008–12.

16. See Edith Pásztor, "La *vita* anonima di Anselmo di Lucca. Una rilettura," in *Sant'Anselmo vescovo di Lucca*, pp. 207–22; Gabriella Severino, "La vita metrica di Anselmo di Lucca scritta da Rangerio. Ideologia e genere letterario," ibid., pp. 223–71; Kathleen G. Cushing, "Events That Led to Sainthood: Sanctity and the Reformers in the Eleventh Century," in *Belief and Culture in the Middle Ages*, ed. Richard Gameson and Henrietta Leyser (Oxford, 2001), pp. 192–96. For the two lives, see *Vita Anselmi episcopi Lucensis*, MGH SS, 12:1–35; *Liber de anulo et baculo MGH LL*, 2:505–33.

17. *Vita sancti Ubaldi episcopi Eugubini*, Acta Sanctorum 15 (May 16), pp. 633, 634; *Vita sancti Brunonis Episcopi*, Acta Sanctorum 30 (July 18), pp. 481, 484; Toubert, *Latium médiéval*, 2:808ff; Anna Benvenuti Papi, "Figure episcopali post-gregoriane: Sant'Ubaldo di Gubbio," in *Pastori di Popolo. Storie e leggende di vescovi e di città nell'Italia medievale* (Florence, 1988), pp. 183–88; Miller, *The Bishop's Palace*, pp. 157–59.

18. Craig B. Fisher, "The Pisan Clergy and an Awakening of Historical Interest in a Medieval Italian Commune," *Studies in Medieval and Renaissance History* 3 (1966): 143–219; Chris Wickham, "The Sense of the Past in Italian Communal Narratives," in *The Perceptions of the Past in Twelfth-Century Europe*, ed. Paul Magdalino (London, 1992), pp. 173–89. For editions of the historical poems, see Edélestand du Méril, ed., *Carmen in Victoriam Pisanorum*, in *Poésies populaires latines du moyen age* (Paris, 1847), pp. 239–51; *De bello Ballearico sive rerum in Majorica Pisanorum*, PL, 163:513–76.

19. Fisher, "The Pisan Clergy," p. 146.

20. Ibid., pp. 213–15.

21. For an introduction to the literature on the chronicle of Genoa and the broader problem of the relation between documents and chronicles, see Alessandro Pratesi, "Cronache e documenti," 1:337–50; Arnaldi, "Cronache con documenti, cronache 'autentiche' e pubblica storiografia," 1:351–74; Arnaldi, "Il notaio-cronista e le cronache cittadine in Italia," pp. 293–309; Ortalli, "Cronache e documentazione," pp. 509–39; Wickham, "The Sense of the Past in Italian Communal Narratives," pp. 173–89. For an edition of the chronicle, see Luigi Tommaso Belgrano, ed., *Annali Genovesi di Caffaro e de' suoi continuatori, Fonti per la storia d'Italia* (Rome, 1890), 11:1–124.

22. See Cammarosano, *Italia medievale*, p. 301.

23. For a discussion of Ranerio's family, see Lucio Riccetti, "La cronaca di Ranerio vescovo di Orvieto," p. 508.

24. AVO Cod B 82v; Polock, *Der Prozess*, p. 114.

25. AVO Cod B 69r, 89r, 103r, 103v, 106r, 107r, 107v, 108v, 111r.

26. AVO Cod B 98v.

27. Fumi, *Codice Diplomatico*, XC, p. 65.

28. AVO Cod B 73r; Perali, *La cronaca*, IV, p. 7.

29. Ibid.

30. AVO Cod B 69v; Perali, *La cronaca*, I, p. 5.

31. AVO Cod B 73r; Perali, *La cronaca*, IV, p. 7.

32. AVO Cod B 69v; Perali, *La cronaca*, II, p. 6.

33. Ibid.

34. AVO Cod B 78r; Perali, *La cronaca*, V, p. 9.

35. AVO Cod B 62r.

36. AVO Cod B 103r; Fumi, *Codice Diplomatico*, LIII, p. 36.

37. As archdeacon, he appears as a witness in various documents (AVO Cod B 64r, 68r, 70r, 98v, 110v). His earliest appearance as archdeacon is dated 1201 (AVO Cod B 98v).

38. *PL*, 215:673, 1086–87.

39. AVO Cod B 96v; Fumi, *Codice Diplomatico*, XCII, pp. 65–66.

40. AVO Cod B 71r, 99r.

41. AVO Cod B 69r, 86v, 87r, 89r.

42. Riccetti, "La cronaca di Ranerio," pp. 499–503. The text is edited by Michele Maccarrone, "La notizia della visita di Innocenzo III ad Orvieto nel cod. M465 della Morgan Library di New York," *Studi su Innocenzo III* (Padua, 1972), pp. 8–9.

43. Maccarrone, "La notizia della visita di Innocenzo III ad Orvieto," p. 8.

44. Waley, *Mediaeval Orvieto*, pp. 18–19.

45. See Fumi, "Cronaca Potestatum (1194–1322)," *Ephemerides*, p. 137, n. 1.

46. AVO Cod B 92v.

47. AVO Cod B 78r; Perali, *La cronaca*, V, p. 9.

CHAPTER 8. THE CONVERGENCE OF ECCLESIASTICAL
REFORM AND COMMUNAL CULTURE

1. *Die Register Innocenz III, Pontifikatsjahr 1198/1199*, 1:401, 600.

2. *PL*, 216:823–24.

3. *COD*, pp. 206ff. Also see Raymonde Foreville, *Latran I, II, III, et Latran IV* (Paris, 1965).

4. For a history of the four Lateran Councils, see Foreville, *Latran I, II, III, et Latran IV*.

5. AVO Cod B 87v; Perali, *La cronaca*, VIII, p. 11.

6. Natalini, *Pietro Parenzo*, p. 159. For *Ad abolendam*, see *PL*, 201:1297ff. For canon 27 of the Third Lateran Council, see *COD*, pp. 222–23.

7. Natalini, *Pietro Parenzo*, pp. 160, 170–71.

8. For the reference in the *Passio*, see ibid., p. 167. For the reference to treason in Innocent's bull, see *Die Register Innocenz III, Pontifikatsjahr, 1199/1200*, 2:5. For a detailed discussion of the relation between Innocent's bull, *Vergentis in senium*, and the *Passio*, see Ovidio Capitani, "Patari in Umbria: Lo 'status quaestionis' nella recente storiografia," *Bollettino dell' Istituto Storico Artistico Orvietano* 39 (1983): 37–54.

9. The case is recorded in AVO Cod B 112v. For a more detailed discussion of this case, along with an introduction to the bibliography on marriage and canon law, see Lansing, *Power and Purity*, pp. 120ff. For other marriage cases brought before Bishop Giovanni, see AVO Cod B 110v.

10. AVO Cod B 110v.

11. Because the usual procedure for judicial ordeals demanded the presence of clerics, this prohibition effectively outlawed the ordeal. See Robert Bartlett, *Trial by Fire and Water: The Medieval Judicial Ordeal* (Oxford, 1986).

12. For an introduction to the vast literature on the care of souls, see Bowsky, "*Populus Sancti Laurentii*," 4:147–91; Michele Maccarrone, "Le costituzioni del IV Concilio Lateranense sui religiosi," in *Nuovi Studi su Innocenzo III* (Rome, 1995), pp. 1–45; Ronzani, "L'organizzazione della cura d'anime nella città di Pisa (secoli XII–XIII)," pp. 35–85; Zelina Zafarana, "Cura pastorale, predicazione, aspetti devozionali nella parrocchia del basso medioevo," in *Da Gregorio VII a Bernardino da Siena* (Florence, 1987), pp. 201–47; Enzo Petrucci, "Vescovi e cura d'anime nel Lazio (sec. XIII–XV)," in *Vescovi e diocesi in Italia dal XIV alla metà del XVI secolo*, ed. Giuseppina

de Sandre Gasparini, Antonio Rigon, et al. (Rome, 1990), pp. 429–546; Giovanni Cherubini, "Parroco, parrocchie e *popolo* nelle campagne centro-settentrionali alla fine del medioevo," in *L'Italia rurale del basso medioevo* (Rome, 1984), pp. 217–45.

13. The synod was an important instrument that helped the bishop provide instruction and pastoral direction to the clergy. See Petrucci, "Vescovi e cura d'anime nel Lazio (sec. XIII–XV)," p. 475.

14. AVO Cod B 138r.

15. AVO Cod B 71r.

16. AVO Cod C 181r. See also Sensi, "Sinodi e visite pastorali in Umbria nel '200, '300, e '400," pp. 346ff.

17. AVO Cod B 71r. For the canons prohibiting the granting of tithes to laypersons, see *COD*, *Lat I*, c. 8, p. 167; *Lat II*, c. 10, p. 175; *Lat III*, c. 14, pp. 194–95.

18. ASO Titolario Cod A 55v; Fumi, *Codice Diplomatico*, CLXXV, p. 114.

19. AVO Cod B 78r; Perali, *La cronaca*, V, p. 8.

20. AVO Cod B 114r–v. Pope Honorius sent this same letter to ecclesiastical provinces throughout Europe. Petrus Pressuti, *Regesta Honorii Papae III* (New York, 1978) 1:377, # 2268. Editions that were sent to the Irish church are found in Edmund Martene and Ursino Durand, *Thesaurus novus anecdotorum* (1717; reprint, New York, 1968), I:875; and Johannes Dominicus Mansi, *Sacrorum Conciliorum Nova et Amplissima Collectio* (1767; reprint, Graz, 1961), 22:1098–1100.

21. AVO Cod B 114r–v. For the responsibility of bishops to discipline the clergy, see *COD*, pp. 212–13, cc. 6, 7.

22. AVO Cod B 114r. Regarding the bishop's responsibility in appointing worthy clergy, see *COD*, pp. 23, 25; cc. 26, 30, 31.

23. *COD*, pp. 216–17. See also Michele Maccarrone, "Le constituzioni del IV Concilio Lateranense sui Religiosi," pp. 19ff.

24. AVO Cod B 114r.

25. Ibid. See also *COD*, pp. 209–11, c. 3.

26. AVO Cod B 114r. For the canons concerning the comportment of the clergy, see *COD*, pp. 218–19, 225, cc. 14–17, 30. For the restriction on benefices with care of souls, see *COD*, p. 224, c. 29.

27. AVO Cod B 114r.

28. Ibid.

29. The passages quoted throughout this section are found in AVO Cod B 78r; Perali, *La cronaca*, V, pp. 8–9.

30. Ranerio did not distinguish between those items he found in the chapel and those he found in the episcopal palace. It seems unlikely that he found a lame mule in the chapel.

31. For an interesting parallel, see comments on the Reatine bishop Rainaldo, in Brentano, *A New World in a Small Place*, p. 4.

32. AVO Cod B 62r.

33. AVO Cod B 75r.

34. See Lucio Riccetti, *La città costruita*.

35. See Tabacco, "Vescovi e monasteri," pp. 105–23; Cinzio Violante, "Il monachesimo cluniacense di fronte al mondo politico ed ecclesiastico (secoli X e XI)," in *Spiritualità Cluniacense* (Todi, 1960), pp. 153–242; Ronzani, "L'organizzazione della cura d'anime nella città di Pisa (secoli XII–XIII)," pp. 35–85.

36. AVO Cod B 98v.

37. AVO Cod B 94v.

38. AVO Cod B 93r.

39. AVO Cod B 141r.

40. AVO Cod B 123r–v.

41. AVO Cod B 125r.

42. AVO Cod B 127r.

43. AVO Cod B 137r.

44. AVO Cod B 130v. There is no indication of the nature of Fordivoglia's grievance against the monastery.

45. Ibid.

46. These developments seem to have been fairly typical for central Italy. See Maire Vigueur, *Comuni e signori*, pp. 30–31.

47. AVO Cod B 88r; Fumi, *Codice Diplomatico*, LXXI, p. 49.

48. Osheim, *An Italian Lordship*, pp. 83–84.

49. AVO Cod B 129r.

50. AVO Cod B 133r.

51. AVO Cod B 98v.

52. AVO Cod B 97r, 98r, 98v, 122v, 131r, 133r, 136v, 138v.

53. AVO Cod B 89r, 94v, 123r, 125r, 131r, 133r, 136v, 137v, 138r.

54. For a remarkably close parallel to these developments, see Brentano, *A New World in a Small Place*, pp. 86–90.

55. San Giovanni of Monte Paglano, Santa Maria of Ficulle, San Donato, Morrano, San Giovanni in Silvolis, Santa Felice, Santa Maria of Rasa, Mimiano, Santa Maria of Stiolo, San Fortunato of Porano, Montelungo.

56. AVO Cod B 73rff, 72r–v, 78v.

57. Ranerio's inventory concentrated on episcopal revenues in the cathedral district (the one remaining area in the city where the bishop held extensive revenues), the castle of Parrano, and Bolsena. AVO Cod B 56vff.

58. AVO Cod B 117r.

59. AVO Cod B 123v.

60. AVO Cod B 78r.

61. ACO Codice di San Costanzo 8r. See also 9r, 10r, 11r.

62. Quoted in John F. McGovern, "Private Property and Individual Rights in the Commentaries of the Jurists, A.D. 1200–1550," in *In Iure Veritas: Studies in Canon Law in Memory of Schafer Williams*, ed. Steven B. Bowman and Blanche E. Cody (Cincinnati, 1991), p. 138.

63. Ibid.

64. ACO Codice di San Costanzo 12v.

65. Natalini, "Il capitolo," p. 184.

66. AVO Cod B 83r, 85v; Perali, *La cronaca*, VI, p. 10; VII, p. 10.

67. See Waley, *Mediaeval Orvieto*, pp. 27–32.

68. Waley, *The Papal State*, pp. 129, 135–40; Carocci, "Barone e podestà," p. 859.

69. Fumi, *Codice Diplomatico*, CXCVI, pp. 130–31.

70. Fumi, *Codice Diplomatico*, CCII, p. 138.

71. Waley, *Mediaeval Orvieto*, p. 28.

72. Fumi, *Cronaca Potestatum*, p. 149.

73. Carocci, "Barone e podestà," p. 853.

74. Lansing, *Power and Purity*, pp. 57–59.

75. For the events surrounding the deteriorating relation between Gregory and Frederick, see David Abulafia, *Frederick II: A Medieval Emperor* (Oxford, 1988), pp. 290ff.

76. See Waley, *Mediaeval Orvieto*, p. 32

77. Fumi, "Cronaca Potestatum (1194–1322)," *Ephemerides*, p. 150.

78. "Processus Canonizationis B. Ambrosii Massanii," p. 567. See also Lansing, *Power and Purity*, pp. 129ff.

79. "Processus Canonizationis B. Ambrosii Massanii," p. 574.

80. Ibid.

81. Fumi, *Codice Diplomatico*, CCII, pp. 135–36.

82. It is unclear where Costantino received his training. See Cesare Cenci, "Il commento al Vangelo di S. Luca di Fr. Costantino da Orvieto, O.P., fonte di S. Bernardino da Siena," *Archivium Franciscanum Historicum* (January–June 1981): 103–45.

83. Quoted in Cenci, "Il commento al Vangelo di S. Luca di Fr. Costantino da Orvieto, O.P., fonte di S. Bernardino da Siena," p. 113.

84. Ibid., p. 137.

85. The second *quaternus* compiled by Costantino is found in AVO Cod C 171v–183r. He began a third *quaternus*, which he left unfinished. AVO Cod C 125v–128r.

86. AVO Cod C 171v. Eleven years earlier, Ranerio appealed to the commune for help in defending San Vito against the counts of Rota Castello.

87. AVO Cod C 181r. The abbot of Monte Amiata claimed that the church belonged to his monastery and tried to withdraw the church from the

authority of the Orvietan bishop. Several months after Costantino's visit, the abbot of Monte Amiata gave the prior of San Gregorio a physical beating for submitting to the Orvietan bishop. AVO Cod C 182v.

88. AVO Cod C 182v.

89. By the early fourteenth century, vicars were omnipresent in Orvietan episcopal administration, as the bishops were increasingly absent on papal business. For a discussion of vicars, see Brentano, *A New World in a Small Place*, pp. 137ff; Osheim, *An Italian Lordship*, pp. 43–44.

90. Along these same lines, Cinzio Violante has commented that spirituality and institutions are too often separated, as if the history of Christianity and the history of the church were two distinct topics. Violante, "Sistemi organizzativi della cura d'anime in Italia tra Medioevo e Rinascimento. Discorso introduttivo," in *Pievi e parrocchie in Italia nel basso medioevo (sec. XIII–XV)*, AH: del VI convegno di storia della chiesa in Italia (Rome, 1984), p. 10.

CONCLUSION

1. "Processus Canonizationis B. Ambrosii Massanii," p. 574.

2. See the testimony of Fra Tobias. Ibid., p. 573.

3. See *COD, Lat I*, c. 8, p. 167; *Lat II*, c. 10, 25, pp. 175, 178; *Lat III*, c. 14, pp. 194–95.

4. For this transformation of the church's attitude toward violence, see Maurice Keen, *Chivalry* (New Haven, 1984), pp. 44ff. Also see Barbara Rosenwein, "Feudal War and Monastic Peace: Cluniac Liturgy as Ritual Aggression," *Viator* 2 (1971): 145–52.

5. See Najemy, "The Dialogue of Power in Florentine Politics."

APPENDIX

1. See Natalini, *Pietro Parenzo*, pp. 64–75.

2. See AVO Cod B 102v (also Fumi, *Codice Diplomatico*, LVI, p. 37). For other references to Maestro Giovanni, see AVO Cod B 81v, 101r (Fumi, LI, p. 35); 103r (Fumi, L, LIII, pp. 34, 36); 107r (Fumi, XLIX, p. 34); 108r (Fumi, LII, p. 35); 108v (Fumi, XLVIII, p. 33).

3. Ferdinando Ughelli, *Italia Sacra*, 10 vols. (Venice, 1717–1722) 1:1468.

4. F. Marabottini, *Cathologus Episcoporum Urbisveteris* (Rome, 1650), p. 6.

5. AVO Cod B 73r. See also Perali, *La cronaca*, III, p. 6.

6. AVO Cod B 78r.

WORKS CITED

MANUSCRIPT SOURCES

Archivio Vescovile di Orvieto
  Codice A
  Codice B
  Codice C

Archivio Capitolare di Orvieto
  Codice di San Costanzo

Archivio di Stato di Orvieto
  Istrumentari 865: Titolario A

PUBLISHED SOURCES

Primary Sources

Balzani, Ugo, ed. *Chronicon Farfense di Gregorio di Catino.* Vols. 33–34, *Fonti per la storia d'Italia.* Rome, 1903.
Belgrano, Luigi Tommaso, ed. *Annali Genovesi di Caffaro e de' suoi continuatori.* Vol. 11, *Fonti per la storia d'Italia.* Rome, 1890.
Boretius, Alfred, ed. *Capitularia Regum Francorum. Monumenta Germaniae Historica. Legum Sectio II.* 2 Vols. 1888. Reprint, Hannover, 1984.
Boso. "Vita Hadriani IV." *Le Liber Pontificalis.* Ed. Louis Duchesne and Cyrille Vogel. Bibliothèque des Ecoles française d'Athènes et de Rome, ser. 2. Vol. 2. Paris, 1955.
———. "Vita Alexandri III." *Le Liber Pontificalis.* Ed. Louis Duchesne and Cyrille Vogel. Bibliothèque des Ecoles française d'Athènes et de Rome, ser. 2. Vol. 2. Paris, 1955.

Bluhme, Friedrich, ed. *Leges Langobardorum. Monumenta Germaniae Historica. Leges.* Vol. 4. 1868. Reprint, Stuttgart, 1984.

Carmen in Victoriam Pisanorum. Ed. Edélestand du Méril. In *Poésies populaires latines du moyen age.* Paris, 1847.

Ciacci, Gaspero, ed. *Gli Aldobrandeschi nella storia e nella divina commedia.* 2 vols. Rome, 1935.

Conciliorum oecumenicorum decreta. Ed. Giuseppe Alberigo. 3d ed. Bologna, 1973.

Daniele, I. "L'Historia inventionis sanctorum Maximi, Iuliani, Felicitatis et Innocentum." *Atti e memorie dell'Accademia patavina di scienze, lettere ed arti,* n.s. 95 (1982–1983): 183–207.

De bello Ballearico sive rerum in Majorica Pisanorum. Ed. Jacques-Paul Migne. Vol. 163, *Patrologia cursus completus, Series Latina.* Paris, 1844–1891.

Drew, Katherine Fischer, trans. *The Lombard Laws.* Philadelphia, 1973.

Fabre, Paul, and Louis Duchesne, eds. *Le Liber Censuum de l'Eglise romaine.* Bibliothèque des Ecoles française d'Athènes et de Rome, ser. 2. 3 vols. Paris, 1889–1952.

Frederici, Vincenzo, ed. *Chronicon Vulturnense del monaco Giovanni.* Vols. 58–60, *Fonti per la storia d'Italia.* Rome, 1925–1938.

Fumi, Luigi, ed. *Codice Diplomatico della città d'Orvieto: Documenti e regesti dal secolo XI al XV e la carta del popolo.* Documenti di Storia Italiana. Vol. 8. Florence, 1884.

———, ed. *Ephemerides Urbevetanae dal Cod.Vaticano Urbinate 1745. Rerum Italicarum Scriptores.* Ed. Ludovico A. Muratori. Vol. 15, part 5. Città di Castello, 1903.

Hageneder, Othmar, Anton Haidacher, et al., eds. *Die Register Innocenz III, Pontifikatsjahr 1198/1199.* 6 vols. Vienna, 1964.

Jaffe, Philip, and L. Loewenfeld, eds. *Regesta pontificum Romanorum.* 2 vols. Leipzig, 1888.

Kehr, Paul, ed. *Karoli III. Diplomata. Monumenta Germaniae Historica. Diplomata Regum Germaniae Ex Stirpe Karolinorum.* Vol. 2. Berlin, 1937.

Liber de anulo et baculo. Vol. 2, *Monumenta Germaniae Historica, Libelli de lite imperatorum et pontificum.* Hannover, 1891–1897.

Loewenfeld, S., ed. *Epistolae Pontificium Romanorum ineditae.* Leipzig, 1885.

Maccarrone, Michele. "La notizia della visita di Innocenzo III ad Orvieto nel cod. M465 della Morgan Library di New York." *Studi su Innocenzo III.* Padua, 1972.

Manaresi, Cesare, ed. *I placiti del 'regnum Italiae'.* Vols. 92, 96, 97, *Fonti per la storia d'Italia.* Rome, 1955–1960.

Mansi, Johannes Dominicus. *Sacrorum Conciliorum Nova et Amplissima Collectio.* 53 vols. 1767. Reprint, Graz, 1961.

Martène, Edmund, and Ursino Durand, eds. *Thesaurus novus anecdotorum.* 5 vols. 1717. Reprint, New York, 1968.

Monumenta Germaniae Historica. Constitutiones et Acta Publica Imperatorum et Regum. Ed. Ludwig Weiland. 2 vols. (1893; reprint, Hannover, 1999).

Mühlbacher, Engelbert, ed. *Die Urkunden Pippins, Karlmanns und Karls des Grossen. Monumenta Germaniae Historica. Diplomata Karolinorum.* Vol. 1. 1906. Reprint, Munich, 1991.

Natalini, Vincenzo, ed. *San Pietro Parenzo. La leggenda scritta dal Maestro Giovanni canonico d'Orvieto.* Rome, 1936.

Patrologia cursus completus, Series Latina. Ed. Jacques-Paul Migne. Paris, 1844–1891. Vols. 201, 214–216.

Paul the Deacon. *Gesta episcoporum Mettensium.* Ed. Georg Heinrich Pertz. Vol. 2, *Monumenta Germaniae Historica. Scriptores.* Hannover, 1829.

Perali, Pericle, ed. *La cronaca del vescovado orvietano 1029–1239 scritta dal vescovo Ranerio: cronachette, notizie e inventari.* Orvieto, 1907.

Polock, Marlene, ed. "Der Prozess von 1194 zwischen Orvieto und Sovana um das Val di Lago." *Quellen und Forschungen aus Italienischen Archiven und Bibliotheken* 70 (1990): 46–150.

Pressuti, Petrus. *Regesta Honorii Papae III.* 2 vols. New York, 1978.

"Processus Canonizationis B. Ambrosii Massanii." Vol. 66 (10 November), *Acta Sanctorum.* Paris, 1863–1919.

Schiaparelli, Luigi, ed. *I Diplomi di Berengario I.* Vol. 35, *Fonti per la storia d'Italia.* Rome, 1903.

Ughelli, Ferdinando. *Italia Sacra.* Venice, 1717–1722.

Vita sancti Brunonis Episcopi. Vol. 30 (18 July), *Acta Sanctorum.* Paris, 1863–1919.

Vita sancti Mauri episcopi Caesenatis et confessoris. Ed. Jacques-Paul Migne. Vol. 144, *Patrologia cursus completus, Series Latina.* Paris, 1844–1891.

Vita sancti Rodulphi episcopi Eugubini. Ed. Jacques-Paul Migne. Vol. 144, *Patrologia cursus completus, Series Latina.* Paris, 1844–1891.

Vita sancti Ubaldi episcopi Eugubini. Vol. 15 (16 May), *Acta Sanctorum.* Paris, 1863–1919.

Wanner, Konrad, ed. *Die Urkunden Ludwigs II. Monumenta Germaniae Historica. Diplomata Karolinorum.* Vol. 4. Munich, 1994.

Secondary Sources

Abulafia, David. *Frederick II: A Medieval Emperor.* Oxford, 1988.

Amelotti, Mario, and Giorgio Costamagna. *Alle origini del notariato italiano.* Studi storici sul notariato italiano. Rome, 1975.

Arnaldi, Girolami. "Il notaio-cronista e le cronache cittadine in Italia." In *La storia del diritto nel quadro delle scienze storiche*. Atti del I congresso internazionale della Società italiana di storia del diritto. Florence, 1966.

———. "Cronache con documenti, cronache 'autentiche' e pubblica storiografia." In *Fonti medioevali e problematica storiografica*. Istituto Storico Italiano per il Medio Evo. 2 vols. Rome, 1976.

Baldwin, John W. *The Government of Philip Augustus: Foundations of French Royal Power in the Middle Ages*. Berkeley, 1986.

Bartlett, Robert. *Trial by Fire and Water: The Medieval Judicial Ordeal*. Oxford, 1986.

Bertolini, Ottorino. "I vescovi del 'regnum Langobardorum' al tempo dei Carolingi." In *Vescovi e diocesi in Italia nel medioevo (sec. IX–XIII)*. Atti del II Convegno di storia della Chiesa in Italia. Padua, 1964.

Bougard, François. *La justice dans le royaume d'Italie de la fin du VIIIe siècle au début du XIe siècle*. Rome, 1995.

Bourdieu, Pierre. *Outline of a Theory of Practice*. Trans. Richard Nice. Cambridge, 1977.

———, and Loïc J. D. Wacquat. *An Invitation to Reflexive Sociology*. Chicago, 1992.

Bowsky, William M. "*Populus Sancti Laurentii*: Care of Souls, a Parish, and a Priest." In *Miscellanea Domenico Maffei*. Ed. Antonio Garcia y Garcia and Peter Weimar. Goldbach, 1995. Vol. 4:147–91.

Boyd, Catherine. *Tithes and Parishes in Medieval Italy: The Historical Roots of a Modern Problem*. Ithaca, 1952.

Brentano, Robert. "The Bishops' Books of Città di Castello." *Traditio* 16 (1960): 241–54.

———. *Two Churches: England and Italy in the Thirteenth Century*. 2d ed. Berkeley, 1988.

———. *A New World in a Small Place: Church and Religion in the Diocese of Rieti, 1188–1378*. Berkeley, 1994.

Bresslau, Harry. *Manuale di diplomatica per la Germania e l'Italia*. Trans. Anna Maria Voci-Roth. Rome, 1998.

Brezzi, Paolo. *Roma e l'impero medioevale, 774–1252*. Bologna, 1947.

Brundage, James A. *Medieval Canon Law*. London, 1995.

Buccolini, Geralberto. "Serie critica dei Vescovi di Bolsena e di Orvieto." *Bollettino della regia Deputazione di Storia patria per l'Umbria* 33 (1941): 5–130.

Cammarosano, Paolo. *La Familia dei Berardenghi: Contributo alla storia della società senese nei secoli XI–XIII*. Spoleto, 1974.

———. *Italia medievale. Struttura e geografia delle fonti scritte*. 3d ed. Rome, 1995.

Cancian, Patrizia, ed. *La memoria delle chiese: Cancellerie vescovili e culture notarili nell'Italia centro-settentrionale (secoli X–XIII)*. Turin, 1995.

Capitani, Ovidio. "Esiste un 'età gregoriana'?" *Rivista di storia e letteratura e religiosa* I (1965): 454–81.

———. "Patari in Umbria: Lo 'status quaestionis' nella recente storiografia." *Bollettino dell' Istituto Storico Artistico Orvietano*. 39 (1983): 37–54.

Carocci, Sandro. "Le *comunalie* di Orvieto fra la fine del XII e la metà del XIV secolo." *Mélanges de l'École française de Rome, moyen âge–temps modernes* 99 (1987): 701–28.

———. "Barone e podestà. L'aristocrazia Romana e gli uffici comunali nel due-trecento." In *I podestà dell'Italia comunale*, Parte I: *Reclutamento e circolazione degli ufficiali forestieri (fine XII sec.–metà XIV sec.)*. Ed. Jean-Claude Maire Vigueur. Rome, 2000.

Carpentier, Elisabeth. *Une ville devant la peste. Orvieto et la peste noire de 1348*. Paris, 1962.

———. *Orvieto à la fin du XIIIe siècle: Ville et campagne dans le cadastre de 1292*. Paris, 1986.

Castagnetti, Andrea. "Il peso delle istituzioni: Strutture ecclesiastiche e mondo rurale. L'esempio Veronese." In *Le campagne italiane prima e dopo il mille. Una società in trasformazione*. Ed. Bruno Andreolli, Vito Fumagalli, and Massimo Montanari. Bologna, 1985.

———. "Il potere sui contadini. Dalla signoria fondiaria alla signoria territoriale. Comunità rurali e comuni cittadini." In *Le campagne italiane prima e dopo il mille. Una società in trasformazione*. Ed. Bruno Andreolli, Vito Fumagalli, and Massimo Montanari. Bologna, 1985.

Cenci, Cesare. "Il commento al Vangelo di S. Luca di Fr. Costantino da Orvieto, O.P., fonte di S. Bernardino da Siena." *Archivium Franciscanum Historicum* (January–June 1981): 103–45.

Cherubini, Giovanni. "Parroco, parrocchie e popolo nelle campagne centro-settentrionali alla fine del medioevo." In *L'Italia rurale del basso medioevo*. Rome, 1984.

Cherubini, Wanda. "Movimenti Patarinici in Orvieto." *Bollettino dell' Istituto Storico Artistico Orvietano* 15 (1959): 3–42.

Chittolini, Giorgio, and Giovanni Miccoli, eds. *La Chiesa e il potere politico dal medioevo all'età contemporanea*. Vol. 9, *Storia d'Italia, Annali*. Turin, 1986.

Civiltà comunale: Libro, Scrittura, Documento. Atti della società Ligure di storia patria, n. s., no. 29. Genoa, 1989.

Clanchy, M. T. *From Memory to Written Record: England 1066–1307*. 2d ed. Oxford, 1993.

Constable, Giles. *The Reformation of the Twelfth Century.* Cambridge, 1996.

Cortese, Ennio. *Il diritto nella storia medievale.* 2 vols. Rome, 1995.

Crosby, Everett. *Bishop and Chapter in Twelfth-Century England: A Study of the Mensa Episcopalis.* Cambridge, 1994.

Cushing, Kathleen G. "Events That Led to Sainthood: Sanctity and the Reformers in the Eleventh Century." In *Belief and Culture in the Middle Ages.* Ed. Richard Gameson and Henrietta Leyser. Oxford, 2001.

Dameron, George. *Episcopal Power and Florentine Society, 1000–1320.* Cambridge, Mass., 1991.

Delumeau, Jean Pierre. *Arezzo: Espace et sociétés, 715–1230. Recherches sur Arezzo et son contado du VIIIe au début du XIIIe siècle.* 2 vols. Rome, 1996.

Duby, Georges. "Les chanoines reguliers et la vie économique des XIe et XIIe siècles." In *La vita comune del clero nei secoli XI e XII.* Atti della Settimana di studio: Mendola, settembre 1959. Milan, 1962.

Egger, Carlo. "Le regole seguite dai canonici regolari nei secoli XI e XII." In *La vita comune del clero nei secoli XI e XII.* Atti della Settimana di studio: Mendola, settembre 1959. Milan, 1962.

Fichtenau, Heinrich. *Heretics and Scholars in the High Middle Ages, 1000–1200.* Trans. Denise A. Kaiser. University Park, Pa., 1998.

Fisher, Craig B. "The Pisan Clergy and an Awakening of Historical Interest in a Medieval Italian Commune." *Studies in Medieval and Renaissance History* 3 (1966): 143–219.

Fissore, Gian Giacomo. "Problemi della documentazione vescovile astigiana per i secoli X–XII." *La memoria delle chiese: Cancellerie vescovili e culture notarili nell'Italia centro-settentrionale (secoli X–XIII).* Ed. Patrizia Cancian. Turin, 1995.

Fonseca, Cosimo Damiano. "Canoniche regolari, capitoli cattedrali e 'cura animarum'." *Pievi e parrocchie in Italia nel basso medioevo sec. XIII–XV.* Vol. 1:257–78. Rome, 1984.

———. " 'Ecclesia Matrix' e 'conventus civium': L'ideologia della cattedrale nell'età comunale." In *La pace di Costanza, 1183.* Bologna, 1984.

Foreville, Raymonde. *Latran I, II, III, et Latran IV.* Paris, 1965.

Fuhrman, Horst. *Germany in the High Middle Ages, c. 1050–1200.* Trans. Timothy Reuter. Cambridge, 1986.

Fumi, Luigi. "L'assedio di Enrico VI di Svevia Re de' Romani contro la Città di Orvieto (1186)." *Bollettino di Storia Patria* 12 (n.d.): 203–16.

Geary, Patrick J. *Phantoms of Remembrance: Memory and Oblivion at the End of the First Millennium.* Princeton, 1994.

Gilchrist, John. "Was There a Gregorian Reform Movement in the Eleventh Century?" *Canadian Catholic Historical Association: Study Sessions* 37 (1970): 1–10.

Hubert, Étienne. *Espace urban et habitat à Rome du Xe siècle à la fin du XIIIe siècle*. Rome, 1990.

Jaeger, C. Stephen. *The Envy of Angels: Cathedral Schools and Social Ideals in Medieval Europe, 950–1200*. Philadelphia, 1994.

Jones, Philip. *The Italian City-State: From Commune to Signoria*. Oxford, 1977.

Keen, Maurice. *Chivalry*. New Haven, 1984.

Keller, Hagen. "Der Gerichtsort in oberitalienischen und toskanischen Städten. Untersuchungen zur Stellung der Stadt im Herrschaftssystem des Regnum Italicum vom 9. bis 11. Jahrhundert." *Quellen und Forschungen aus italienischen Archiven und Bibliotheken* 49 (1969): 1–72.

———. "I placiti nella storiografia degli ultimi cento anni." *Fonti medioevali e problematica storiografica*. Atti del congresso internazionale tenuto in occasione del 90 anniversario della fondazione dell' istituto storico italiano. Rome, 1976.

———. *Signori e Vassali Nell'Italia Delle Città (secoli IX–XII)*. Trans. Andrea Piazza. Turin, 1995.

Koenig, John. *Il popolo dell'Italia del Nord nel XIII secolo*. Bologna, 1986.

Kurze, Wilhelm. "I momenti principali della storia di S. Salvatore e Monte Amiata." In *L'Amiata nel medioevo*. Ed. Mario Ascheri and Wilhelm Kurze. Rome, 1989.

Lambert, Malcolm. *Medieval Heresy: Popular Movements from the Gregorian Reform to the Reformation*. 2nd ed. Oxford, 1992.

———. *The Cathars*. Oxford, 1998.

Lansing, Carol. *Power and Purity: Cathar Heresy in Medieval Italy*. Oxford, 1997.

Lawrence, C. H. *Medieval Monasticism: Forms of Religious Life in Western Europe in the Middle Ages*. New York, 1984.

Leclercq, Jean. "La spiritualité des chanoines réguliers." In *La vita comune del clero nei secoli XI e XII*. Atti della Settimana di studio: Mendola, settembre 1959. Milan, 1962.

Leicht, P. S. "Influenze di scuola in documenti toscani dei secoli XI–XII." *Bullettino Senese di Storia Patria* 16 (1909): 174–90.

Maccarrone, Michele. "I papi del secolo XII e la vita comune e regolare del clero." In *La vita comune del clero nei secoli XI e XII*. Atti della Settimana di studio: Mendola, settembre 1959. Milan, 1962.

———. "Orvieto e la predicazione della crociata." In *Studi su Innocenzo III*. Padua, 1972.

———. "Le constituzioni del IV Concilio Lateranense sui Religiosi." In *Nuovi Studi su Innocenzo III*. Rome, 1995.

Maire Vigueur, Jean-Claude. *Comuni e signorie in Umbria, Marche, e Lazio*. Turin, 1987.

———. "Nello stato della chiesa: Da una pluralità di circuiti al trionfo del guelfismo." In *I podestà dell'Italia comunale*, Parte I: *Reclutamento e circolazione degli ufficiali forestieri (fine XII sec.–metà XIV sec.)*. Ed. Jean-Claude Maire Vigueur. Rome, 2000.

Marabottini, F. *Cathologus Episcoporum Urbisveteris*. Rome, 1650.

Marchal, Guy P. "De la mémoire communicative à la mémoire culturelle. La passé dans les témoignages d'Arezzo et de Sienne (1177–1180)." *Annales* 56:3 (May–June 2001): 563–89.

Martines, Lauro. *Lawyers and Statecraft in Renaissance Florence*. Princeton, 1968.

McGovern, John F. "Private Property and Individual Rights in the Commentaries of the Jurists, A.D. 1200–1550." In *In Iure Veritas: Studies in Canon Law in Memory of Schafer Williams*. Ed. Steven B. Bowman and Blanche E. Cody. Cincinnati, 1991.

McKitterick, Rosamond. *The Frankish Kingdoms under the Carolingians, 751–987*. New York, 1983.

Miccoli, Giovanni. "Pier Damiani e la vita comune del clero." In *La vita comune del clero nei secoli XI e XII*. Atti della Settimana di studio: Mendola, settembre 1959. Milan 1962.

Miller, Maureen. *The Formation of a Medieval Church: Ecclesiastical Change in Verona, 950–1150*. Ithaca, 1993.

———. *The Bishop's Palace: Architecture and Authority in Medieval Italy*. Ithaca, 2000.

Milo, Yoram. "From Imperial Hegemony to the Commune: Reform in Pistoia's Cathedral Chapter and its Political Impact." In *Istituzioni ecclesiastiche della toscana medioevale*. Lecce, 1980.

Mochi Onory, S. *Ricerche sui poteri civili dei vescovi nelle città umbre durante l'alto medioevo*. Bologna, 1930.

Mor, Carlo Guido, and Heinrich Schmidinger, eds. *I poteri temporali dei vescovi in Italia e in Germania*. Bologna, 1979.

Morandi, Ubaldo. "Il notaio all'origine del comune medioevale senese," In *Il notariato nella civiltà Toscana*. Studi storici sul notariato italiano, no. 8. Rome, 1985.

Muir, Edward. "The Sources of Civil Society in Italy." *Journal of Interdisciplinary History* 29:3 (Winter 1999): 379–406.

Najemy, John M. "The Dialogue of Power in Florentine Politics." In *City States in Classical Antiquity and Medieval Italy*. Ed. Anthony Molho, Kurt Raaflaub, and Julia Emlen. Ann Arbor, 1991.

Natalini, Vincenzo. "Il capitolo del duomo di Orvieto ed i suoi statuti inediti 1260–1458." *Rivista di storia della chiesa in Italia* 9 (1955): 177–232.

Nelson, Janet. "Literacy in Carolingian Government." In *The Uses of Literacy in Early Medieval Europe.* Ed. Rosamond McKitterick. Cambridge, 1990.

Nicolaj, Giovanna. "Storie di vescovi e di notai ad Arezzo fra XI e XII secolo." In *La memoria delle chiese: Cancellerie vescovili e culture notarili nell'Italia centro-settentrionale (secoli X–XIII).* Ed. Patrizia Cancian. Turin, 1995.

Nobili, Mario. "Il *Liber de Anulo et Baculo* del vescovo di Lucca Rangerio, Matilda e la lotta per le investiture negli anni 1110–1111." In *Sant'Anselmo vescovo di Lucca (1073–1086) nel quadro delle trasformazioni sociali e della riforma ecclesiastica.* Ed. Cinzio Violante. Nuovo Studi Storici, 13. Rome, 1992.

Noble, Thomas F. X. *The Republic of St. Peter: The Birth of the Papal State, 680–825.* Philadelphia, 1984.

Il notariato nella civiltà Toscana. Studi storici sul notariato italiano, no. 8. Rome, 1985.

Ortalli, Gherardo. "Cronache e documentazione." In *Civiltà comunale: Libro, scrittura, documento.* Atti della società ligure di storia patria. Genoa, 1988.

Osheim, Duane. *An Italian Lordship: The Bishopric of Lucca in the Late Middle Ages.* Berkeley, 1977.

Paolini, Lorenzo. "Italian Catharism and Written Culture." In *Heresy and Literacy, 1000–1350.* Ed. Peter Biller and Anne Hudson. Cambridge, 1994.

Papi, Anna Benvenuti. "Figure episcopali post-gregoriane: Sant'Ubaldo di Gubbio." In *Pastori di Popolo. Storie e leggende di vescovi e di città nell'Italia medievale.* Florence, 1988.

Partner, Peter. *The Lands of St. Peter: The Papal State in the Middle Ages and the Early Renaissance.* London, 1972.

Pásztor, Edith. "La *vita* anonima di Anselmo di Lucca. Una rilettura." In *Sant'Anselmo vescovo di Lucca (1073–1086) nel quadro delle trasformazioni sociali e della riforma ecclesiastica.* Ed. Cinzio Violante. Rome, 1992.

Petersohn, Jürgen. "Kaiser, Papst und Praefectura Urbis zwischen Alexander III. und Innocenz III. Probleme der Besetzung und Chronologie der römischen Präfektur im letzten Viertel des 12 Jahrhunderts." *Quellen und Forschungen aus italienischen Archiven und Bibliotheken* 60 (1980): 157–88.

Petrucci, Armando. "Il notariato italiano dalle origini al secolo XIV." In *Notarii. Documenti per la storia del notariato italiano.* Milan, 1958.

———. "Modello Notarile e testualità." In *Notariato nella civiltà Toscana. Studi storici sul notariato italiano*, no. 8. Rome, 1985.

Petrucci, Enzo. "Attraverso I poteri civili dei vescovi nel medioevo. A propositi degli atti di un recente convengo." *Rivista di storia della chiesa in Italia* 32:2 (1980): 518–45.

———. "Vescovi e cura d'anime nel Lazio sec. XIII–XV." In *Vescovi e diocesi in Italia dal XIV alla metà del XVI secolo*. Ed. Giuseppina de Sandre Gasparini, Antonio Rigon, Francesco Trolese, and Gian Maria Varanini. Rome, 1990.

Picard, Jean-Charles. *Le souvenir des évêques: Sepultures, listes épiscopales et culte des évêques en Italie du Nord des origins au Xe siècle*. Rome, 1988.

Poly, J. P., and E. Bournazel. *The Feudal Transformation, 900–1200*. Trans. Caroline Higgit. London, 1991.

Pratesi, Alessandro. "Cronache e documenti." In *Fonti medioevali e problematica storiografica*. Istituto Storico Italiano per il Medio Evo. 2 vols. Rome, 1976.

Racine, Pierre. "Evêque et cité dans la royaume d'Italie: Aux origines des comunes italiennes." *Cahiers de Civilisation Médiévale* 27:1–2 (1984): 129–39.

———. "Città e contado in Emilia e Lombardia nel secolo XI." In *L'evoluzione delle città italiane nell'XI secolo*. Ed. Renato Bordone and Jörg Jarnut. Bologna, 1988.

Radding, Charles. *The Origins of Medieval Jurisprudence: Pavia and Bologna, 850–1150*. New Haven, 1988.

Remensnyder, Amy G. "Pollution, Purity, and Peace: An Aspect of Social Reform between the Late Tenth Century and 1076." In *The Peace of God: Social Violence and Religious Response in France around the Year 1000*. Ed. Thomas Head and Richard Landes. Ithaca, 1992.

———. *Remembering Kings Past: Monastic Foundation Legends in Medieval Southern France*. Ithaca, 1995.

Reuter, Timothy. *Germany in the Early Middle Ages, 800–1056*. New York, 1991.

Reynolds, Susan. *Fiefs and Vassals: The Medieval Evidence Reinterpreted*. Oxford, 1994.

———. *Kingdoms and Communities in Western Europe, 900–1300*. 2d ed. Oxford, 1997.

Riccetti, Lucio. "La cronaca di Ranerio vescovo di Orvieto (1228–1248). Una prima ricognizione." *Rivista di storia della chiesa in Italia* 43:2 (July–December 1989): 480–509.

———. *La città costruita: Lavori pubblici e immagine in Orvieto medievale*. Florence, 1992.

Riché, Pierre. *Education and Culture in the Barbarian West from the Sixth through the Eighth Century.* Trans. John J. Contreni. Columbia, S.C., 1976.

———. *The Carolingians: A Family Who Forged Europe.* Trans. Michael Idomir Allen. Philadelphia, 1993.

Rigon, Antonio. "L'identità difficile: Il clero secolare tra l'universalità e particolarismi." In *Vita religiosa e identità politiche: universalità e particolarismi nell'Europa del tardo medioevo.* Ed. Sergio Gensini. Pisa, 1998.

Robinson, Ian S. *The Papacy, 1073–1198: Continuity and Innovation.* Cambridge, 1990.

Ronzani, Mauro. "L'organizzazione della cura d'anime nella città di Pisa secoli XII–XIII." In *Istituzioni ecclesiastiche della toscana medioevale.* Lecce, 1980.

———. "Aspetti e problemi della pievi e delle parrocchie cittadine nell'Italia centro-settentrionale." In *Pievi e parrocchie in Italia nel basso medioevo sec. XIII–XV.* Rome, 1984.

———. "La plebs città. La problematica della *pieve* urbana in Italia centro-settentrionale fra il IX e il XIV secolo." In *Chiesa e città.* Ed. Cosimo Damiano Fonseca and Cinzio Violante. Potenza, 1990.

Rosenwein, Barbara. "Feudal War and Monastic Peace: Cluniac Liturgy as Ritual Aggression." *Viator* 2 (1971): 129–57.

Rossetti, Gabriella. "Gli Aldobrandeschi." In *I ceti dirigenti in Toscana nell'età precomunale.* Comitato di studi sulla storia di ceti dirigenti in Toscana. Pisa, 1981.

Rossi Caponeri, Marilena, and Lucio Riccetti, eds. *Chiese e conventi degli ordini mendicanti in Umbria nei secoli XIII–XIV. Inventario delle fonti archivistiche e catologo delle informazioni documentarie.* Perugia, 1987.

Rovere, Antonella. "I 'libri iurium' dell'Italia comunale." In *Civiltà Comunale: Libro, Scrittura, Documento.* Atti della società ligure di storia patria, n.s. no. 29. Genoa, 1989.

Satoli, Alberto. "Peculiarità dell'urbanistica orvietana nel medioevo." *Bolletino dell'Istituto storico-artistico orvietano* 24 (1968): 3–69.

Schimmelpfennig, Bernard. *The Papacy.* Trans. James Sievert. New York, 1992.

Sensi, Mario. "Sinodi e visite pastorali in Umbria nel '200, '300, e '400." In *Vescovi e diocesi in Italia dal XIV alla metà del XVI secolo.* Ed. Giuseppina de Sandre Gasparini, Antonio Rigon, Francesco Trolese, and Gian Maria Varanini. Rome, 1990.

Sergi, Giuseppe. "Vescovi, monastery, aristocrazia militare." In *La Chiesa e il potere politico dal medioevo all'età contemporanea. Storia d'Italia, annali* 9. Ed. Giorgio Chittolini and Giovanni Miccoli. Turin, 1986.

Severino, Gabriella. "La vita metrica di Anselmo di Lucca scritta da Rangerio. Ideologia e genere letterario." *Sant'Anselmo vescovo di Lucca (1073–1086) nel quadro delle trasformazioni sociali e della riforma ecclesiastica.* Ed. Cinzio Violante. Rome, 1992.

Signorelli, G. *Viterbo nella storia della chiesa.* 2 vols. Viterbo, 1907.

Sot, Michel. *Gesta Episcoporum, Gesta Abbatum.* Vol. 37, Typologie des sources du moyen âge occidental. Turnhout, 1981.

Spicciani, Amleto. "I Farolfingi: Conti di Chiusi e Conti di Orvieto." *Bullettino Senese di Storia Patria* 92 (1985): 7–65.

Stopani, Renato. *La Via Francigena: Una strada europea nell'Italia del medioevo.* Florence, 1988.

Tabacco, Giovanni. "Vescovi e monasteri." In *Il monachesimo e la riforma ecclesiastica 1049–1122.* Milan, 1971.

———. "L'ambiguità delle istituzioni nell'Europa costruita dai Franchi." *Rivista storica italiana* (1975): 401–38.

———. "Vescovi e comuni in Italia." In *I poteri temporali dei vescovi in Italia e in Germania.* Ed. Carlo Guido Mor and Heinrich Schmidinger. Bologna, 1979.

———. *The Struggle for Power in Medieval Italy: Structures of Political Rule.* Trans. Rosalind Brown Jensen. Cambridge, 1989.

———. "La Toscana meridionale nel medioevo." In *L'Amiata nel medioevo.* Ed. Mario Ascheri and Wilhelm Kurze. Rome, 1989.

Tellenbach, Gerd. *The Church in Western Europe from the Tenth to the Early Twelfth Century.* Trans. Timothy Reuter. Cambridge, 1993.

Theseider, Eugenio Dupré. "Vescovi e città nell'Italia precomunale." In *Vescovi e diocesi in Italia nel Medioevo sec IX–XIII.* Atti del II convegno di storia della chiesa in Italia. Rome, 1964.

Thouzellier, Charles. "Heresie et pauvreté à la fin du XIIe et au début du XIIIe siècle." In *Études sur l'histoire de la pauvreté. Moyen Age–XVIe siècle.* Ed. Michel Mollat. Paris, 1974.

Tilatii, Andrea. "Dall'agiografia alla cronaca. Le *inventiones* degli antichi patroni padovanni. Fra interpretazione storiografia e sviluppo di una coscienza civica (secc. XI–XII)." In *La religion civique à l'epoque médiévale e moderne (Chrétienté et Islam).* Ed. André Vauchez. Rome, 1995.

Toubert, Pierre. *Les structures du Latium medieval: Le Latium méridional et la Sabine du IXe à la fin du XIIe siècle.* Ecole française de Rome. Rome, 1973.

Vauchez, André. "Il culto dei 'nuovi' santi in Umbria nei secoli XIII e XIV." In *Ordini mendicanti e società italiana, XIII–XV secolo.* Milan, 1990.

Violante, Cinzio. "Il monachesimo cluniacense di fronte al mondo politico ed ecclesiastico secoli X e XI." In *Spiritualità cluniacense.* Convegni del centro di studi sulla spiritualità medievale, 2. Todi, 1960.

——. "Pievi e parrocchie nell'Italia centrosettentrionale durante i secoli XI e XII." In *Le istituzioni ecclesiastiche della "societas christiana" dei secoli XI–XII. Diocesi, pievi, e parrocchie.* Milan, 1977.

——. "Quelques caractéristiques des structures familiales en Lombardie, Emile et Toscane aux XIe et XIIe siècles." In *Famille et parenté dans l'occident médiéval.* Ed. Georges Duby and Jacques Le Goff. Rome, 1977.

——. "Sistemi organizzativi della cura d'anime in Italia tra Medioevo e Rinascimento. Discorso introduttivo." In *Pievi e parrocchie in Italia nel basso medioevo sec. XIII–XV.* Atti del VI convegno di storia della chiesa in Italia. Rome, 1984.

——. "La réforme ecclésiastique du XIe siècle: Une synthèse progressive d'idées et de structures opposes." *Le Moyen Age* 97:3–4 (1991): 355–65.

——. "Il concetto di 'Chiesa feudale' nella storiografia." In *Chiesa e mondo feudale nei secoli X–XII.* Atti della dodicesima Settimana internazionale di studio, Mendola. Milan, 1995.

La vita comune del clero nei secoli XI e XII. Atti della Settimana di studio: Mendola, settembre 1959. 2 vols. Milan, 1962.

Waley, Daniel. *Mediaeval Orvieto: The Political History of an Italian City-State, 1157–1334.* Cambridge, 1957.

——. *The Papal State in the Thirteenth Century.* London, 1961.

——. *The Italian City-Republics.* 3d ed. New York, 1988.

Wallace-Hadrill, J. M. *The Frankish Church.* Oxford, 1983.

Weber, Max. *Economy and Society.* Ed. and trans. Guenther Roth and Claus Wittich. 2 vols. Berkeley, 1978.

Wickham, Chris. "The Other Transition: From the Ancient World to Feudalism." *Past and Present* 103 (1984): 3–36.

——. *Il problema dell'incastellamento nell'Italia centrale: L'esempio de San Vincenzo al Volturno.* Florence, 1985.

——. "Land disputes and Their Social Framework in Lombard-Carolingian Italy, 700–900." In *The Settlement of Disputes in Early Medieval Europe,* pp. 105–24. Ed. Wendy Davies and Paul Fouracre. New York, 1986.

——. *The Mountains and the City: The Tuscan Appennines in the Early Middle Ages.* Oxford, 1988.

——. *Early Medieval Italy: Central Power and Local Society 400–1000.* Ann Arbor, 1989.

——. "Paesaggi sepolti: Insediamento e incastellamento sull'Amiata, 750–1250." In *L'Amiata nel medioevo.* Ed. Mario Ascheri and Wilhelm Kurze. Rome, 1989.

————. "The Sense of the Past in Italian Communal Narratives." In *The Perceptions of the Past in Twelfth-Century Europe.* Ed. Paul Magdalino. London, 1992.

————. "Debate: The Feudal Revolution." *Past and Present* 155 (1997): 196–208.

Zafarana, Zelina. "Cura pastorale, predicazione, aspetti devozionali nella parrocchia del basso medioevo." In *Da Gregorio VII a Bernardino da Siena. Saggi di storia medievale.* Ed. Ovidio Capitani. Florence, 1987.

Zanella, Gabrielle. "L'eresia catara fra XII e XIV secolo: in margine al disagio di una storiografia." *Bollettino dell'istituto storico italiano per il medio evo e archivio muratoriano* 88 (1979): 239–58.

INDEX